ABOUT THIS PUBLICATION

FOR SERVICE ASSISTANCE

Customer Service
1.704.898.0770

North Carolina General Statues is published by The Muliti-Media Group of Greater Charlotte in Charlotte, North Carolina. Copyright 2015 by the Multi-Media Group of Greater Charlotte. This book or parts thereof may not be reproduced in any form, stored in a retrieval system, or transmitted in any form by any means—electronic, mechanical, photocopy, recording or otherwise—without prior written permission of the publisher, except as provided by United States of America copyright law.

The records required by U.S. Code 2257(a) through (c) and the pertinent regulations 28 C.F.R. Cli. 1, Part 75 with respect to this publication and all materials associated with such records are maintained by The Multi-Media Group of Greater Charlotte, Publisher and available for review by Attorney General.

www.visionbooks.org

Copyright © 2015 by MMGGC
All rights reserved!

TID: 5061690
ISBN (10) digit: 1502915111
ISBN (13) digit: 978-1502915115
123-4-56789-01239-Paperback
123-4-56789-01239-Hardback

First Edition

090520140547

Printed in the United States of America

2015 EDITION

North Carolina Criminal Law And Procedure-Pamphlet # 46

Printed In conjunction with the Administration of the Courts

North Carolina Criminal Law and Procedure
Pamphlet Reference Guide

Chapters	Pamphlet
Chapter 1 Civil Procedure	1
Chapter 1 Civil Procedure (Continue)	2
Chapter 1A Rules of Civil Procedure	2
Chapter 1B Contribution.	2
Chapter 1C Enforcement of Judgments.	2
Chapter 1D Punitive Damages.	2
Chapter 1E Eastern Band of Cherokee Indians.	2
Chapter 1F North Carolina Uniform Interstate Depositions and Discovery Act.	2
Chapter 2 - Clerk of Superior Court [Repealed and Transferred.]	3
Chapter 3 - Commissioners of Affidavits and Deeds [Repealed.]	3
Chapter 4 - Common Law	3
Chapter 5 - Contempt [Repealed.]	3
Chapter 5A - Contempt	3
Chapter 6 - Liability for Court Costs	3
Chapter 7 - Courts [Repealed and Transferred.]	3
Chapter 7A – Judicial Department	3
Chapter 7A – Continuation (Judicial Department)	4
Chapter 7A – Continuation (Judicial Department)	5
Chapter 7B - Juvenile Code	5
Chapter 8 - Evidence	6
Chapter 8A - Interpreters for Deaf Persons [Recodified.]	6
Chapter 8B - Interpreters for Deaf Persons	6
Chapter 8C - Evidence Code	6
Chapter 9 - Jurors	6
Chapter 10 - Notaries [Repealed.]	6
Chapter 10A - Notaries [Recodified.]	6
Chapter 10B - Notaries	6
Chapter 11 - Oaths	6
Chapter 12 - Statutory Construction	6
Chapter 13 - Citizenship Restored	6
Chapter 14 - Criminal Law	7
Chapter 14 –Criminal Law (Continuation)	8
Chapter 15 - Criminal Procedure	9
Chapter 15A - Criminal Procedure Act (Continuation)	10
Chapter 15A - Criminal Procedure Act (Continuation)	11
Chapter 15B - Victims Compensation	11
Chapter 15C - Address Confidentiality Program	11
Chapter 16 - Gaming Contracts and Futures	11
Chapter 17 - Habeas Corpus	11

Chapter 17A - Law-Enforcement Officers [Recodified.]	11
Chapter 17B - North Carolina Criminal Justice Education and Training System [Recodified.] Chapter 17C - North Carolina Criminal Justice Education and Training Standards Commission	11
	11
Chapter 17D - North Carolina Justice Academy	11
Chapter 17E - North Carolina Sheriffs' Education and Training Standards Commission	11
Chapter 18 - Regulation of Intoxicating Liquors [Repealed.]	12
Chapter 18A - Regulation of Intoxicating Liquors [Repealed.]	12
Chapter 18B - Regulation of Alcoholic Beverages	12
Chapter 18C - North Carolina State Lottery	12
Chapter 19 - Offenses against Public Morals	12
Chapter 19A - Protection of Animals	12
Chapter 20 - Motor Vehicles	13
Chapter 20 - Motor Vehicles (Continuation)	14
Chapter 20 - Motor Vehicles (Continuation)	15
Chapter 20 - Motor Vehicles (Continuation)	16
Chapter 21 - Bills of Lading	17
Chapter 22 - Contracts Requiring Writing	17
Chapter 22A - Signatures	17
Chapter 22B - Contracts Against Public Policy	17
Chapter 22C - Payments to Subcontractors	17
Chapter 23 - Debtor and Creditor	17
Chapter 24 – Interest	17
Chapter 25 – Uniform Commercial Code	18
Chapter 25 – Uniform Commercial Code (Continuation)	19
Chapter 25A – Retail Installment Sales Act	20
Chapter 25B - Credit	20
Chapter 25C - Sales of Artwork	20
Chapter 26 - Suretyship	20
Chapter 27 - Warehouse Receipts [Repealed.]	20
Chapter 28 - Administration [Repealed.]	20
Chapter 28A - Administration of Decedents' Estates	20
Chapter 28B - Estates of Absentees in Military Service	20
Chapter 28C - Estates of Missing Persons	20
Chapter 29 - Intestate Succession	21
Chapter 30 - Surviving Spouses	21
Chapter 31 - Wills	21
Chapter 31A - Acts Barring Property Rights	21
Chapter 31B - Renunciation of Property and Renunciation of Fiduciary Powers Act	21
Chapter 31C - Uniform Disposition of Community Property Rights at Death Act	21
Chapter 32 - Fiduciaries	21
Chapter 32A - Powers of Attorney	21
Chapter 33 - Guardian and Ward [Repealed and Recodified.]	21

Chapter 33A - North Carolina Uniform Transfers to Minors Act	21
Chapter 33B - North Carolina Uniform Custodial Trust Act	21
Chapter 34 - Veterans' Guardianship Act	22
Chapter 35 - Sterilization Procedures	22
Chapter 35A - Incompetency and Guardianship	22
Chapter 36 - Trusts and Trustees [Repealed.]	22
Chapter 36A - Trusts and Trustees	22
Chapter 36B - Uniform Management of Institutional Funds Act [Repealed.]	22
Chapter 36C - North Carolina Uniform Trust Code	22
Chapter 36D - North Carolina Community Third Party Trusts, Pooled Trusts	23
Chapter 36E - Uniform Prudent Management of Institutional Funds Act	23
Chapter 37 - Allocation of Principal and Income [Repealed.]	23
Chapter 37A - Uniform Principal and Income Act	23
Chapter 38 - Boundaries	23
Chapter 38A - Landowner Liability	23
Chapter 39 - Conveyances	23
Chapter 39A - Transfer Fee Covenants Prohibited	23
Chapter 40 - Eminent Domain [Repealed.]	23
Chapter 40A - Eminent Domain	23
Chapter 41 - Estates	23
Chapter 41A - State Fair Housing Act	23
Chapter 42 - Landlord and Tenant	23
Chapter 42A - Vacation Rental Act	23
Chapter 43 - Land Registration	23
Chapter 44 - Liens	24
Chapter 44A - Statutory Liens and Charges	24
Chapter 45 - Mortgages and Deeds of Trust	24
Chapter 45A - Good Funds Settlement Act	24
Chapter 46 - Partition	24
Chapter 47 - Probate and Registration	25
Chapter 47A - Unit Ownership	25
Chapter 47B - Real Property Marketable Title Act	25
Chapter 47C - North Carolina Condominium Act	25
Chapter 47D - Notice of Settlement Act [Expired.]	25
Chapter 47E - Residential Property Disclosure Act	25
Chapter 47F - North Carolina Planned Community Act	25
Chapter 47G - Option to Purchase Contracts	25
Chapter 47H - Contracts for Deed	25
Chapter 48 - Adoptions +	26
Chapter 48A - Minors	26
Chapter 49 - Bastardy	26
Chapter 49A - Rights of Children	26
Chapter 50 - Divorce and Alimony	26
Chapter 50A - Uniform Child-Custody Jurisdiction and	

Enforcement Act	26
Chapter 50B - Domestic Violence	26
Chapter 50C - Civil No-Contact Orders	26
Chapter 51 - Marriage	26
Chapter 52 - Powers and Liabilities of Married Persons	27
Chapter 52A - Uniform Reciprocal Enforcement of Support Act [Repealed.]	27
Chapter 52B - Uniform Premarital Agreement Act	27
Chapter 52C - Uniform Interstate Family Support Act	27
Chapter 53 - Banks	27
Chapter 53A - Business Development Corporations and North Carolina Capital Resource Corporations	28
Chapter 53B - Financial Privacy Act	28
Chapter 54 - Cooperative Organizations	28
Chapter 54A - Capital Stock Savings and Loan Associations [Repealed.]	28
Chapter 54B - Savings and Loan Associations	29
Chapter 54C - Savings Banks	29
Chapter 55 - North Carolina Business Corporation Act	30
Chapter 55A - North Carolina Nonprofit Corporation Act	31
Chapter 55B - Professional Corporation Act	31
Chapter 55C - Foreign Trade Zones	31
Chapter 55D - Filings, Names, and Registered Agents for Corporations, Nonprofit Corporations, and Partnerships	31
Chapter 56 - Electric, Telegraph and Power Companies [Repealed.]	31
Chapter 57 - Hospital, Medical and Dental Service Corporations [Recodified.]	31
Chapter 57A - Health Maintenance Organization Act [Recodified.]	31
Chapter 57B - Health Maintenance Organization Act [Recodified.]	31
Chapter 57C - North Carolina Limited Liability Company Act.	31
Chapter 58 - Insurance.	32
Chapter 58 - Insurance (Continuation)	33
Chapter 58 - Insurance (Continuation)	34
Chapter 58 - Insurance (Continuation)	35
Chapter 58 - Insurance (Continuation)	36
Chapter 58 - Insurance (Continuation)	37
Chapter 58 - Insurance (Continuation)	38
Chapter 58A - North Carolina Health Insurance Trust Commission [Recodified.]	38
Chapter 59 - Partnership.	39
Chapter 59B - Uniform Unincorporated Nonprofit Association Act.	39
Chapter 60 - Railroads and Other Carriers [Repealed and Transferred.]	39
Chapter 61 - Religious Societies	39
Chapter 62 - Public Utilities	39

Chapter 62 - Public Utilities (Continuation)	40
Chapter 62A - Public Safety Telephone Service And Wireless Telephone Service	40
Chapter 63 - Aeronautics	40
Chapter 63A - North Carolina Global TransPark Authority	40
Chapter 64 - Aliens	40
Chapter 65 – Cemeteries	40
Chapter 66 - Commerce and Business	41
Chapter 67 - Dogs	41
Chapter 68 - Fences and Stock Law	41
Chapter 69 - Fire Protection	41
Chapter 70 - Indian Antiquities, Archaeological Resources and Unmarked Human Skeletal Remains Protection	42
Chapter 71 - Indians [Repealed.]	42
Chapter 71A - Indians	42
Chapter 72 - Inns, Hotels and Restaurants	42
Chapter 73 - Mills	42
Chapter 74 - Mines and Quarries	42
Chapter 74A - Company Police [Repealed.]	42
Chapter 74B - Private Protective Services Act [Repealed.]	42
Chapter 74C - Private Protective Services	42
Chapter 74D - Alarm Systems	42
Chapter 74E - Company Police Act	42
Chapter 74F - Locksmith Licensing Act	42
Chapter 74G - Campus Police Act	42
Chapter 75 - Monopolies, Trusts and Consumer Protection	42
Chapter 75A - Boating and Water Safety	43
Chapter 75B - Discrimination in Business	43
Chapter 75C - Motion Picture Fair Competition Act	43
Chapter 75D - Racketeer Influenced and Corrupt Organizations	43
Chapter 75E - Unlawful Activities in Connection With Certain Corporate Transactions	43
Chapter 76 - Navigation	43
Chapter 76A - Navigation and Pilotage Commissions	43
Chapter 77 - Rivers, Creeks, and Coastal Waters	43
Chapter 78 - Securities Law [Repealed.]	43
Chapter 78A - North Carolina Securities Act	43
Chapter 78B - Tender Offer Disclosure Act [Repealed.]	43
Chapter 78C - Investment Advisers	43
Chapter 78D - Commodities Act	43
Chapter 79 - Strays [Repealed.]	43
Chapter 80 - Trademarks, Brands, etc.	44
Chapter 81 - Weights and Measures [Recodified.]	44
Chapter 81A - Weights and Measures Act of 1975.	44
Chapter 82 - Wrecks [Repealed.]	44
Chapter 83 - Architects [Recodified.]	44

Chapter 83A - Architects	44
Chapter 84 - Attorneys-at-Law	44
Chapter 84A - Foreign Legal Consultants	44
Chapter 85 - Auctions and Auctioneers [Repealed.]	44
Chapter 85A - Bail Bondsmen and Runners [Recodified.]	44
Chapter 85B - Auctions and Auctioneers	44
Chapter 85C - Bail Bondsmen and Runners [Recodified.]	44
Chapter 86 - Barbers [Recodified.]	44
Chapter 86A - Barbers	44
Chapter 87 - Contractors	44
Chapter 88 - Cosmetic Art [Repealed.]	44
Chapter 88A - Electrolysis Practice Act	44
Chapter 88B - Cosmetic Art	45
Chapter 89 - Engineering and Land Surveying [Recodified.]	45
Chapter 89A - Landscape Architects	45
Chapter 89B - Foresters	45
Chapter 89C - Engineering and Land Surveying	45
Chapter 89D - Landscape Contractors	45
Chapter 89E - Geologists Licensing Act	45
Chapter 89F - North Carolina Soil Scientist Licensing Act	45
Chapter 89G - Irrigation Contractors	45
Chapter 90 - Medicine and Allied Occupations	45
Chapter 90 - Medicine and Allied Occupations (Continuation)	46
Chapter 90 - Medicine and Allied Occupations (Continuation)	47
Chapter 90 - Medicine and Allied Occupations (Continuation)	48
Chapter 90A - Sanitarians and Water and Wastewater Treatment Facility Operators	48
Chapter 90B - Social Worker Certification and Licensure Act	48
Chapter 90C - North Carolina Recreational Therapy Licensure Act	48
Chapter 90D - Interpreters and Transliterators	48
Chapter 91 - Pawnbrokers [Repealed.]	48
Chapter 91A - Pawnbrokers Modernization Act of 1989	48
Chapter 92 - Photographers [Deleted.]	48
Chapter 93 - Certified Public Accountants	48
Chapter 93A - Real Estate License Law	49
Chapter 93B - Occupational Licensing Boards	49
Chapter 93C - Watchmakers [Repealed.]	49
Chapter 93D - North Carolina State Hearing Aid Dealers and Fitters Board.	49
Chapter 93E - North Carolina Appraisers Act	49
Chapter 94 - Apprenticeship	49
Chapter 95 - Department of Labor and Labor Regulations	49
Chapter 95 - Department of Labor and Labor Regulations (Continuation)	50
Chapter 96 - Employment Security	50
Chapter 97 - Workers' Compensation Act	50
Chapter 97 - Workers' Compensation Act (Continuation)	51

Chapter 98 - Burnt and Lost Records	51
Chapter 99 - Libel and Slander	51
Chapter 99A - Civil Remedies for Criminal Actions	51
Chapter 99B - Products Liability	51
Chapter 99C - Actions Relating to Winter Sports Safety and Accidents	51
Chapter 99D - Civil Rights	51
Chapter 99E - Special Liability Provisions	51
Chapter 100 - Monuments, Memorials and Parks	51
Chapter 101 - Names of Persons	51
Chapter 102 - Official Survey Base	51
Chapter 103 - Sundays, Holidays and Special Days	51
Chapter 104 - United States Lands	51
Chapter 104A - Degrees of Kinship	51
Chapter 104B - Hurricanes or Other Acts of Nature	51
Chapter 104C - Atomic Energy, Radioactivity and Ionizing Radiation [Repealed and Recodified.]	51
Chapter 104D - Southern States Energy Compact	51
Chapter 104E - North Carolina Radiation Protection Act	51
Chapter 104F - Southeast Interstate Low-Level Radioactive Waste Management Compact [Repealed]	51
Chapter 104G - North Carolina Low-Level Radioactive Waste Management Authority Act of 1987 [Repealed]	51
Chapter 105 - Taxation	51
Chapter 105 - Taxation (Continuation)	52
Chapter 105 - Taxation (Continuation)	53
Chapter 105 - Taxation (Continuation)	54
Chapter 105A - Setoff Debt Collection Act	55
Chapter 105B - Defaulted Student Loan Recovery Act	55
Chapter 106 - Agriculture	55
Chapter 106 - Agriculture (Continue)	56
Chapter 106 - Agriculture (Continue)	57
Chapter 107 - Agricultural Development Districts [Repealed.]	57
Chapter 108 - Social Services [Repealed and Recodified.]	57
Chapter 108A - Social Services	57
Chapter 108B - Community Action Programs	58
Chapter 108C Medicaid and Health Choice Provider Requirements.	58
Chapter 108D Medicaid Managed Care for Behavioral Health Services.	58
Chapter 109 - Bonds [Recodified.]	58
Chapter 110 - Child Welfare	58
Chapter 111 - Aid to the Blind	58
Chapter 112 - Confederate Homes and Pensions [Repealed.]	58
Chapter 113 - Conservation and Development	58
Chapter 113 - Conservation and Development (Continuation)	59

Chapter 113A - Pollution Control and Environment	59
Chapter 113A - Pollution Control and Environment (Continuation)	60
Chapter 113B - North Carolina Energy Policy Act of 1975	60
Chapter 114 - Department of Justice	60
Chapter 115 - Elementary and Secondary Education [Repealed.]	60
Chapter 115A - Community Colleges, Technical Institutes, and Industrial Education Centers [Repealed.]	60
Chapter 115B - Tuition and Fee Waivers	60
Chapter 115C - Elementary and Secondary Education	60
Chapter 115C - Elementary and Secondary Education (Continuation)	61
Chapter 115C - Elementary and Secondary Education (Continuation)	62
Chapter 115C - Elementary and Secondary Education (Continuation)	63
Chapter 115D - Community Colleges	63
Chapter 115E - Private Educational Facilities Finance Act [Recodified]	63
Chapter 116 - Higher Education	63
Chapter 116 - Higher Education (Continuation)	63
Chapter 116A - Escheats and Abandoned Property [Repealed.]	64
Chapter 116B - Escheats and Abandoned Property	64
Chapter 116C - Continuum of Education Programs	64
Chapter 116D - Higher Education Bonds	64
Chapter 117 - Electrification	64
Chapter 118 - Firemen's and Rescue Squad Workers' Relief and Pension Funds [Recodified.]	64
Chapter 118A - Firemen's Death Benefit Act [Repealed.]	64
Chapter 118B - Members of a Rescue Squad Death Benefit Act [Repealed.]	64
Chapter 119 - Gasoline and Oil Inspection and Regulation	64
Chapter 120 - General Assembly	65
Chapter 120 - General Assembly (Continuation)	66
Chapter 120 - General Assembly (Continuation)	67
Chapter 120C - Lobbying	67
Chapter 121 - Archives and History	67
Chapter 122 - Hospitals for the Mentally Disordered [Repealed.]	67
Chapter 122A - North Carolina Housing Finance Agency	67
Chapter 122B - North Carolina Agricultural Facilities Finance Act [Repealed.]	67
Chapter 122C - Mental Health, Developmental Disabilities, and Substance Abuse Act of 1985	67
Chapter 122C - Mental Health, Developmental Disabilities, and Substance Abuse Act of 1985 (Continuation)	68
Chapter 122D - North Carolina Agricultural Finance Act	68

Chapter 122E - North Carolina Housing Trust and Oil Overcharge Act	68
Chapter 123 - Impeachment	69
Chapter 123A - Industrial Development [Repealed.]	69
Chapter 124 - Internal Improvements	69
Chapter 125 - Libraries	69
Chapter 126 - State Personnel System	69
Chapter 127 - Militia [Repealed.]	69
Chapter 127A - Militia	69
Chapter 127B - Military Affairs	69
Chapter 127C - Advisory Commission on Military Affairs	69
Chapter 128 - Offices and Public Officers	69
Chapter 128 - Offices and Public Officers (Continuation)	70
Chapter 129 - Public Buildings and Grounds	70
Chapter 130 - Public Health [Repealed.]	70
Chapter 130A - Public Health	70
Chapter 130A - Public Health (Continuation)	71
Chapter 130A - Public Health (Continuation)	72
Chapter 130B - Hazardous Waste Management Commission [Repealed.]	72
Chapter 131 - Public Hospitals [Repealed.]	72
Chapter 131A - Health Care Facilities Finance Act	72
Chapter 131B - Licensing of Ambulatory Surgical Facilities [Repealed.]	72
Chapter 131C - Charitable Solicitation Licensure Act [Repealed.]	72
Chapter 131D - Inspection and Licensing of Facilities	72
Chapter 131E - Health Care Facilities and Services	72
Chapter 131E - Health Care Facilities and Services (Continuation)	73
Chapter 131F - Solicitation of Contributions	73
Chapter 132 - Public Records	73
Chapter 133 - Public Works	74
Chapter 134 - Youth Development [Recodified.]	74
Chapter 134A - Youth Services [Repealed.]	74
Chapter 135 - Retirement System for Teachers and State Employees; Social Security; Health Insurance Program for Children	74
Chapter 135 - Retirement System for Teachers and State Employees; Social Security; Health Insurance Program for Children	75
Chapter 136 - Transportation	75
Chapter 136 - Transportation (Continuation)	76
Chapter 137 - Rural Rehabilitation [Repealed.]	76
Chapter 138 - Salaries, Fees and Allowances	76
Chapter 138A - State Government Ethics Act	76
Chapter 139 - Soil and Water Conservation Districts	76

Chapter 140 - State Art Museum; Symphony and Art Societies	76
Chapter 140A - State Awards System	76
Chapter 141 - State Boundaries	76
Chapter 142 - State Debt	76
Chapter 143 - State Departments, Institutions, and Commissions	77
Chapter 143 - State Departments, Institutions, and Commissions (Continuation)	78
Chapter 143 - State Departments, Institutions, and Commissions (Continuation)	79
Chapter 143 - State Departments, Institutions, and Commissions (Continuation)	80
Chapter 143A - State Government Reorganization	80
Chapter 143B - Executive Organization Act of 1973	80
Chapter 143B - Executive Organization Act of 1973 (Continuation)	81
Chapter 143B - Executive Organization Act of 1973 (Continuation)	82
Chapter 143C - State Budget Act	83
Chapter 143D - The State Governmental Accountability and Internal Control Act	83
Chapter 144 - State Flag, Official Governmental Flags, Motto, and Colors	83
Chapter 145 - State Symbols and Other Official Adoptions.	83
Chapter 146 - State Lands	83
Chapter 147 - State Officers	83
Chapter 148 - State Prison System	84
Chapter 149 - State Song and Toast	84
Chapter 150 - Uniform Revocation of Licenses [Repealed.]	84
Chapter 150A - Administrative Procedure Act [Recodified.]	84
Chapter 150B - Administrative Procedure Act	84
Chapter 151 - Constables [Repealed.]	84
Chapter 152 - Coroners	84
Chapter 152A - County Medical Examiner [Repealed.]	84
Chapter 152A - County Medical Examiner [Repealed.] (Continuation)	85
Chapter 153 - Counties and County Commissioners [Repealed.]	85
Chapter 153A - Counties	85
Chapter 153B - Mountain Resources Planning Act	85
Chapter 153C - Uwharrie Regional Resources Act	85
Chapter 154 - County Surveyor [Repealed.]	85
Chapter 155 - County Treasurer [Repealed.]	85
Chapter 156 - Drainage	85
Chapter 156 – Drainage (Continuation)	86

Chapter 157 - Housing Authorities and Projects	86
Chapter 157A - Historic Properties Commissions [Transferred.]	86
Chapter 158 - Local Development	86
Chapter 159 - Local Government Finance	86
Chapter 159 - Local Government Finance (Continuation)	87
Chapter 159A - Pollution Abatement and Industrial Facilities Financing Act [Unconstitutional.]	87
Chapter 159B - Joint Municipal Electric Power and Energy Act	87
Chapter 159C - Industrial and Pollution Control Facilities Financing Act	87
Chapter 159D - The North Carolina Capital Facilities Financing Act	87
Chapter 159E - Registered Public Obligations Act	87
Chapter 159F - North Carolina Energy Development Authority [Repealed.]	87
Chapter 159G - Water Infrastructure	87
Chapter 159H - [Reserved.]	87
Chapter 159I - Solid Waste Management Loan Program and Local Government Special Obligation Bonds	87
Chapter 160 - Municipal Corporations [Repealed And Transferred.]	87
Chapter 160A - Cities and Towns	88
Chapter 160A - Cities and Towns (Continuation)	89
Chapter 160B - Consolidated City-County Act	89
Chapter 160C - Baseball Park Districts [Repealed.]	90
Chapter 161 - Register of Deeds	90
Chapter 162 - Sheriff	90
Chapter 162A - Water and Sewer Systems	90
Chapter 162B Continuity of Local Government in Emergency.	90
Chapter 163 Elections and Election Laws.	90
Chapter 163 Elections and Election Laws. (Continuation)	91
Chapter 164 Concerning the General Statutes of North Carolina.	92
Chapter 165 Veterans.	92
Chapter 166 Civil Preparedness Agencies [Repealed.]	92
Chapter 166A North Carolina Emergency Management Act.	92
Chapter 167 State Civil Air Patrol [Repealed.]	92
Chapter 168 Persons with Disabilities.	92
Chapter 168A Persons With Disabilities Protection Act.	92

§ 90-38. Licensing former dentists who have moved back into State or resumed practice.

Any person who shall have been licensed by the North Carolina State Board of Dental Examiners to practice dentistry in this State who shall have retired from practice or who shall have moved from the State and shall have returned to the State, may, upon a satisfactory showing to said Board of his proficiency in the profession of dentistry and his good moral character during the period of his retirement, be granted by said Board a license to resume the practice of dentistry upon making application to the said Board in such form as it may require. The license to resume practice, after issuance thereof, shall be subject to all the provisions of this Article. (1935, c. 66, s. 11; 1953, c. 564, s. 2.)

§ 90-39. Fees.

In order to provide the means of carrying out and enforcing the provisions of this Article and the duties devolving upon the North Carolina State Board of Dental Examiners, it is authorized to charge and collect fees established by its rules not exceeding the following:

(1)   Each application for general dentistry license.. $1,200

(2)   Each general dentistry license renewal, which fee shall be annually fixed by the Board and not later than November 30 of each year it shall give written notice of the amount of the renewal fee to each dentist licensed to practice in this State by mailing such notice to the last address of record with the Board of each such dentist... 600.00

(2a)   Penalty for late renewal of any license or permit... 100.00

(3)   Each provisional license.. 300.00

(4)   Each intern permit or renewal thereof... 500.00

(5)   Each certificate of license to a resident dentist desiring to change to another state or territory... 75.00

(6)   Repealed by Session Laws 1995, (Reg. Sess., 1996), c. 584, s. 1.

(7)   Each license to resume the practice issued to a dentist who has retired from and returned to this State... 500.00

(8)   Each instructor's license or renewal thereof.. 500.00

(9)   With each renewal of a dentistry license, an annual fee to help fund special peer review organizations for impaired dentists.. 100.00

(10)   Each duplicate of any license, permit, or certificate issued by the Board.... 75.00

(11)   Each office inspection for general anesthesia and parenteral sedation permits 750.00

(12)   Each general anesthesia and parenteral sedation permit application or renewal of permit 100.00

(13)   Each application for license by credentials... 3,000.00

(14)   Each application for limited volunteer dental license............................... 200.00

(15)   Each limited volunteer dental license annual renewal................................. 50.00.

(1935, c. 66, s. 12; 1953, c. 564, s. 1; 1961, c. 446, s. 8; 1965, c. 163, s. 3; 1971, c. 755, s. 8; 1979, 2nd Sess., c. 1195, s. 12; 1987, c. 555, s. 1; 1993, c. 420, s. 1; 1995 (Reg. Sess., 1996), c. 584, s. 1; 2002-37, s. 5; 2003-348, s. 1; 2005-366, s. 2.)

§ 90-40. Unauthorized practice; penalty.

If any person shall practice or attempt to practice dentistry in this State without first having passed the examination and obtained a license from the North Carolina Board of Dental Examiners or having obtained a provisional license from said Board; or if he shall practice dentistry after March 31 of each year without applying for a certificate of renewal of license, as provided in G.S. 90-31; or shall practice or attempt to practice dentistry while his license is revoked, or suspended, or when a certificate of renewal of license has been refused; or shall violate any of the provisions of this Article for which no specific penalty has been provided; or shall practice or attempt to practice, dentistry in violation of the provisions of this Article; or shall practice dentistry under any name other than his own name, said person shall be guilty of a Class 1 misdemeanor. Each day's violation of this Article shall constitute a separate offense. (1935, c. 66, s. 13; 1953, c. 564, s. 6; 1957, c. 592, s. 4; 1965, c. 163, s. 6; 1969, c. 804, s. 2; 1993, c. 539, s. 619; 1994, Ex. Sess., c. 24, s. 14(c).)

§ 90-40.1. Enjoining unlawful acts.

(a) The practice of dentistry by any person who has not been duly licensed so as to practice or whose license has been suspended or revoked, or the doing, committing or continuing of any of the acts prohibited by this Article by any person or persons, whether licensed dentists or not, is hereby declared to be inimical to public health and welfare and to constitute a public nuisance. The Attorney General for the State of North Carolina, the district attorney of any of the superior courts, the North Carolina State Board of Dental Examiners in its own name, or any resident citizen may maintain an action in the name of the State of North Carolina to perpetually enjoin any person from so unlawfully practicing dentistry and from the doing, committing or continuing of such unlawful act. This proceeding shall be in addition to and not in lieu of criminal prosecutions or proceedings to revoke or suspend licenses as authorized by this Article.

(b) In an action brought under this section the final judgment, if in favor of the plaintiff, shall perpetually restrain the defendant or defendants from the commission or continuance of the act or acts complained of. A temporary injunction to restrain the commission or continuance thereof may be granted upon proof or by affidavit that the defendant or defendants have violated any of the laws or statutes applicable to unauthorized or unlawful practice of dentistry. The provisions of the statutes or rules relating generally to injunctions as provisional remedies in actions shall apply to such a temporary injunction and the proceedings thereunder.

(c)   The venue for actions brought under this section shall be the superior court of any county in which such acts constituting unlicensed or unlawful practice of dentistry are alleged to have been committed or in which there appear reasonable grounds to believe that they will be committed, in the county where the defendants in such action reside, or in Wake County.

(d)   The plaintiff in such action shall be entitled to examination of the adverse party and witnesses before filing complaint and before trial in the same manner as provided by law for the examination of the parties. (1957, c. 592, s. 5; 1973, c. 47, s. 2; 2012-195, s. 2.)

§ 90-40.2. Management arrangements.

(a)   The following definitions apply in this section:

(1)   Ancillary personnel. - Dental hygienists or dental assistants who assist licensed dentists in providing direct patient care.

(2)   Clinical. - Of or relating to the activities of a dentist as described in G.S. 90-29(b)(1)-(10).

(3)   Management arrangement. - Any one or more agreements or arrangements, alone or together, whether written or oral, between a management company and a dentist or professional entity whereby the management company provides services to assist in the development, promotion, delivery, financing, support, or administration of the dentist's or professional entity's dental practice.

(4)   Management company. - Any individual, business corporation, nonprofit corporation, partnership, limited liability company, limited partnership, or other legal entity that is not a professional entity or dentist which provides through one or more contractual arrangements any combination of management or business support services, including, but not limited to, accounting and financial services; collection, billing, and payment services; file and records maintenance; human resources services; assistance with the acquisition of fixed assets, including the locating and procurement of office space, facilities, and equipment;

maintenance of offices, equipment, furniture, and fixtures; marketing and practice development; information technology; compliance with applicable federal, State, and local laws; and clerical services.

(5) Professional entity. - A professional corporation, nonprofit corporation, partnership, professional limited liability company, professional limited partnership, or other entity or aggregation of individuals that is licensed or certified or otherwise explicitly permitted to practice dentistry under North Carolina General Statutes.

(6) Unlicensed person. - Any person or entity other than a dentist licensed in this State or registered professional entity authorized to provide dental services under this Article.

(b) A management arrangement executed on or after January 1, 2013, is invalid unless there appears on the instrument evidencing, directly above or below the space or spaces provided for the signature of the parties, in such type size or distinctive marking that it appears more clearly and conspicuously than anything else on the document:

"WARNING - YOU HAVE THE RIGHT AND ARE ENCOURAGED TO HAVE THIS CONTRACT REVIEWED BY YOUR OWN LEGAL COUNSEL PRIOR TO SIGNING."

(c) No member of the Board shall be subject to examination in connection with any investigation, inquiry, or interview related to the Board's review of any management arrangement.

(d) For actions brought under G.S. 90-40.1, the venue shall be the superior court of any county in which acts constituting unlicensed or unlawful practice of dentistry are alleged to have been committed or in which there appear reasonable grounds to believe that they will be committed, in the county where at least one defendant in the action resides, or in Wake County.

(e) If investigative information in the possession of the Board, its employees, or agents indicates that a crime may have been committed, the Board may report the information to the appropriate law enforcement agency or district attorney of the district in which the offense was committed.

(f) The Board shall cooperate with and assist law enforcement agencies and the district attorney conducting a criminal investigation or prosecution of a licensee or person engaged in the unauthorized practice of dentistry, including a management company, by providing information that is relevant to the criminal investigation or prosecution to the investigating agency or district attorney. Information disclosed by the Board to an investigative agency or district attorney remains confidential and may not be disclosed by the investigating agency except as necessary to further the investigation.

(g) Nothing in this section shall affect the validity of any of the Board's rules or regulations which were in effect as of the effective date of this section, except to the extent that such rules or regulations directly conflict with the provisions of this section. (2012-195, s. 1.)

§ 90-41. Disciplinary action.

(a) The North Carolina State Board of Dental Examiners shall have the power and authority to (i) Refuse to issue a license to practice dentistry; (ii) Refuse to issue a certificate of renewal of a license to practice dentistry; (iii) Revoke or suspend a license to practice dentistry; and (iv) Invoke such other disciplinary measures, censure, or probative terms against a licensee as it deems fit and proper;

in any instance or instances in which the Board is satisfied that such applicant or licensee:

(1) Has engaged in any act or acts of fraud, deceit or misrepresentation in obtaining or attempting to obtain a license or the renewal thereof;

(2) Is a chronic or persistent user of intoxicants, drugs or narcotics to the extent that the same impairs his ability to practice dentistry;

(3) Has been convicted of any of the criminal provisions of this Article or has entered a plea of guilty or nolo contendere to any charge or charges arising therefrom;

(4) Has been convicted of or entered a plea of guilty or nolo contendere to any felony charge or to any misdemeanor charge involving moral turpitude;

(5) Has been convicted of or entered a plea of guilty or nolo contendere to any charge of violation of any state or federal narcotic or barbiturate law;

(6) Has engaged in any act or practice violative of any of the provisions of this Article or violative of any of the rules and regulations promulgated and adopted by the Board, or has aided, abetted or assisted any other person or entity in the violation of the same;

(7) Is mentally, emotionally, or physically unfit to practice dentistry or is afflicted with such a physical or mental disability as to be deemed dangerous to the health and welfare of his patients. An adjudication of mental incompetency in a court of competent jurisdiction or a determination thereof by other lawful means shall be conclusive proof of unfitness to practice dentistry unless or until such person shall have been subsequently lawfully declared to be mentally competent;

(8) Has conducted in-person solicitation of professional patronage or has employed or procured any person to conduct such solicitation by personal contact with potential patients, except to the extent that informal advice may be permitted by regulations issued by the Board of Dental Examiners;

(9) Has permitted the use of his name, diploma or license by another person either in the illegal practice of dentistry or in attempting to fraudulently obtain a license to practice dentistry;

(10) Has engaged in such immoral conduct as to discredit the dental profession;

(11) Has obtained or collected or attempted to obtain or collect any fee through fraud, misrepresentation, or deceit;

(12) Has been negligent in the practice of dentistry;

(13) Has employed a person not licensed in this State to do or perform any act or service, or has aided, abetted or assisted any such unlicensed person to do or perform any act or service which under this Article or under Article 16 of this Chapter, can lawfully be done or performed only by a dentist or a dental hygienist licensed in this State;

(14) Is incompetent in the practice of dentistry;

(15) Has practiced any fraud, deceit or misrepresentation upon the public or upon any individual in an effort to acquire or retain any patient or patients;

(16) Has made fraudulent or misleading statements pertaining to his skill, knowledge, or method of treatment or practice;

(17) Has committed any fraudulent or misleading acts in the practice of dentistry;

(18) Has, directly or indirectly, published or caused to be published or disseminated any advertisement for professional patronage or business which is untruthful, fraudulent, misleading, or in any way inconsistent with rules and regulations issued by the Board of Dental Examiners governing the time, place, or manner of such advertisements;

(19) Has, in the practice of dentistry, committed an act or acts constituting malpractice;

(20) Repealed by Session Laws 1981, c. 751, s. 7.

(21) Has permitted a dental hygienist or a dental assistant in his employ or under his supervision to do or perform any act or acts violative of this Article, or of Article 16 of this Chapter, or of the rules and regulations promulgated by the Board;

(22) Has wrongfully or fraudulently or falsely held himself out to be or represented himself to be qualified as a specialist in any branch of dentistry;

(23) Has persistently maintained, in the practice of dentistry, unsanitary offices, practices, or techniques;

(24) Is a menace to the public health by reason of having a serious communicable disease;

(25) Has distributed or caused to be distributed any intoxicant, drug or narcotic for any other than a lawful purpose; or

(26) Has engaged in any unprofessional conduct as the same may be, from time to time, defined by the rules and regulations of the Board.

(b) If any person engages in or attempts to engage in the practice of dentistry while his license is suspended, his license to practice dentistry in the State of North Carolina may be permanently revoked.

(c) The Board may, on its own motion, initiate the appropriate legal proceedings against any person, firm or corporation when it is made to appear to the Board that such person, firm or corporation has violated any of the provisions of this Article or of Article 16.

(d) The Board may appoint, employ or retain an investigator or investigators for the purpose of examining or inquiring into any practices committed in this State that might violate any of the provisions of this Article or of Article 16 or any of the rules and regulations promulgated by the Board.

(e) The Board may employ or retain legal counsel for such matters and purposes as may seem fit and proper to said Board.

(f) As used in this section the term "licensee" includes licensees, provisional licensees and holders of intern permits, and the term "license" includes license, provisional license, instructor's license, and intern permit.

(g) Records, papers, and other documents containing information collected or compiled by the Board, or its members or employees, as a result of investigations, inquiries, or interviews conducted in connection with a licensing or disciplinary matter, shall not be considered public records within the meaning of Chapter 132 of the General Statutes; provided, however, that any notice or statement of charges against any licensee, or any notice to any licensee of a hearing in any proceeding, shall be a public record within the meaning of Chapter 132 of the General Statutes, notwithstanding that it may contain information collected and compiled as a result of any investigation, inquiry, or interview; and provided, further, that if any record, paper, or other document containing information collected and compiled by the Board is received and admitted into evidence in any hearing before the Board, it shall then be a public record within the meaning of Chapter 132 of the General Statutes. (1935, c. 66, s. 14; 1957, c. 592, s. 7; 1965, c. 163, s. 4; 1967, c. 451, s. 1; 1971, c. 755, s. 9; 1979, 2nd Sess., c. 1195, ss. 7, 8; 1981, c. 751, s. 7; 1989, c. 442; 1997-456, s. 27; 2002-37, s. 9.)

§ 90-41.1. Hearings.

(a) With the exception of applicants for license by comity and applicants for reinstatement after revocation, every licensee, provisional licensee, intern, or applicant for license, shall be afforded notice and opportunity to be heard before the North Carolina State Board of Dental Examiners shall take any action, the effect of which would be:

(1)   To deny permission to take an examination for licensing for which application has been duly made; or

(2)   To deny a license after examination for any cause other than failure to pass an examination; or

(3)   To withhold the renewal of a license for any cause other than failure to pay a statutory renewal fee; or

(4)   To suspend a license; or

(5)   To revoke a license; or

(6)   To revoke or suspend a provisional license or an intern permit; or

(7)   To invoke any other disciplinary measures, censure, or probative terms against a licensee, a provisional licensee, or an intern,

such proceedings to be conducted in accordance with the provisions of Chapter 150B of the General Statutes of North Carolina.

(b)   In lieu of or as a part of such hearing and subsequent proceedings, the Board is authorized and empowered to enter any consent order relative to the discipline, censure, or probation of a licensee, provisional licensee, an intern, or an applicant for a license, or relative to the revocation or suspension of a license, provisional license, or intern permit.

(c)   Following the service of the notice of hearing as required by Chapter 150B of the General Statutes, the Board and the person upon whom such notice is served shall have the right to conduct adverse examinations, take depositions, and engage in such further discovery proceedings as are permitted by the laws of this State in civil matters. The Board is hereby authorized and empowered to issue such orders, commissions, notices, subpoenas, or other process as might be necessary or proper to effect the purposes of this subsection; provided, however, that no member of the Board shall be subject to examination hereunder. (1967, c. 451, s. 2; 1969, c. 804, s. 3; 1971, c. 755, s. 10; 1973, c. 1331, s. 3; 1987, c. 827, s. 1.)

§ 90-42. Restoration of revoked license.

Whenever any dentist has been deprived of his license, the North Carolina State Board of Dental Examiners, in its discretion, may restore said license upon due notice being given and hearing had, and satisfactory evidence produced of proper reformation of the licentiate, before restoration. (1935, c. 66, s. 14.)

§ 90-43. Compensation and expenses of Board.

Notwithstanding G.S. 93B-5(a), each member of the North Carolina State Board of Dental Examiners shall receive as compensation for his services in the performance of his duties under this Article a sum not exceeding one hundred dollars ($100.00) for each day actually engaged in the performance of the duties of his office, said per diem to be fixed by said Board, and all legitimate and necessary expenses incurred in attending meetings of the said Board.

The Board is authorized and empowered to expend from funds collected hereunder such additional sum or sums as it may determine necessary in the administration and enforcement of this Article, and employ such personnel as it may deem requisite to assist in carrying out the administrative functions required by this Article and by the Board. (1935, c. 66, s. 15; 1965, c. 163, s. 5; 1971, c. 755, s. 11; 1979, 2nd Sess., c. 1195, s. 9; 1989 (Reg. Sess., 1990), c. 892.)

§ 90-44. Annual report of Board.

Said Board shall, on or before the fifteenth day of February in each year, make an annual report as of the thirty-first day of December of the year preceding, of its proceedings, showing therein the examinations given, the fees received, the expenses incurred, the hearings conducted and the result thereof, which said report shall be filed with the Governor of the State of North Carolina. (1935, c. 66, s. 15.)

§ 90-45. Repealed by Session Laws 1967, c. 218, s. 4.

§ 90-46. Filling prescriptions.

Legally licensed druggists of this State may fill prescriptions of dentists duly licensed by the North Carolina State Board of Dental Examiners. (1935, c. 66, s. 17.)

§ 90-47. Repealed by Session Laws 1979, 2nd Sess., c. 1195, s. 13.

§ 90-48. Rules and regulations of Board; violation a misdemeanor.

The North Carolina State Board of Dental Examiners shall be and is hereby vested, as an agency of the State, with full power and authority to enact rules and regulations governing the practice of dentistry within the State, provided such rules and regulations are not inconsistent with the provisions of this Article. Such rules and regulations shall become effective 30 days after passage, and the same may be proven, as evidence, by the president and/or the secretary-treasurer of the Board, and/or by certified copy under the hand and official seal of the secretary-treasurer. A certified copy of any rule or regulation shall be receivable in all courts as prima facie evidence thereof if otherwise competent, and any person, firm, or corporation violating any such rule, regulation, or bylaw shall be guilty of a Class 2 misdemeanor, and each day that this section is violated shall be considered a separate offense.

The Board shall issue every two years to each licensed dentist a compilation or supplement of the Dental Practice Act and the Board rules and regulations, and upon written request therefor by such licensed dentist, a directory of dentists. (1935, c. 66, s. 19; 1957, c. 592, s. 6; 1971, c. 755, s. 12; 1993, c. 539, s. 620; 1994, Ex. Sess., c. 24, s. 14(c).)

§ 90-48.1. Free choice by patient guaranteed.

No agency of the State, county or municipality, nor any commission or clinic, nor any board administering relief, social security, health insurance or health service under the laws of the State of North Carolina shall deny to the recipients or beneficiaries of their aid or services the freedom to choose a duly licensed dentist as the provider of care or services which are within the scope of practice of the profession of dentistry as defined in this Chapter. (1965, c. 1169, s. 3.)

§ 90-48.2. Board agreements with special peer review organizations for impaired dentists.

(a) The State Board of Dental Examiners may, under rules adopted by the Board in compliance with Chapter 150B of the General Statutes, enter into agreements with special impaired dentist peer review organizations formed by the North Carolina Dental Society. The organizations shall be made up of Dental Society members designated by the Society, the Board, and the Dental School of the University of North Carolina. Peer review activities to be covered by such agreements shall include investigation, review and evaluation of records, reports, complaints, litigation, and other information about the practices and practice patterns of dentists licensed by the Board, as such matters may relate to impaired dentists. Special impaired dentist peer review organizations may include a statewide supervisory committee and various regional and local components or subgroups. The statewide supervisory committee shall consist of representatives from the North Carolina Dental Society, the UNC School of Dentistry, and the Board. When the statewide supervisory committee considers activities and programs that relate to impaired dental hygienists pursuant to G.S. 90-48.3, its membership shall be expanded to include two dental hygienists appointed upon the recommendation of the dental hygienist member of the Board.

(b) Agreements authorized under this section shall include provisions for the impaired dentist peer review organizations to receive relevant information from the Board and other sources, conduct any investigation, review, and evaluation in an expeditious manner, provide assurance of confidentiality of nonpublic information and of the peer review process, make reports of investigations and evaluations to the Board, and to do other related activities for operating and promoting a coordinated and effective peer review process. The agreements shall include provisions assuring basic due process for dentists that become involved.

(c) The impaired dentist peer review organizations that enter into agreements with the Board shall establish and maintain a program for impaired dentists licensed by the Board for the purpose of identifying, reviewing and evaluating the ability of those dentists to function as dentists, and to provide programs for treatment and rehabilitation. The Board may provide funds for the administration of these impaired dentist peer review programs. The Board shall adopt rules to apply to the operation of impaired dentist peer review programs, with provisions for: definitions of impairment; guidelines for program elements; procedures for receipt and use of information of suspected impairment; procedures for intervention and referral; arrangements for monitoring treatment, rehabilitation, posttreatment support and performance; reports of individual cases to the Board; periodic reporting of statistical information; and assurance of confidentiality of nonpublic information and of the peer review process.

(d) Upon investigation and review of a dentist licensed by the Board, or upon receipt of a complaint or other information, an impaired dentist peer review organization that enters into a peer review agreement with the Board shall report immediately to the Board detailed information about any dentist licensed by the Board, if:

(1) The dentist constitutes an imminent danger to the public or himself;

(2) The dentist refuses to cooperate with the program, refuses to submit to treatment, or is still impaired after treatment and exhibits professional incompetence; or

(3) It reasonably appears that there are other grounds for disciplinary action.

(e) Impaired dentist peer review organizations operating pursuant to this section shall have the same protections and responsibilities as traditional State and local dental society peer review committees under Article 2A of this Chapter. In addition, any confidential patient information and other nonpublic information acquired, created, or used in good faith by an impaired dentist peer review organization pursuant to this section shall remain confidential and shall not be subject to discovery or subpoena in a civil case. No person participating in good faith in an impaired dentist peer review program developed under this section shall be required in a civil case to disclose any information (including opinions, recommendations, or evaluations) acquired or developed solely in the course of participating in the program.

(f) Impaired dentist peer review activities conducted in good faith pursuant to any program developed under this section shall not be grounds for civil action under the laws of this State, and the activities are deemed to be State directed and sanctioned and shall constitute "State action" for the purposes of application of antitrust laws. (1993, c. 420, s. 2; 1999-382, s. 4.)

§ 90-48.3. Board authority to include impaired dental hygienists in programs developed for impaired dentists.

The Board may enter into agreements with special impaired dentist peer review organizations to include programs for impaired dental hygienists, and the provisions of G.S. 90-48.2 shall apply to any such agreements and programs. Special impaired dentist peer review organizations shall have the authority to appoint to the organizations, upon the recommendation of the dental hygienist member of the Board, one additional member who is a licensed dental hygienist and the member shall participate in activities and programs as they relate to impaired dental hygienists. Peer liaisons and volunteers participating in programs for impaired dental hygienists shall be dental hygienists. Dental hygienists who work with special impaired dentist peer review organizations in conducting programs for impaired dental hygienists shall have the same protections and responsibilities as members of traditional State and local dental society peer review committees under Article 2A of this Chapter and as provided in G.S. 90-48.2. The provisions of G.S. 90-48.2 regarding confidentiality shall also be applicable to all dental hygienist activities authorized under this section. (1999-382, s. 1.)

§§ 90-48.4 through 90-48.6. Reserved for future codification purposes.

Article 2A.

Dental Peer Review Protection Act.

§ 90-48.7. Title.

General Statutes 90-48.7 through G.S. 90-48.11 may be cited as the "Dental Peer Review Protection Act." (1979, 2nd Sess., c. 1192, s. 1.)

§ 90-48.8. Immunity of a member.

No member of a dental peer review committee of a State or local dental society shall be held liable in damages to any person for any action taken or recommendation made within the scope of the functions of that committee, except with regard to Medicare and Medicaid charges or payments if the committee member acts without malice and in reasonable belief that the action or recommendation was warranted by the facts known to him after reasonable effort to obtain the facts of the matter as to which the action was taken or recommendation was made. (1979, 2nd Sess., c. 1192, s. 1.)

§ 90-48.9. Immunity of witnesses before dental peer review committee.

Notwithstanding any other provision of law, no person providing information to any dental peer review committee or organization shall be held, by reason of having provided such information, to have violated any criminal law, or to be civilly liable under any law unless:

(1)   The information is unrelated to the performance of the duty or function of the peer review committee or organization, or

(2)   The information is false, and the person providing the information knew, or had good reason to believe that the information was false. (1979, 2nd Sess., c. 1192, s. 1.)

§ 90-48.10. Confidentiality of review organization's proceedings and records.

The proceedings and records of a dental review committee except those concerning the investigation and consideration of Medicare and Medicaid charges or payments, shall be held in confidence and shall not be subject to discovery or introduction into evidence in any civil action arising out of the matters which are the subject of evaluation and review by the committee; and no person who was in attendance at a meeting of the committee shall be permitted or required to testify in any civil action as to any evidence or other matters produced or presented during the proceedings of the committee or as to any findings, recommendations, evaluations, opinions, or other actions of the committee or any members thereof, except with regard to Medicare and Medicaid charges or payments: Provided, however, that information, documents or records otherwise available from original sources are not to be construed as immune from discovery or use in any civil action merely because they were presented during proceedings of a committee, nor should any person who testifies before a committee or who is a member of a committee be prevented from testifying as to matters within his knowledge, but the witness shall not be asked about his testimony before a committee or opinions formed by him as a result of the committee hearings, except with regard to Medicare and Medicaid charges or payments. (1979, 2nd Sess., c. 1192, s. 1.)

§ 90-48.11. No limitation on previous privileges and immunities.

Nothing in this G.S. 90-48.7 through G.S. 90-48.11 shall be deemed to annul, abridge, or limit in any manner any privileges or immunities heretofore existing under the laws of this State. (1979, 2nd Sess., c. 1192, s. 1.)

Article 3.

The Licensing of Mouth Hygienists to Teach and Practice Mouth Hygiene in Public Institutions.

§§ 90-49 through 90-52. Repealed by Session Laws 1945, c. 639, s. 14.

Article 4.

Pharmacy.

Part 1. Practice of Pharmacy.

§§ 90-53 through 90-75. Recodified as §§ 90-85.2 to 90-85.26, 90-85.32 to 90-85.40.

§ 90-76. Repealed by Session Laws 1979, c. 1017, s. 1, effective January 1, 1980.

Part 1A. Drug Product Selection.

§§ 90-76.1 through 90-76.5: Recodified as §§ 90-85.27 to 90-85.31 pursuant to Session Laws 1981 (Regular Session, 1982), c. 1188, s. 3.

§ 90-76.6. Repealed by Session Laws 1981 (Regular Session, 1982), c. 1188, s. 4, effective July 1, 1982.

Part 2. Dealing in Specific Drugs Regulated.

§§ 90-77 through 90-80.1. Repealed by Session Laws 1981 (Regular Session, 1982), c. 1188, s. 5, effective July 1, 1982.

§§ 90-81 through 90-85. Repealed by Session Laws 1955, c. 1330, s. 8.

§ 90-85.1. Repealed by Session Laws 1981 (Regular Session, 1982), c. 1188, s.5.

Article 4A.

North Carolina Pharmacy Practice Act.

Part 1. North Carolina Pharmacy Practice Act.

§ 90-85.2. Legislative findings.

The General Assembly of North Carolina finds that mandatory licensure of all who engage in the practice of pharmacy is necessary to insure minimum standards of competency and to protect the public from those who might otherwise present a danger to the public health, safety and welfare. (1981 (Reg. Sess., 1982), c. 1188, s. 1.)

§ 90-85.3. Definitions.

(a)   "Administer" means the direct application of a drug to the body of a patient by injection, inhalation, ingestion or other means.

(b)   "Board" means the North Carolina Board of Pharmacy.

(b1)   "Certified pharmacy technician" means a pharmacy technician who (i) has passed a nationally recognized pharmacy technician certification board examination, or its equivalent, that has been approved by the Board and (ii) obtains and maintains certification from a nationally recognized pharmacy technician certification board that has been approved by the Board.

(b2)   "Clinical pharmacist practitioner" means a licensed pharmacist who meets the guidelines and criteria for such title established by the joint subcommittee of the North Carolina Medical Board and the North Carolina Board of Pharmacy and is authorized to enter into drug therapy management agreements with physicians in accordance with the provisions of G.S. 90-18.4.

(c)   "Compounding" means taking two or more ingredients and combining them into a dosage form of a drug, exclusive of compounding by a drug manufacturer, distributor, or packer.

(d)   "Deliver" means the actual, constructive or attempted transfer of a drug, a device, or medical equipment from one person to another.

(e) "Device" means an instrument, apparatus, implement, machine, contrivance, implant, in vitro reagent or other similar or related article including any component part or accessory, whose label or labeling bears the statement "Caution: federal law requires dispensing by or on the order of a physician." The term does not include:

(1) Devices used in the normal course of treating patients by health care facilities and agencies licensed under Chapter 131E or Article 2 of Chapter 122C of the General Statutes;

(2) Devices used or provided in the treatment of patients by medical doctors, dentists, physical therapists, occupational therapists, speech pathologists, optometrists, chiropractors, podiatrists, and nurses licensed under Chapter 90 of the General Statutes, provided they do not dispense devices used to administer or dispense drugs.

(f) "Dispense" means preparing and packaging a prescription drug or device in a container and labeling the container with information required by State and federal law. Filling or refilling drug containers with prescription drugs for subsequent use by a patient is "dispensing". Providing quantities of unit dose prescription drugs for subsequent administration is "dispensing".

(g) "Drug" means:

(1) Any article recognized as a drug in the United States Pharmacopeia, or in any other drug compendium or any supplement thereto, or an article recognized as a drug by the United States Food and Drug Administration;

(2) Any article, other than food or devices, intended for use in the diagnosis, cure, mitigation, treatment or prevention of disease in man or other animals;

(3) Any article, other than food or devices, intended to affect the structure or any function of the body of man or other animals; and

(4) Any article intended for use as a component of any articles specified in clause (1), (2) or (3) of this subsection.

(h) "Emancipated minor" means any person under the age of 18 who is or has been married or who is or has been a parent; or whose parents or guardians have surrendered their rights to the minor's services and earnings as well as their right to custody and control of the minor's person; or who has been emancipated by an appropriate court order.

(i) "Health care provider" means any licensed health care professional; any agent or employee of any health care institution, health care insurer, health care professional school; or a member of any allied health profession.

(i1) "Immunizing pharmacist" means a licensed pharmacist who meets all of the following qualifications:

(1) Holds a current provider level cardiopulmonary resuscitation certification issued by the American Heart Association or the American Red Cross, or an equivalent certification.

(2) Has successfully completed a certificate program in vaccine administration accredited by the Centers for Disease Control and Prevention, the Accreditation Council for Pharmacy Education, or a similar health authority or professional body approved by the Board.

(3) Maintains documentation of three hours of continuing education every two years, designed to maintain competency in the disease states, drugs, and vaccine administration.

(4) Has successfully completed training approved by the Division of Public Health's Immunization Branch for participation in the North Carolina Immunization Registry.

(5) Has notified the North Carolina Board of Pharmacy and the North Carolina Medical Board of immunizing pharmacist status.

(6) Administers vaccines or immunizations in accordance with G.S. 90-18.15B.

(j) "Label" means a display of written, printed or graphic matter upon the immediate or outside container of any drug.

(k) "Labeling" means preparing and affixing a label to any drug container, exclusive of labeling by a manufacturer, packer or distributor of a nonprescription drug or a commercially packaged prescription drug or device.

(l) "License" means a license to practice pharmacy including a renewal license issued by the Board.

(l1) "Medical equipment" means any of the following items that are intended for use by the consumer in the consumer's place of residence:

(1) A device.

(2) Ambulation assistance equipment.

(3) Mobility equipment.

(4) Rehabilitation seating.

(5) Oxygen and respiratory care equipment.

(6) Rehabilitation environmental control equipment.

(7) Diagnostic equipment.

(8) A bed prescribed by a physician to treat or alleviate a medical condition.

The term "medical equipment" does not include (i) medical equipment used or dispensed in the normal course of treating patients by or on behalf of home care agencies, hospitals, and nursing facilities licensed under Chapter 131E of the General Statutes or hospitals or agencies licensed under Article 2 of Chapter 122C of the General Statutes; (ii) medical equipment used or dispensed by professionals licensed under Chapters 90 or 93D of the General Statutes, provided the professional is practicing within the scope of that professional's practice act; (iii) upper and lower extremity prosthetics and related orthotics; or (iv) canes, crutches, walkers, and bathtub grab bars.

(l2) "Mobile pharmacy" means a pharmacy that meets all of the following conditions:

(1) Is either self-propelled or moveable by another vehicle that is self-propelled.

(2) Is operated by a nonprofit corporation.

(3) Dispenses prescription drugs at no charge or at a reduced charge to persons whose family income is less than two hundred percent (200%) of the federal poverty level and who do not receive reimbursement for the cost of the dispensed prescription drugs from Medicare, Medicaid, a private insurance company, or a governmental unit.

(m) "Permit" means a permit to operate a pharmacy, deliver medical equipment, or dispense devices, including a renewal license issued by the Board.

(n) "Person" means an individual, corporation, partnership, association, unit of government, or other legal entity.

(o) "Person in loco parentis" means the person who has assumed parental responsibilities for a child.

(p) "Pharmacist" means a person licensed under this Article to practice pharmacy.

(q) "Pharmacy" means any place where prescription drugs are dispensed or compounded.

(q1) "Pharmacy personnel" means pharmacists and pharmacy technicians.

(q2) "Pharmacy technician" means a person who may, under the supervision of a pharmacist, perform technical functions to assist the pharmacist in preparing and dispensing prescription medications.

(r) "Practice of pharmacy" is as specified in G.S. 90-85.3A.

(s) "Prescription drug" means a drug that under federal law is required, prior to being dispensed or delivered, to be labeled with the following statement:

"Caution: Federal law prohibits dispensing without prescription."

(t) "Prescription order" means a written or verbal order for a prescription drug, prescription device, or pharmaceutical service from a person authorized by law to prescribe such drug, device, or service. A prescription order includes an order entered in a chart or other medical record of a patient.

(u) "Unit dose medication system" means a system in which each dose of medication is individually packaged in a properly sealed and properly labeled container. (1981 (Reg. Sess., 1982), c. 1188, s. 1; 1983, c. 196, ss. 1-3; 1991, c. 578, s. 1; 1993 (Reg. Sess., 1994), c. 692, s. 2; 1995, c. 94, s. 24; 1999-246, s. 1; 1999-290, ss. 4, 5; 2001-375, s. 1; 2002-159, s. 37; 2013-246, ss. 1, 2; 2013-379, s. 1.)

§ 90-85.3A. Practice of pharmacy.

(a) A pharmacist is responsible for interpreting and evaluating drug orders, including prescription orders; compounding, dispensing, and labeling prescription drugs and devices; properly and safely storing drugs and devices; maintaining proper records; and controlling pharmacy goods and services.

(b) A pharmacist may advise and educate patients and health care providers concerning therapeutic values, content, uses, and significant problems of drugs and devices; assess, record, and report adverse drug and device reactions; take and record patient histories relating to drug and device therapy; monitor, record, and report drug therapy and device usage; perform drug utilization reviews; and participate in drug and drug source selection and device and device source selection as provided in G.S. 90-85.27 through G.S. 90-85.31.

(c) An immunizing pharmacist is authorized and permitted to administer drugs as provided in G.S. 90-85.15B, and in accordance with rules adopted by each of the Board of Pharmacy, the Board of Nursing, and the North Carolina Medical Board. These rules shall be designed to ensure the safety and health of the patients for whom such drugs are administered.

(d) An approved clinical pharmacist practitioner may collaborate with physicians in determining the appropriate health care for a patient subject to the provisions of G.S. 90-18.4. (2013-246, s. 3.)

§ 90-85.4. North Carolina Pharmaceutical Association.

The North Carolina Pharmaceutical Association, and the persons composing it, shall continue to be a body politic and corporate under the name and style of the

North Carolina Pharmaceutical Association, and by that name have the right to sue and be sued, to plead and be impleaded, to purchase and hold real estate and grant the same, to have and to use a common seal, and to do any other things and perform any other acts as appertain to bodies corporate and politic not inconsistent with the Constitution and laws of the State. (1881, c. 355, s. 1; Code, s. 3135; Rev., s. 4471; C.S., s. 6650; 1981 (Reg. Sess., 1982), c. 1188, s. 1.)

§ 90-85.5. Objective of Pharmaceutical Association.

The objective of the Association is to unite the pharmacists of this State for mutual aid, encouragement, and improvement; to encourage scientific research, develop pharmaceutical talent and to elevate the standard of professional thought. (1881, c. 355, s. 2; Code, s. 3136; Rev., s. 4472; C.S., s. 6651; 1981 (Reg. Sess., 1982), c. 1188, s. 1; 1991, c. 125, s. 1.)

§ 90-85.6. Board of Pharmacy; creation; membership; qualification of members.

(a)   Creation. - The responsibility for enforcing the provisions of this Article and the laws pertaining to the distribution and use of drugs is vested in the Board. The Board shall adopt reasonable rules for the performance of its duties. The Board shall have all of the duties, powers and authorities specifically granted by and necessary for the enforcement of this Article, as well as any other duties, powers and authorities that may be granted from time to time by other appropriate statutes. The Board may establish a program for the purpose of aiding in the recovery and rehabilitation of pharmacists who have become addicted to controlled substances or alcohol, and the Board may use money collected as fees to fund such a program.

(b)   Membership. - The Board shall consist of six members, one of whom shall be a representative of the public, and the remainder of whom shall be pharmacists.

(c)   Qualifications. - The public member of the Board shall not be a health care provider or the spouse of a health care provider. He shall not be enrolled in a program to prepare him to be a health care provider. The public member of the Board shall be a resident of this State at the time of his appointment and while serving as a Board member. The pharmacist members of the Board shall be residents of this State at the time of their appointment and while serving as Board members. (1905, c. 108, ss. 5-7, 9; Rev., ss. 4473, 4475; 1907, c. 113, s. 1; C.S., ss. 6652, 6654; 1945, c. 572, s. 1; 1981, c. 717, s. 1; 1981 (Reg. Sess., 1982), c. 1188, s. 1; 1997-177, s. 1.)

§ 90-85.7. Board of Pharmacy; selection; vacancies; commission; term; per diem; removal.

(a) The Board of Pharmacy shall consist of six persons. Five of the members shall be licensed as pharmacists within this State and shall be elected and commissioned by the Governor as hereinafter provided. Pharmacist members shall be chosen in an election held as hereinafter provided in which every person licensed to practice pharmacy in North Carolina and residing in North Carolina shall be entitled to vote. Each pharmacist member of said Board shall be elected for a term of five years and until his successor shall be elected and shall qualify. Members chosen by election under this section shall be elected upon the expiration of the respective terms of the members of the present Board of Pharmacy. No pharmacist shall be nominated for membership on said Board, or shall be elected to membership on said Board, unless, at the time of such nomination, and at the time of such election, he is licensed to practice pharmacy in North Carolina. In case of death, resignation or removal from the State of any pharmacist member of said Board, the pharmacist members of the Board shall elect in his place a pharmacist who meets the criteria set forth in this section to fill the unexpired term.

One member of the Board shall be a person who is not a pharmacist and who represents the interest of the public at large. The Governor shall appoint this member.

All Board members serving on June 30, 1989, shall be eligible to complete their respective terms. No member appointed or elected to a term on or after July 1, 1989, shall serve more than two complete consecutive five-year terms. The Governor may remove any member appointed by him for good cause shown and may appoint persons to fill unexpired terms of members appointed by him.

It shall be the duty of a member of the Board of Pharmacy, within 10 days after receipt of notification of his appointment and commission, to appear before the clerk of the superior court of the county in which he resides and take and subscribe an oath to properly and faithfully discharge the duties of his office according to law.

(b) All nominations and elections of pharmacist members of the Board shall be conducted by the Board of Pharmacy, which is hereby constituted a Board of Pharmacy Elections. Every pharmacist with a current North Carolina license residing in this State shall be eligible to vote in all elections. The list of pharmacists shall constitute the registration list for elections. The Board of Pharmacy Elections is authorized to make rules and regulations relative to the conduct of these elections, provided such rules and regulations are not in conflict with the provisions of this section and provided that notice shall be given to all pharmacists residing in North Carolina. All such rules and regulations shall be adopted subject to the procedures of Chapter 150B of the General Statutes of North Carolina. From any decision of the Board of Pharmacy Elections relative to the conduct of such elections, appeal may be taken to the courts in the manner otherwise provided by Chapter 150B of the General Statutes.

(c) All rules, regulations, and bylaws of the North Carolina Board of Pharmacy so far as they are not inconsistent with the provisions of this Article, shall continue in effect.

(d) Notwithstanding G.S. 93B-5, Board members shall receive as compensation for their services per diem not to exceed one hundred dollars ($100.00) for each day during which they are engaged in the official business of the Board. (1905, c. 108, ss. 5-7; Rev., s. 4473; C.S., s. 6652; 1981, c. 717, s. 1; 1981 (Reg. Sess., 1982), c. 1188, s. 1; 1983, c. 196, s. 4; 1989, c. 118; 1989 (Reg. Sess., 1990), c. 825.)

§ 90-85.8. Organization.

The Board shall elect from its members a president, vice-president, and other officers as it deems necessary. The officers shall serve one-year terms and until their successors have been elected and qualified. (1905, c. 108, s. 8; Rev., s. 4474; C.S., s. 6653; 1923, c. 82; 1981 (Reg. Sess., 1982), c. 1188, s. 1.)

§ 90-85.9. Meetings.

The Board shall meet at least twice annually for the purpose of administering examinations and conducting other business. Four Board members constitute a quorum. The Board shall keep a record of its proceedings, a register of all licensed persons, and a register of all persons to whom permits have been issued. The Board shall report, in writing, annually to the Governor and the presiding officer of each house of the General Assembly. (1905, c. 108, s. 8; Rev., s. 4474; C.S., s. 6653; 1923, c. 82; 1981 (Reg. Sess., 1982), c. 1188, s. 1.)

§ 90-85.10. Employees; Executive Director.

The Board shall employ as Executive Director a pharmacist to serve as a full-time employee of the Board. The Executive Director shall serve as secretary and treasurer of the Board and shall perform administrative functions as authorized by the Board. The Board shall have the authority to employ other personnel as it may deem necessary to carry out the requirements of this Article. (1905, c. 108, s. 9; Rev., s. 4475; 1907, c. 113, s. 1; C.S., s. 6654; 1945, c. 572, s. 1; 1981 (Reg. Sess., 1982), c. 1188, s. 1.)

§ 90-85.11. Compensation of employees.

The Board shall determine the compensation of its employees. Employees shall be reimbursed for all necessary expenses incurred in the performance of their official duties. (1981 (Reg. Sess., 1982), c. 1188, s. 1.)

§ 90-85.11A. Acquisition of real property; equipment; liability insurance.

(a) The Board shall have the power to acquire, hold, rent, encumber, alienate, and otherwise deal with real property in the same manner as a private person or corporation, subject only to approval of the Governor and the Council of State. Collateral pledged by the Board for an encumbrance is limited to the assets, income, and revenues of the Board.

(b) The Board may purchase, rent, or lease equipment and supplies and purchase liability insurance or other insurance to cover the activities of the Board, its operations, or its employees. (2001-407, s. 1.)

§ 90-85.12. Executive Director to make investigations and prosecute.

(a) Upon receiving information concerning a violation of this Article that is a threat to the public safety, health, or welfare, the Executive Director shall promptly conduct an investigation, and if he finds evidence of the violation, he may file a complaint and prosecute the offender in a Board hearing. If the Executive Director receives information concerning a violation of this Article that does not pose a threat to the public safety, health, or welfare, the Executive Director may conduct an investigation, and if he finds evidence of the violation, he may file a complaint and prosecute the offender in a Board hearing.

(b) In all prosecutions of unlicensed persons for the violation of any of the provisions of this Article, a certificate signed under oath by the Executive Director shall be competent and admissible evidence in any court of this State that the person is not licensed, as required by law. (1905, c. 108, s. 11; Rev., s. 4477; C.S., s. 6656; 1923, c. 74, s. 1; 1981 (Reg. Sess., 1982), c. 1188, s. 1; 2005-402, s. 1.2.)

§ 90-85.13. Approval of schools and colleges of pharmacy.

The Board shall approve schools and colleges of pharmacy upon a finding that students successfully completing the course of study offered by the school or college can reasonably be expected to practice pharmacy safely and properly. (1981 (Reg. Sess., 1982), c. 1188, s. 1.)

§ 90-85.14. Practical experience program.

The Board shall issue regulations governing a practical experience program. These regulations shall assure that the person successfully completing the program will have gained practical experience that will enable him to safely and properly practice pharmacy. (1981 (Reg. Sess., 1982), c. 1188, s. 1.)

§ 90-85.15. Application and examination for licensure as a pharmacist; prerequisites.

(a) Any person who desires to be licensed as a pharmacist shall file an application with the Executive Director on the form furnished by the Board, verified under oath, setting forth the applicant's name, age, the place at which and the time that he has spent in the study of pharmacy, and his experience in compounding and dispensing prescriptions under the supervision of a pharmacist. The applicant shall also appear at a time and place designated by the Board and submit to an examination as to his qualifications for being licensed. The applicant must demonstrate to the Board his physical and mental competency to practice pharmacy.

(b) On or after July 1, 1982, all applicants shall have received an undergraduate degree from a school of pharmacy approved by the Board. Applicants shall be required to have had up to one year of experience, approved by the Board, under the supervision of a pharmacist and shall pass the required examination offered by the Board. Upon completing these requirements and upon paying the required fee, the applicant shall be licensed.

(c) The Department of Justice may provide a criminal record check to the Board for a person who has applied for a license through the Board. The Board shall provide to the Department of Justice, along with the request, the fingerprints of the applicant, any additional information required by the Department of Justice, and a form signed by the applicant consenting to the check of the criminal record and to the use of the fingerprints and other identifying information required by the State or national repositories. The applicant's fingerprints shall be forwarded to the State Bureau of Investigation for a search of the State's criminal history record file, and the State Bureau of Investigation shall forward a set of the fingerprints to the Federal Bureau of Investigation for a national criminal history check. The Board shall keep all information pursuant to this subsection privileged, in accordance with applicable State law and federal guidelines, and the information shall be confidential and shall not be a public record under Chapter 132 of the General Statutes.

The Department of Justice may charge each applicant a fee for conducting the checks of criminal history records authorized by this subsection. (1905, c. 108, s. 13; Rev., ss. 4479, 4480; 1915, c. 165; C.S., s. 6658; 1921, c. 52; 1933, c.

206, ss. 1, 2; 1935, c. 181; 1937, c. 94; 1971, c. 481; 1981, c. 717, s. 4; 1981 (Reg. Sess., 1982), c. 1188, s. 1; 1983, c. 196, s. 5; 2002-147, s. 8.)

§ 90-85.15A. Pharmacy technicians.

(a) Registration, Generally. - A registration program for pharmacy technicians is established for the purposes of identifying those persons who are employed or are eligible for employment as pharmacy technicians. The Board must maintain a registry of pharmacy technicians that contains the name of each pharmacy technician, the name and location of a pharmacy in which the pharmacy technician works, the pharmacist-manager who employs the pharmacy technician, and the dates of that employment.

(a1) Registration of Noncertified Pharmacy Technicians. - The Board must register a pharmacy technician who pays the fee required under G.S. 90-85.24, is employed by a pharmacy holding a valid permit under this Article, and completes a required training program provided by the supervising pharmacist-manager as specified in subsection (b) of this section. A pharmacy technician must register with the Board within 30 days after the date the pharmacy technician completes a training program provided by the supervising pharmacist-manager. The registration must be renewed annually by paying a registration fee.

(a2) Registration of Certified Pharmacy Technicians. - The Board must register a certified pharmacy technician who pays the fee required under G.S. 90-85.24 and provides proof of current certification. The registration must be renewed annually by paying a registration fee and providing proof of current certification.

(b) Responsibilities of Pharmacist-Manager to Noncertified Pharmacy Technicians. - A pharmacist-manager may hire a person who has a high school diploma or equivalent or is currently enrolled in a program that awards a high school diploma or equivalent to work as a pharmacy technician. Pursuant to G.S. 90-85.21, a pharmacist-manager must notify the Board within 21 days of the date the pharmacy technician began employment. The pharmacist-manager must provide a training program for a pharmacy technician that includes pharmacy terminology, pharmacy calculations, dispensing systems and labeling requirements, pharmacy laws and regulations, record keeping and documentation, and the proper handling and storage of medications. The requirements of a training program may differ depending upon the type of employment. The training program must be provided and completed within 180 days of the date the pharmacy technician began employment.

(b1)   Responsibilities of Pharmacist-Manager to Certified Pharmacy Technicians. - A pharmacist-manager may hire a certified pharmacy technician who has registered with the Board pursuant to subsection (a2) of this section. Pursuant to G.S. 90-85.21, a certified pharmacy technician shall notify the Board within 10 days of beginning employment as a pharmacy technician. The supervising pharmacist-manager and certified pharmacy technician shall be deemed to have satisfied the pharmacy technician training program requirements of subsection (b) of this section.

(c)   Supervision. - A pharmacist may not supervise more than two pharmacy technicians unless the pharmacist-manager receives written approval from the Board. The Board may not allow a pharmacist to supervise more than two pharmacy technicians unless the additional pharmacy technicians are certified pharmacy technicians. The Board must respond to a request from a pharmacist-manager to allow a pharmacist to supervise more than two pharmacy technicians within 60 days of the date it received the request. The Board must respond to the request in one of three ways:

(1)   Approval of the request.

(2)   Approval of the request as amended by the Board.

(3)   Disapproval of the request. A disapproval of a request must include a reasonable explanation of why the request was not approved.

(d)   Disciplinary Action. - The Board may, in accordance with Chapter 150B of the General Statutes and rules adopted by the Board, issue a letter of reprimand or suspend, restrict, revoke, or refuse to grant or renew the registration of a pharmacy technician if the pharmacy technician has done one or more of the following:

(1)   Made false representations or withheld material information in connection with registering as a pharmacy technician.

(2)   Been found guilty of or plead guilty or nolo contendere to a felony involving the use or distribution of drugs.

(3) Indulged in the use of drugs to an extent that it renders the pharmacy technician unfit to assist a pharmacist in preparing and dispensing prescription medications.

(4) Developed a physical or mental disability that renders the pharmacy technician unfit to assist a pharmacist in preparing and dispensing prescription medications.

(4a) Been negligent in assisting a pharmacist in preparing and dispensing prescription medications.

(5) Failed to comply with the laws governing pharmacy technicians, including any provision of this Article or rules adopted by the Board governing pharmacy technicians.

(e) Exemption. - This section does not apply to pharmacy students who are enrolled in a school of pharmacy approved by the Board under G.S. 90-85.13.

(f) Rule-Making Authority. - The Board may adopt rules necessary to implement this section. (2001-375, s. 2; 2013-379, s. 2.)

§ 90-85.15B. Immunizing pharmacists.

(a) Except as provided in subsection (b) and (c) of this section, an immunizing pharmacist may administer vaccinations or immunizations only if the vaccinations or immunizations are recommended or required by the Centers for Disease Control and Prevention and administered to persons at least 18 years of age pursuant to a specific prescription order.

(b) An immunizing pharmacist may administer the vaccinations or immunizations listed in subdivisions (1) through (5) of this subsection to persons at least 18 years of age if the vaccinations or immunizations are administered under written protocols as defined in 21 NCAC 46 .2507(b)(12) and 21 NCAC 32U .0101(b)(12) and in accordance with the supervising physician's responsibilities as defined in 21 NCAC 46 .2507(e) and 21 NCAC 32U .0101(e), and the physician is licensed in and has a practice physically located in North Carolina:

(1) Pneumococcal polysaccharide or pneumococcal conjugate vaccines.

(2)   Herpes zoster vaccine.

(3)   Hepatitis B vaccine.

(4)   Meningococcal polysaccharide or meningococcal conjugate vaccines.

(5)   Tetanus-diphtheria, tetanus and diphtheria toxoids and pertussis, tetanus and diphtheria toxoids and acellular pertussis, or tetanus toxoid vaccines. However, a pharmacist shall not administer any of these vaccines if the patient discloses that the patient has an open wound, puncture, or tissue tear.

(c)   An immunizing pharmacist may administer the influenza vaccine to persons at least 14 years of age pursuant to 21 NCAC 46 .2507 and 21 NCAC 32U .0101.

(d)   An immunizing pharmacist who administers a vaccine or immunization to any patient pursuant to this section shall do all of the following:

(1)   Maintain a record of any vaccine or immunization administered to the patient in a patient profile.

(2)   Within 72 hours after administration of the vaccine or immunization, notify any primary care provider identified by the patient. If the patient does not identify a primary care provider, the immunizing pharmacist shall direct the patient to information describing the benefits to a patient of having a primary care physician, prepared by any of the following: North Carolina Medical Board, North Carolina Academy of Family Physicians, North Carolina Medical Society, or Community Care of North Carolina.

(3)   Except for influenza vaccines administered under G.S. 90-85.15B(b)(6), access the North Carolina Immunization Registry prior to administering the vaccine or immunization and record any vaccine or immunization administered to the patient in the registry within 72 hours after the administration. In the event the registry is not operable, an immunizing pharmacist shall report as soon as reasonably possible. (2013-246, s. 4.)

§ 90-85.16. Examination.

The license examination shall be given by the Board at least twice each year. The Board shall determine the subject matter of each examination and the place, time and date for administering the examination. The Board shall also determine which persons have passed the examination. The examination shall be designed to determine which applicants can reasonably be expected to safely and properly practice pharmacy. (1905, c. 108, s. 13; Rev., ss. 4479, 4480; 1915, c. 165; C.S., s. 6658; 1921, c. 52; 1933, c. 206, ss. 1, 2; 1935, c. 181; 1937, c. 94; 1971, c. 481; 1981, c. 717, s. 4; 1981 (Reg. Sess., 1982), c. 1188, s. 1.)

§ 90-85.17. License renewal.

In accordance with Board regulations, each license to practice pharmacy shall expire on December 31 and shall be renewed annually by filing with the Board on or after December 1 an application for license renewal furnished by the Board, accompanied by the required fee. It shall be unlawful to practice pharmacy more than 60 days after the expiration date without renewing the license. All licensees shall give the Board notice of a change of mailing address or a change of place of employment within 30 days after the change. The Board may require licensees to obtain up to 30 hours of continuing education every two years from Board-approved providers as a condition of license renewal, with a minimum of 10 hours required per year. (1905, c. 108, ss. 18, 19, 27; Rev., ss. 3653, 4484; 1911, c. 48; C.S., s. 6662; 1921, c. 68, s. 2; 1947, c. 781; 1953, c. 1051; 1981 (Reg. Sess., 1982), c. 1188, s. 1; 2005-402, s. 4.)

§ 90-85.18. Approval of continuing education programs.

The Board shall approve providers of continuing education programs upon finding that the provider is competent to and does offer an educational experience designed to enable those who successfully complete the program to more safely and properly practice pharmacy. (1981 (Reg. Sess., 1982), c. 1188, s. 1.)

§ 90-85.19. Reinstatement.

Whenever a pharmacist who has not renewed his license for five or more years seeks to renew or reinstate his license, he must appear before the Board and submit evidence that he can safely and properly practice pharmacy. (1981 (Reg. Sess., 1982), c. 1188, s. 1.)

§ 90-85.20. Licensure without examination.

(a) The Board may issue a license to practice pharmacy, without examination, to any person who is licensed as a pharmacist in another jurisdiction if the applicant shall present satisfactory evidence of possessing the same qualifications as are required of licensees in this State, that he was licensed by examination in such other jurisdiction, and that the standard of competence required by such other jurisdiction is substantially equivalent to that of this State at that time. The Board must be satisfied that a candidate for licensure has a satisfactory understanding of the laws governing the practice of pharmacy and distribution of drugs in this State.

(b) Repealed by Session Laws 1991, c. 125, s. 2. (1905, c. 108, s. 16; Rev., s. 4482; C.S., s. 6660; 1945, c. 572, s. 2; 1971, c. 468; 1977, c. 598; 1981, c. 717, ss. 6, 7; 1981 (Reg. Sess., 1982), c. 1188, s. 1; 1983, c. 196, ss. 6, 7; 1991, c. 125, s. 2.)

§ 90-85.21. Pharmacy permit.

(a) In accordance with Board regulations, each pharmacy in North Carolina shall annually register with the Board on a form provided by the Board. The application shall identify the pharmacist-manager of the pharmacy and all pharmacy personnel employed in the pharmacy. All pharmacist-managers shall notify the Board of any change in pharmacy personnel within 30 days of the change. In addition to identifying the pharmacist-manager, a pharmacy may identify a pharmacy permittee's designated agent that the Board shall notify of any investigation of the pharmacy or a pharmacist employed by the pharmacy. The notice shall include the specific reason for the investigation and be given prior to the initiation of any disciplinary proceedings.

(a1) A mobile pharmacy shall register annually with the Board in the manner prescribed in subsection (a) of this section, and the registration shall be renewed annually. A mobile pharmacy shall be considered a single pharmacy and shall not be required to pay a separate registration fee for each location but shall pay the annual registration fee prescribed in G.S. 90-85.24. A mobile pharmacy shall provide the Board with the address of every location from which prescription drugs will be dispensed by the mobile pharmacy.

(b) Each physician who dispenses prescription drugs, for a fee or other charge, shall annually register with the Board on the form provided by the Board, and with the licensing board having jurisdiction over the physician. Such dispensing shall comply in all respects with the relevant laws and regulations that apply to pharmacists governing the distribution of drugs, including packaging, labeling, and record keeping. Authority and responsibility for disciplining physicians who fail to comply with the provisions of this subsection are vested in the licensing board having jurisdiction over the physician. The form provided by the Board under this subsection shall be as follows:

Application For Registration

With The Pharmacy Board

As A Dispensing Physician

1.	2.
Name and Address of Dispensing Physician	Affix Dispensing Label Here

3. Physician's North Carolina License Number
_____

4. Are you currently practicing in a professional association registered with the North Carolina Medical Board?

_____ Yes _____ No. If yes, enter the name and registration number of the professional corporation:

_____
_____

_____
_____

5. I certify that the information is correct and complete.

_____   _____
Signature   Date

(1927, c. 28, s. 1; 1953, c. 183, s. 2; 1981 (Reg. Sess., 1982), c. 1188, s. 1; 1987, c. 687; 1995, c. 94, s. 25; 1999-246, s. 2; 2001-375, s. 3; 2005-427, s. 1.)

§ 90-85.21A. Applicability to out-of-state operations.

(a) Any pharmacy operating outside the State which ships, mails, or delivers in any manner a dispensed legend drug into this State shall annually register with the Board on a form provided by the Board. In order to satisfy the registration requirements of this subsection, a pharmacy shall certify that the pharmacy employs a pharmacist who is responsible for dispensing, shipping, mailing, or delivering dispensed legend drugs into this State or in a state approved by the Board and has met requirements for licensure equivalent to the requirements for licensure in this State. In order for the pharmacy's certification of the pharmacists to be valid, a pharmacist shall agree in writing, on a form approved by the Board, to be subject to the jurisdiction of the Board, the provisions of this Article, and the rules adopted by the Board. If the Board revokes this certification, the pharmacy shall no longer have authority to dispense, ship, mail, or deliver in any manner a dispensed legend drug into this State.

(b) Any pharmacy subject to this section shall at all times maintain a valid unexpired license, permit, or registration necessary to conduct such pharmacy in compliance with the laws of the state in which such pharmacy is located. No pharmacy operating outside the State may ship, mail, or deliver in any manner a dispensed legend drug into this State unless such drug is lawfully dispensed by a licensed pharmacist in the state where the pharmacy is located.

(c) The Board shall be entitled to charge and collect not more than five hundred dollars ($500.00) for original registration of a pharmacy under this section, and for renewal thereof, not more than two hundred dollars ($200.00), and for reinstatement thereof, not more than two hundred dollars ($200.00).

(d) The Board may deny a nonresident pharmacy registration upon a determination that the pharmacy has a record of being formally disciplined in its home state for violations that relate to the compounding or dispensing of legend drugs and presents a threat to the public health and safety.

(e) Except as otherwise provided in this subsection, the Board may adopt rules to protect the public health and safety that are necessary to implement this section. Notwithstanding G.S. 90-85.6, the Board shall not adopt rules pertaining to the shipment, mailing, or other manner of delivery of dispensed legend drugs by pharmacies required to register under this section that are more restrictive than federal statutes or regulations governing the delivery of prescription medications by mail or common carrier. A pharmacy required to register under this section shall comply with rules adopted pursuant to this section.

(f) The Board may deny, revoke, or suspend a nonresident pharmacy registration for failure to comply with any requirement of this section. (1993, c. 455, s. 1; 1998-212, s. 12.3B(b); 2004-199, s. 25; 2005-402, s. 3.)

§ 90-85.21B. Unlawful practice of pharmacy.

It shall be unlawful for any person, firm, or corporation not licensed or registered under the provisions of this Article to:

(1) Use in a trade name, sign, letter, or advertisement any term, including "drug", "pharmacy", "prescription drugs", "prescription", "Rx", or "apothecary", that would imply that the person, firm, or corporation is licensed or registered to practice pharmacy in this State.

(2) Hold himself or herself out to others as a person, firm, or corporation licensed or registered to practice pharmacy in this State. (2003-284, s. 10.8D.)

§ 90-85.22. Device and medical equipment permits.

(a) Devices. - Each place, whether located in this State or out-of-state, where devices are dispensed or delivered to the user in this State shall register annually with the Board on a form provided by the Board and obtain a device permit. A business that has a current pharmacy permit does not have to register and obtain a device permit. Records of devices dispensed in pharmacies or other places shall be kept in accordance with rules adopted by the Board.

(b) Medical Equipment. - Each place, whether located in this State or out-of-state, that delivers medical equipment to the user of the equipment in this State shall register annually with the Board on a form provided by the Board and obtain a medical equipment permit. A business that has a current pharmacy permit or a current device permit does not have to register and obtain a medical equipment permit. Medical equipment shall be delivered only in accordance with requirements established by rules adopted by the Board.

(c) This section shall not apply to either of the following:

(1) A pharmaceutical manufacturer registered with the Food and Drug Administration.

(2) A wholly owned subsidiary of a pharmaceutical manufacturer registered with the Food and Drug Administration. (1981 (Reg. Sess., 1982), c. 1188, s. 1; 1993 (Reg. Sess., 1994), c. 692, s. 1; 2001-339, s. 1.)

§ 90-85.23. License and permit to be displayed.

Every pharmacist-manager's license, every permit, and every current renewal shall be conspicuously posted in the place of business owned by or employing the person to whom it is issued. The licenses and every last renewal of all other pharmacists employed in the pharmacy must be readily available for inspection by agents of the Board. Failure to display any license or permit and the most recent renewal shall be a violation of this Article and each day that the license or permit or renewal is not displayed shall be a separate and distinct offense. (1905, c. 108, ss. 18, 26; Rev., ss. 3651, 4485; C.S., s. 6663; 1921, c. 68, s. 3; 1953, c. 1051; 1981 (Reg. Sess., 1982), c. 1188, s. 1.)

§ 90-85.24. Fees collectible by Board.

(a) The Board of Pharmacy shall be entitled to charge and collect not more than the following fees:

(1) For the examination of an applicant for license as a pharmacist, two hundred dollars ($200.00), plus the cost of the test material;

(2) For renewing the license as a pharmacist, one hundred thirty-five dollars ($135.00);

(3) For reinstatement of a license as a pharmacist, one hundred thirty-five dollars ($135.00);

(4) For annual registration of a pharmacy technician, thirty dollars ($30.00);

(5) For reinstatement of a registration of a pharmacy technician, thirty dollars ($30.00);

(6) For licenses without examination as provided in G.S. 90-85.20, original, six hundred dollars ($600.00);

(7) For original registration of a pharmacy, five hundred dollars ($500.00), and renewal thereof, two hundred dollars ($200.00);

(8) For reinstatement of the registration of a pharmacy, two hundred dollars ($200.00);

(9)   For annual registration as a dispensing physician under G.S. 90-85.21(b), seventy-five dollars ($75.00);

(10)   For reinstatement of registration as a dispensing physician, seventy-five dollars ($75.00);

(11)   For annual registration as a dispensing physician assistant under G.S. 90-18.1, seventy-five dollars ($75.00);

(12)   For reinstatement of registration as a dispensing physician assistant, seventy-five dollars ($75.00);

(13)   For annual registration as a dispensing nurse practitioner under G.S. 90-18.2, seventy-five dollars ($75.00);

(14)   For reinstatement of registration as a dispensing nurse practitioner, seventy-five dollars ($75.00);

(15)   For registration of any change in pharmacist personnel as required under G.S. 90-85.21(a), thirty-five dollars ($35.00);

(16)   For a duplicate of any license, permit, or registration issued by the Board, twenty-five dollars ($25.00);

(17)   For original registration to dispense devices, deliver medical equipment, or both, five hundred dollars ($500.00);

(18)   For renewal of registration to dispense devices, deliver medical equipment, or both, two hundred dollars ($200.00);

(19)   For reinstatement of a registration to dispense devices, deliver medical equipment, or both, two hundred dollars ($200.00).

(b)   All fees under this section shall be paid before any applicant may be admitted to examination or the applicant's name may be placed upon the register of pharmacists or before any license or permit, or any renewal or reinstatement thereof, may be issued by the Board. (1905, c. 108, s. 12; Rev., s. 4478; C.S., s. 6657; 1921, c. 57, s. 3; 1945, c. 572, s. 3; 1953, c. 183, s. 1; 1965, c. 676, s. 1; 1973, c. 1183; 1981, c. 72; c. 717, s. 3; 1981 (Reg. Sess., 1982), c. 1188, s. 2; 1983, c. 196, s. 8; 1987, c. 260; 1987 (Reg. Sess., 1988),

c. 1039, s. 4; 1993 (Reg. Sess., 1994), c. 692, s. 3; 1997-231, s. 1; 2001-375, s. 4; 2005-402, s. 2.)

§ 90-85.25. Disasters and emergencies.

(a) In the event of an occurrence which the Governor of the State of North Carolina has declared a state of emergency, or in the event of an occurrence for which a county or municipality has enacted an ordinance to deal with states of emergency under G.S. 166A-19.31, or to protect the public health, safety, or welfare of its citizens under G.S. 160A-174(a) or G.S. 153A-121(a), as applicable, the Board may waive the requirements of this Article in order to permit the provision of drugs, devices, and professional services to the public.

(b) The pharmacist in charge of a pharmacy shall report within 10 days to the Board any disaster, accident, theft, or emergency which may affect the strength, purity, or labeling of drugs and devices in the pharmacy. (1981 Reg. Sess., 1982), c. 1188, s. 1; 1998-212, s. 12.3B(a); 2012-12, s. 2(gg).)

§ 90-85.26. Prescription orders preserved.

(a) Every pharmacist-manager of a pharmacy shall maintain for at least three years the original of every prescription order and refill compounded or dispensed at the pharmacy except for prescription orders recorded in a patient's medical record. An automated data processing system may be used for the storage and retrieval of refill information for prescriptions pursuant to the regulations of the Board. A pharmacist-manager may comply with this section by capturing and maintaining an electronic image of a prescription order or refill. An electronic image of a prescription order or refill shall constitute the original prescription order, and a hard copy of the prescription order or refill is not required to be maintained. If a pharmacist-manager elects to maintain prescription orders by capturing electronic images of prescription orders or refills, the pharmacy's computer system must be capable of maintaining, printing, and providing in an electronic or paper format, upon a request by the Board, all of the information required by this Chapter or rules adopted pursuant to this Chapter within 48 hours of such a request.

(b) Every pharmacy permittee's designated agent shall maintain documentation of alleged medication errors and incidents described in G.S. 90-85.47(e)(1) for which the pharmacy permittee has knowledge. (1905, c. 108, s. 21; Rev., s. 4490; C.S., s. 6666; 1981 (Reg. Sess., 1982), c. 1188, s. 1; 2005-427, s. 2; 2007-248, s. 1.)

§ 90-85.26A. Clinical pharmacist practitioners subcommittee.

The North Carolina Board of Pharmacy shall appoint and maintain a subcommittee of the Board consisting of four licensed pharmacists to work jointly with the subcommittee of the North Carolina Medical Board to develop rules to govern the provision of drug therapy management by clinical pharmacist practitioners and to determine reasonable fees to accompany an application for approval or renewal of such approval as provided in G.S. 90-6. The rules developed by this subcommittee shall govern the performance of acts by clinical pharmacist practitioners and shall become effective when they have been adopted by both Boards. (1999-290, s. 6.)

§ 90-85.27. Definitions.

As used in G.S. 90-85.28 through G.S. 90-85.31:

(1) "Equivalent drug product" means a drug product which has the same established name, active ingredient, strength, quantity, and dosage form, and which is therapeutically equivalent to the drug product identified in the prescription;

(2) "Established name" has the meaning given in section 502(e)(3) of the Federal Food, Drug and Cosmetic Act, 21 U.S.C. 352(e)(3);

(3) "Good manufacturing practice" has the meaning given it in Part 211 of Chapter 1 of Title 21 of the Code of Federal Regulations;

(4) "Manufacturer" means the actual manufacturer of the finished dosage form of the drug;

(4a) "Narrow therapeutic index drugs" means those pharmaceuticals having a narrowly defined range between risk and benefit. Such drugs have less than a twofold difference in the minimum toxic concentration and minimum effective concentration in the blood or are those drug product formulations that exhibit limited or erratic absorption, formulation-dependent bioavailability, and wide intrapatient pharmacokinetic variability that requires blood-level monitoring. Drugs identified as having narrow therapeutic indices shall be designated by the North Carolina Secretary of Health and Human Services upon the advice of the State Health Director, North Carolina Board of Pharmacy, and North Carolina Medical Board, as narrow therapeutic index drugs and shall be subject to the provisions of G.S. 90-85.28(b1). The North Carolina Board of Pharmacy shall submit the list of narrow therapeutic index drugs to the Codifier of Rules, in a timely fashion for publication in January of each year in the North Carolina Register.

(5) "Prescriber" means anyone authorized to prescribe drugs pursuant to the laws of this State. (1979, c. 1017, s. 1; 1981 (Reg. Sess., 1982), c. 1188, s. 3; 1983, c. 196, s. 9; 1997-76, s. 1; 1997-443, s. 11A.118(b).)

§ 90-85.28. Selection by pharmacists permissible; prescriber may permit or prohibit selection; price limit on selected drugs.

(a) A pharmacist dispensing a prescription for a drug product prescribed by its brand name may select any equivalent drug product which meets the following standards:

(1) The manufacturer's name and the distributor's name, if different from the manufacturer's name, shall appear on the label of the stock package;

(2) It shall be manufactured in accordance with current good manufacturing practices;

(3) Effective January 1, 1982, all oral solid dosage forms shall have a logo, or other identification mark, or the product name to identify the manufacturer or distributor;

(4) The manufacturer shall have adequate provisions for drug recall; and

(5) The manufacturer shall have adequate provisions for return of outdated drugs, through his distributor or otherwise.

(b) The pharmacist shall not select an equivalent drug product if the prescriber instructs otherwise by one of the following methods:

(1) A prescription form shall be preprinted or stamped with two signature lines at the bottom of the form which read:

"
_____   _____

Product Selection Permitted   Dispense as Written"

On this form, the prescriber shall communicate his instructions to the pharmacist by signing the appropriate line.

(2) In the event the preprinted or stamped prescription form specified in (b)(1) is not readily available, the prescriber may handwrite "Dispense as Written" or words or abbreviations of the same meaning on a prescription form.

(3) When ordering a prescription orally, the prescriber shall specify either that the prescribed drug product be dispensed as written or that product selection is permitted. The pharmacist shall note the instructions on the file copy of the prescription and retain the prescription form for the period prescribed by law.

(b1) A prescription for a narrow therapeutic index drug shall be refilled using only the same drug product by the same manufacturer that the pharmacist last dispensed under the prescription, unless the prescriber is notified by the pharmacist prior to the dispensing of another manufacturer's product, and the prescriber and the patient give documented consent to the dispensing of the other manufacturer's product. For purposes of this subsection, the term "refilled" shall include a new prescription written at the expiration of a prescription which continues the patient's therapy on a narrow therapeutic index drug.

(c) The pharmacist shall not select an equivalent drug product unless its price to the purchaser is less than the price of the prescribed drug product. (1979, c. 1017, s. 1; 1981 (Reg. Sess., 1982), c. 1188, s. 3; 1997-76, s. 2.)

§ 90-85.29. Prescription label.

The prescription label of every drug product dispensed shall contain the brand name of any drug product dispensed, or in the absence of a brand name, the established name. The prescription drug label of every drug product dispensed shall:

(1)   Contain the discard date when dispensed in a container other than the manufacturer's original container. The discard date shall be the earlier of one year from the date dispensed or the manufacturer's expiration date, whichever is earlier, and

(2)   Not obscure the expiration date and storage statement when the product is dispensed in the manufacturer's original container.

As used in this section, "expiration date" means the expiration date printed on the original manufacturer's container, and "discard date" means the date after which the drug product dispensed in a container other than the original manufacturer's container shall not be used. Nothing in this section shall impose liability on the dispensing pharmacist or the prescriber for damages related to or caused by a drug product that loses its effectiveness prior to the expiration or disposal date displayed by the pharmacist or prescriber. (1979, c. 1017, s. 1; 1981 (Reg. Sess., 1982), c. 1188, s. 3; 1993, c. 529, s. 7.5.)

§ 90-85.30. Prescription record.

The pharmacy file copy of every prescription shall include the brand or trade name, if any, or the established name and the manufacturer of the drug product dispensed. (1979, c. 1017, s. 1; 1981 (Reg. Sess., 1982), c. 1188, s. 3.)

§ 90-85.31. Prescriber and pharmacist liability not extended.

The selection of an equivalent drug product pursuant to this Article shall impose no greater liability upon the pharmacist for selecting the dispensed drug product or upon the prescriber of the same than would be incurred by either for dispensing the drug product specified in the prescription. (1979, c. 1017, s. 1; 1981 (Reg. Sess., 1982), c. 1188, s. 3.)

§ 90-85.32. Rules pertaining to filling, refilling, transfer, and mail or common-carrier delivery of prescription orders.

(a) Except as otherwise provided in this section, the Board may adopt rules governing the filling, refilling and transfer of prescription orders not inconsistent with other provisions of law regarding the distribution of drugs and devices. The rules shall assure the safe and secure distribution of drugs and devices. Prescriptions marked PRN shall not be refilled more than one year after the date issued by the prescriber unless otherwise specified.

(b) Notwithstanding G.S. 90-85.6, the Board shall not adopt rules pertaining to the shipment, mailing, or other manner of delivery of dispensed legend drugs that are more restrictive than federal statutes or regulations governing the delivery of prescription medications by mail or common carrier. (1981 (Reg. Sess., 1982), c. 1188, s. 1; 1998-212, s. 12.3B(c).)

§ 90-85.33. Unit dose medication systems.

The Board may adopt regulations governing pharmacists providing unit dose medication systems. The regulations shall ensure the safe and proper distribution of drugs in the patient's best health interests. (1981 (Reg. Sess., 1982), c. 1188, s. 1.)

§ 90-85.34. Unique pharmacy practice.

Consistent with the provisions of this Article, the Board may regulate unique pharmacy practices including, but not limited to, nuclear pharmacy and clinical pharmacy, to ensure the best interests of patient health and safety. (1981 (Reg. Sess., 1982), c. 1188, s. 1.)

§ 90-85.34A. Public health pharmacy practice.

(a) A registered nurse in a local health department clinic may dispense prescription drugs and devices, other than controlled substances as defined in G.S. 90-87, under the following conditions:

(1) The registered nurse has training acceptable to the Board in the labeling and packaging of prescription drugs and devices;

(2) Dispensing by the registered nurse shall occur only at a local health department clinic;

(3) Only prescription drugs and devices contained in a formulary recommended by the Department of Health and Human Services and approved by the Board shall be dispensed;

(4) The local health department clinic shall obtain a pharmacy permit in accordance with G.S. 90-85.21;

(5) Written procedures for the storage, packaging, labeling and delivery of prescription drugs and devices shall be approved by the Board; and

(6) The pharmacist-manager, or another pharmacist at his direction, shall review dispensing records at least weekly, provide consultation where appropriate, and be responsible to the Board for all dispensing activity at the local health department clinic.

(b) This section is applicable only to prescriptions issued on behalf of persons receiving local health department clinic services and issued by an individual authorized by law to prescribe drugs and devices.

(c) This section does not affect the practice of nurse practitioners pursuant to G.S. 90-18.2 or of physician assistants pursuant to G.S. 90-18.1. (1985, c. 359; 1989 (Reg. Sess., 1990), c. 1004, s. 2; 1997-443, s. 11A.22.)

§ 90-85.35. Availability of patient records.

Pharmacists employed in health care facilities shall have access to patient records maintained by those facilities when necessary for the pharmacist to provide pharmaceutical services. The pharmacist shall make appropriate entries in patient records. (1981 (Reg. Sess., 1982), c. 1188, s. 1.)

§ 90-85.36. Availability of pharmacy records.

(a) Except as provided in subsections (b) and (c) below, written or electronic prescription orders on file in a pharmacy or other place where prescriptions are dispensed are not public records and any person having custody of or access to the prescription orders may divulge the contents or provide a copy only to the following persons:

(1) An adult patient for whom the prescription was issued or a person who is legally appointed guardian of that person;

(2) An emancipated minor patient for whom the prescription order was issued or a person who is the legally appointed guardian of that patient;

(3) An unemancipated minor patient for whom the prescription order was issued when the minor's consent is sufficient to authorize treatment of the condition for which the prescription was issued;

(4) A parent or person in loco parentis of an unemancipated minor patient for whom the prescription order was issued when the minor's consent is not sufficient to authorize treatment for the condition for which the prescription is issued;

(5) The licensed practitioner who issued the prescription;

(6) The licensed practitioner who is treating the patient for whom the prescription was issued;

(7) A pharmacist who is providing pharmacy services to the patient for whom the prescription was issued;

(8) Anyone who presents a written authorization for the release of pharmacy information signed by the patient or his legal representative;

(9) Any person authorized by subpoena, court order or statute;

(10) Any firm, association, partnership, business trust, corporation or company charged by law or by contract with the responsibility of providing for or

paying for medical care for the patient for whom the prescription order was issued;

(11)   A member or designated employee of the Board;

(12)   The executor, administrator or spouse of a deceased patient for whom the prescription order was issued;

(13)   Researchers and surveyors who have approval from the Board. The Board shall issue this approval when it determines that there are adequate safeguards to protect the confidentiality of the information contained in the prescription orders and that the researchers or surveyors will not publicly disclose any information that identifies any person;

(14)   The person owning the pharmacy or his authorized agent; or

(15)   A HIPAA covered entity, or business associate described in 45 C.F.R. § 160.103, or a health care provider who is not a covered entity, for purposes of treatment, payment, or health care operations to the extent that disclosure is permitted or required by applicable State or federal law.

(b)   A pharmacist may disclose any information to any person only when he reasonably determines that the disclosure is necessary to protect the life or health of any person.

(c)   Records required to be kept by G.S. 90-93(d) (Schedule V) are not public records and shall be disclosed at the pharmacist's discretion. (1905, c. 108, s. 21; Rev., s. 4490; C.S., s. 6666; 1981 (Reg. Sess., 1982), c. 1188, s. 1; 1991, c. 125, s. 3; 2011-314, s. 1.)

§ 90-85.37. Embargo.

Notwithstanding any other provisions of law, whenever an authorized representative of the Board has reasonable cause to believe that any drug or device presents a danger to the public health, he shall affix to the drug or device a notice that the article is suspected of being dangerous to the public health and warning all persons not to remove or dispose of the article. Whenever an authorized representative of the Board has reasonable cause to believe that any drug or device presents a danger to the public health and that there are reasonable grounds to believe that it might be disposed of pending a judicial resolution of the matter, he shall seize the article and take it to a safe and secure place. When an article has been embargoed under this section, the Board shall, as soon as practical, file a petition in Orange County District Court for a condemnation order for such article. If the judge determines after hearing, that the article is not dangerous to the public health, the Board shall direct the immediate removal of the tag or other marking, and where appropriate, shall direct that the article be returned to its owner. If the judge finds the article is dangerous to the public health, he shall order its destruction at the owner's expense and under the Board's supervision. If the judge determines that the article is dangerous to the public health, he shall order the owner of the article to pay all court costs, reasonable attorney's fees, storage fees, and all other costs incident to the proceeding. (1981 (Reg. Sess., 1982), c. 1188, s. 1.)

§ 90-85.38. Disciplinary authority.

(a) The Board may, in accordance with Chapter 150B of the General Statutes, issue a letter of reprimand or suspend, restrict, revoke, or refuse to grant or renew a license to practice pharmacy, or require licensees to successfully complete remedial education if the licensee has done any of the following:

(1) Made false representations or withheld material information in connection with securing a license or permit.

(2) Been found guilty of or plead guilty or nolo contendere to any felony in connection with the practice of pharmacy or the distribution of drugs.

(3) Indulged in the use of drugs to an extent that renders the pharmacist unfit to practice pharmacy.

(4) Made false representations in connection with the practice of pharmacy that endanger or are likely to endanger the health or safety of the public, or that defraud any person.

(5) Developed a physical or mental disability that renders the pharmacist unfit to practice pharmacy with reasonable skill, competence and safety to the public.

(6)   Failed to comply with the laws governing the practice of pharmacy and the distribution of drugs.

(7)   Failed to comply with any provision of this Article or rules adopted by the Board.

(8)   Engaged in, or aided and abetted an individual to engage in, the practice of pharmacy without a license.

(9)   Been negligent in the practice of pharmacy.

(b)   The Board, in accordance with Chapter 150B of the General Statutes, may suspend, revoke, or refuse to grant or renew any permit for the same conduct as stated in subsection (a). The administration of required lethal substances or any assistance whatsoever rendered with an execution under Article 19 of Chapter 15 of the General Statutes does not constitute the practice of pharmacy under this Article, and any assistance rendered with an execution under Article 19 of Chapter 15 of the General Statutes shall not be the cause for disciplinary action under this Article.

(c)   Any license or permit obtained through false representation or withholding of material information shall be void and of no effect. (1905, c. 108, ss. 17, 25; Rev., s. 4483; C.S., s. 6661; 1967, c. 807; 1973, c. 138; 1981, c. 412, s. 4; c. 717, s. 8; c. 747, s. 66; 1981 (Reg. Sess., 1982), c. 1188, s. 1; 1987, c. 827, s. 1; 2001-375, s. 5; 2013-154, s. 1(c).)

§ 90-85.39. Injunctive authority.

The Board may apply to any court for an injunction to prevent violations of this Article or of any rules enacted pursuant to it. The court is empowered to grant the injunctions regardless of whether criminal prosecution or other action has been or may be instituted as a result of the violation. (1981 (Reg. Sess., 1982), c. 1188, s. 1.)

§ 90-85.40. Violations.

(a) It shall be unlawful for any owner or manager of a pharmacy or other place to allow or cause anyone other than a pharmacist to dispense or compound any prescription drug unless that person is a pharmacy technician or a pharmacy student who is enrolled in a school of pharmacy approved by the Board and is working under the supervision of a pharmacist.

(b) Every person lawfully authorized to compound or dispense prescription drugs shall comply with all the laws and regulations governing the labeling and packaging of such drugs by pharmacists.

(c) It shall be unlawful for any person not licensed as a pharmacist to compound or dispense any prescription drug, unless that person is a pharmacy technician or a pharmacy student who is enrolled in a school of pharmacy approved by the Board and is working under the supervision of a pharmacist.

(d) It shall be unlawful for any person to manage any place of business where devices are dispensed or sold at retail without a permit as required by this Article.

(d1) It is unlawful for a person to own or manage a place of business from which medical equipment is delivered without a permit as required by this Article.

(e) It shall be unlawful for any person without legal authorization to dispose of an article that has been embargoed under this Article.

(f) It shall be unlawful to violate any provision of this Article or of any rules or regulations enacted pursuant to it.

(g) This Article shall not be construed to prohibit any person from performing an act that person is authorized to perform pursuant to North Carolina law. Health care providers who are authorized to prescribe drugs without supervision are authorized to dispense drugs without supervision.

(h) A violation of this Article shall be a Class 1 misdemeanor. (1905, c. 108, ss. 4, 23, 24; Rev., ss. 3649, 3650, 4487; C.S., ss. 6667, 6668, 6669; 1921, c. 68, ss. 6, 7; Ex. Sess. 1924, c. 116; 1953, c. 1051; 1957, c. 617; 1959, c. 1222; 1981 (Reg. Sess., 1982), c. 1188, s. 1; 1993, c. 539, s. 621; 1994, Ex. Sess., c. 24, s. 14(c); 1993 (Reg. Sess., 1994), c. 692, s. 4; 2001-375, ss. 6, 7.)

§ 90-85.41. Board agreements with special peer review organizations for impaired pharmacy personnel.

(a) The North Carolina Board of Pharmacy may, under rules adopted by the Board in compliance with Chapter 150B of the General Statutes, enter into agreements with special impaired pharmacy personnel peer review organizations. Peer review activities to be covered by such agreements shall include investigation, review and evaluation of records, reports, complaints, litigation, and other information about the practices and practice patterns of pharmacy personnel licensed or registered by the Board, as such matters may relate to impaired pharmacy personnel. Special impaired pharmacy personnel peer review organizations may include a statewide supervisory committee and various regional and local components or subgroups.

(b) Agreements authorized under this section shall include provisions for the impaired pharmacy personnel peer review organizations to receive relevant information from the Board and other sources, conduct any investigation, review, and evaluation in an expeditious manner, provide assurance of confidentiality of nonpublic information and of the peer review process, make reports of investigations and evaluations to the Board, and to do other related activities for operating and promoting a coordinated and effective peer review process. The agreements shall include provisions assuring basic due process for pharmacy personnel that become involved.

(c) The impaired pharmacy personnel peer review organizations that enter into agreements with the Board shall establish and maintain a program for impaired pharmacy personnel licensed or registered by the Board for the purpose of identifying, reviewing, and evaluating the ability of those pharmacists to function as pharmacists, and pharmacy technicians to function as pharmacy technicians, and to provide programs for treatment and rehabilitation. The Board may provide funds for the administration of these impaired pharmacy personnel peer review programs. The Board shall adopt rules to apply to the operation of impaired pharmacy personnel peer review programs, with provisions for: (i) definitions of impairment; (ii) guidelines for program elements; (iii) procedures for receipt and use of information of suspected impairment; (iv) procedures for intervention and referral; (v) arrangements for monitoring treatment, rehabilitation, posttreatment support, and performance; (vi) reports of individual cases to the Board; (vii) periodic reporting of statistical information; and (viii) assurance of confidentiality of nonpublic information and of the peer review process.

(d) Upon investigation and review of a pharmacist licensed by the Board, or a pharmacy technician registered with the Board, or upon receipt of a complaint or other information, an impaired pharmacy personnel peer review organization that enters into a peer review agreement with the Board shall report immediately to the Board detailed information about any pharmacist licensed or pharmacy technician registered by the Board, if:

(1) The pharmacist or pharmacy technician constitutes an imminent danger to the public or himself or herself.

(2) The pharmacist or pharmacy technician refuses to cooperate with the program, refuses to submit to treatment, or is still impaired after treatment and exhibits professional incompetence.

(3) It reasonably appears that there are other grounds for disciplinary action.

(e) Any confidential patient information and other nonpublic information acquired, created, or used in good faith by an impaired pharmacy personnel peer review organization pursuant to this section shall remain confidential and shall not be subject to discovery or subpoena in a civil case. No person participating in good faith in an impaired pharmacy personnel peer review program developed under this section shall be required in a civil case to disclose any information (including opinions, recommendations, or evaluations) acquired or developed solely in the course of participating in the program.

(f) Impaired pharmacy personnel peer review activities conducted in good faith pursuant to any program developed under this section shall not be grounds for civil action under the laws of this State, and the activities are deemed to be State directed and sanctioned and shall constitute "State action" for the purposes of application of antitrust laws. (1999-81, s. 1; 2001-375, s. 8.)

§ 90-85.42. Reserved for future codification purposes.

§ 90-85.43. Reserved for future codification purposes.

Part 2. Drug, Supplies, and Medical Device Repository Program.

§ 90-85.44. Drug, Supplies, and Medical Device Repository Program established.

(a) Definitions. - As used in this section unless the context clearly requires otherwise, the following definitions apply:

(1) Board. - As defined in G.S. 90-85.3.

(2) Dispense. - As defined in G.S. 90-85.3.

(3) Drug. - As defined in G.S. 90-85.3.

(4) Eligible donor. - The following are eligible donors under the Program:

a. A patient or the patient's family member.

b. A manufacturer, wholesaler, or supplier of drugs, supplies, or medical devices.

c. A pharmacy, free clinic, hospital, or a hospice care program.

(5) Eligible patient. - An uninsured or underinsured patient who meets the eligibility criteria established by the Board, free clinic, or pharmacy.

(6) Free clinic. - A private, nonprofit, community-based organization that provides health care services at little or no charge to low-income, uninsured, and underinsured persons through the use of volunteer health care professionals.

(7) Medical device. - A device as defined in G.S. 90-85.3(e).

(8) Pharmacist. - As defined in G.S. 90-85.3.

(9) Pharmacy. - As defined in G.S. 90-85.3.

(10) Practitioner. - A physician or other provider of health services licensed or otherwise permitted to distribute, dispense, or administer drugs, supplies, or medical devices.

(11) Program. - The Drug, Supplies, and Medical Device Repository Program established under this act.

(12) Supplies. - Supplies associated with or necessary for the administration of a drug.

(b) Program Purpose. - The Board shall establish and administer the Program. The purpose of the Program is to allow an eligible donor to donate unused drugs, supplies, and medical devices to uninsured and underinsured patients in this State. The unused drugs, supplies, and medical devices shall be donated to a free clinic or pharmacy that elects to participate in the Program. A free clinic that receives a donated unused drug, supplies, or medical device under the Program may distribute the drug, supplies, or medical device to another free clinic or pharmacy for use under the Program.

(c) Requirements of Participating Pharmacists or Free Clinics. - A pharmacist may accept and dispense drugs, supplies, and medical devices donated to the Program to eligible patients if all of the following requirements are met:

(1) The drug, supplies, or medical device is in the original, unopened, sealed, and tamper-evident packaging or, if packaged in single-unit doses, the single-unit dose packaging is unopened.

(2) The pharmacist has determined that the drug, supplies, or medical device is safe for redistribution.

(3) The drug bears an expiration date that is later than six months after the date that the drug was donated.

(4) The drug, supplies, or medical device is not adulterated or misbranded, as determined by a pharmacist.

(5) The drug, supplies, or medical device is prescribed by a practitioner for use by an eligible patient and is dispensed by a pharmacist.

(d) Fee. - A participating pharmacist or free clinic shall not resell a drug, supplies, or a medical device donated to the Program. A pharmacist or free clinic may charge an eligible patient a handling fee to receive a donated drug, supplies, or medical device, which shall not exceed the amount specified in rules adopted by the Board.

(e) Program Participation Voluntary. - Nothing in this section requires a free clinic or pharmacy to participate in the Program.

(f) Eligible Patient. - The Board shall establish eligibility criteria for individuals to receive donated drugs, supplies, or medical devices. Board eligibility criteria shall provide that individuals meeting free clinic or pharmacy eligibility criteria are eligible patients. Dispensing shall be prioritized to patients who are uninsured or underinsured. Dispensing to other patients shall be permitted if an uninsured or underinsured patient is not available.

(g) Rules. - The Board shall adopt rules necessary for the implementation of the Program. Rules adopted by the Board shall provide for the following:

(1) Requirements for free clinics and pharmacies to accept and dispense donated drugs, supplies, and medical devices pursuant to the Program, including eligibility criteria, confidentiality of donors, and standards and procedures for a free clinic or pharmacy to accept and safely store and dispense donated drugs, supplies, and medical devices.

(2) The amount of the maximum handling fee that a free clinic or pharmacy may charge for distributing or dispensing donated drugs, supplies, or medical devices.

(3) A list of drugs, supplies, and medical devices, arranged either by category or by individual drug, supply, or medical device, that the Program will accept for dispensing.

(h) Immunity. - The following limited immunities apply under the Program:

(1) Unless a pharmaceutical manufacturer exercises bad faith, the manufacturer is not subject to criminal or civil liability for injury, death, or loss to a person or property for matters related to the donation, acceptance, or dispensing of a drug or medical device manufactured by the manufacturer that is donated by any person under the Program, including liability for failure to

transfer or communicate product or consumer information or the expiration date of the donated drug or medical device.

(2) The following individuals or entities are immune from civil liability for an act or omission that causes injury to or the death of an individual to whom the drug, supplies, or medical device is dispensed under the Program, and no disciplinary action may be taken against a pharmacist or practitioner as long as the drug, supplies, or medical device is donated in accordance with the requirements of this section:

a. A pharmacy or free clinic participating in the Program.

b. A pharmacist dispensing a drug, supplies, or medical device pursuant to the Program.

c. A practitioner administering a drug, supplies, or medical devices pursuant to the Program.

d. An eligible donor who has donated a drug, supplies, or a medical device pursuant to the Program. (2009-423, s. 2.)

Article 4B.

Pharmacy Quality Assurance Protection Act.

§ 90-85.45. Legislative intent.

It is the intent of the General Assembly to require pharmacy quality assurance programs to further contribute to and enhance the quality of health care and reduce medication errors in this State by facilitating a process for the continuous review of the practice of pharmacy. (2005-427, s. 3.)

§ 90-85.46. Definitions.

The following definitions shall apply in this Article:

(1) Board. - The North Carolina Board of Pharmacy.

(2) Pharmacy quality assurance program. - A program pertaining to one of the following:

a. A pharmacy association created under G.S. 90-85.4 or incorporated under Chapter 55A of the General Statutes that evaluates the quality of pharmacy services and alleged medication errors and incidents and makes recommendations to improve the quality of pharmacy services.

b. A program established by a person or entity holding a valid pharmacy permit pursuant to G.S. 90-85.21 or G.S. 90-85.21A to evaluate the quality of pharmacy services and alleged medication errors and incidents and make recommendations to improve the quality of pharmacy services.

c. A quality assurance committee or medical or peer review committee established by a health care provider licensed under this Chapter or a health care facility licensed under Chapter 122C, 131D, or 131E of the General Statutes that includes evaluation of the quality of pharmacy services and alleged medication errors and incidents and makes recommendations to improve the quality of pharmacy services. (2005-427, s. 3; 2006-259, s. 16(a).)

§ 90-85.47. Pharmacy quality assurance program required; limited liability; discovery.

(a) Every person or entity holding a valid pharmacy permit pursuant to G.S. 90-85.21 or G.S. 90-85.21A shall establish or participate in a pharmacy quality assurance program as defined under G.S. 90-85.46(2), to evaluate the following:

(1) The quality of the practice of pharmacy.

(2) The cause of alleged medication errors and incidents.

(3) Pharmaceutical care outcomes.

(4) Possible improvements for the practice of pharmacy.

(5) Methods to reduce alleged medication errors and incidents.

(b) There shall be no monetary liability on the part of, or no cause of action for damages arising against, any member of a duly appointed pharmacy quality assurance program or any pharmacy or pharmacist furnishing information to a pharmacy quality assurance program or any person, including a person acting as a witness or incident reporter to or investigator for a pharmacy quality assurance program, for any act or proceeding undertaken or performed within the scope of the functions of the pharmacy quality assurance program.

(c) This section shall not be construed to confer immunity from liability on any professional association, pharmacy or pharmacist, or health care provider while performing services other than as a member of a pharmacy quality assurance program or upon any person, including a person acting as a witness or incident reporter to or investigator for a pharmacy quality assurance program, for any act or proceeding undertaken or performed outside the scope of the functions of the pharmacy quality assurance program. Except as provided in subsection (a) or (b) of this section, where a cause of action would arise against a pharmacy, pharmacist, or an individual health care provider, the cause of action shall remain in effect.

(d) The proceedings of a pharmacy quality assurance program, the records and materials it produces, and the materials it considers shall be confidential and not considered public records within the meaning of G.S. 132-1 or G.S. 58-2-100 and shall not be subject to discovery or introduction into evidence in any civil action, administrative hearing or Board investigation against a pharmacy, pharmacist, pharmacy technician, a pharmacist manager or a permittee or a hospital licensed under Chapter 122C or Chapter 131E of the General Statutes or that is owned or operated by the State, which civil action, administrative hearing or Board Investigation results from matters that are the subject of evaluation and review by the pharmacy quality assurance program. No person who was in attendance at a meeting of the pharmacy quality assurance program shall be required to testify in any civil action, administrative hearing or Board investigation as to any evidence or other matters produced or presented during the proceedings of the pharmacy quality assurance program or as to any findings, recommendations, evaluations, opinions, or other actions of the pharmacy quality assurance program or its members. However, information, documents, or records otherwise available are not immune from discovery or use in a civil action merely because they were presented during proceedings of the pharmacy quality assurance program. Documents otherwise available as public records within the meaning of G.S. 132-1 do not lose their status as public records merely because they were presented or considered during proceedings of the pharmacy quality assurance program. A member of the pharmacy quality assurance program may testify in a civil or administrative action but cannot be asked about the person's testimony before the pharmacy quality assurance program or any opinions formed as a result of the pharmacy quality assurance program. Nothing in this subsection shall preclude:

(1) A pharmacy, pharmacist, pharmacy technician, or other person or any agent or representative of a pharmacy, pharmacist, pharmacy technician or other person participating on a pharmacy quality assurance program may use otherwise privileged, confidential information for legitimate internal business or professional purposes of the pharmacy quality assurance program.

(2) A pharmacy, pharmacist, pharmacy technician, other person participating on the committee, or any person or organization named as a defendant in a civil action, a respondent in an administrative proceeding, or a pharmacy, pharmacist, or pharmacy technician subject to a Board investigation as a result of participation in the pharmacy quality assurance program may use otherwise privileged, confidential information in the pharmacy quality assurance program or person's own defense. A plaintiff in the civil action or the agency in the administrative proceeding may disclose records or determinations of or communications to the pharmacy quality assurance program in rebuttal to information given by the defendant, respondent, or pharmacist subject to Board investigation.

(e) Upon the Board providing written notice to the pharmacy permittee's designated agent under G.S. 90-85.21(a) and pharmacist of an investigation against the pharmacist, including the specific reason for the Board investigation, the pharmacy permittee's designated agent shall compile and provide documentation within 10 days of the receipt of the notice of any alleged medication error or incident committed by the pharmacist in the 12 months preceding the receipt of the notice, that the pharmacy permittee has knowledge of, when:

(1) The alleged medication error or incident resulted in any of the following:

a. A visit to a physician or an emergency room attributed to the alleged medication incident or error.

b. Hospitalization requiring an overnight stay or longer.

c. A fatality.

(2) The Board has initiated a disciplinary proceeding against the pharmacist as a result of the investigation. Unless the documentation relates to an alleged medication error or incident that was specifically the cause of the investigation, the Board may review the documentation only after the Board has made findings of fact and conclusions of law pursuant to G.S. 150B-42(a) and may use the documentation in determining the remedial action the pharmacist shall undergo as part of the disciplinary action imposed by the Board. The documentation shall be released only to the Board or its designated employees pursuant to this subsection and shall not otherwise be released except as required by law.

The documentation provided to the Board shall not include the proceedings and records of a pharmacy quality assurance program or information prepared by the pharmacy solely for consideration by or upon request of a pharmacy quality assurance program.

(f) Nothing in this section shall preclude the Board from obtaining information concerning a specific alleged medication error or incident that is the subject of a Board investigation resulting from a complaint to the Board. (2005-427, s. 3; 2006-259, s. 16(b).)

§ 90-85.48: Reserved for future codification purposes.

§ 90-85.49: Reserved for future codification purposes.

Article 4C.

Pharmacy Audit Rights.

§ 90-85.50. Declaration of pharmacy rights during audit.

(a) The following definitions apply in this Article:

(1) "Pharmacy" means a person or entity holding a valid pharmacy permit pursuant to G.S. 90-85.21 or G.S. 90-85.21A.

(2) "Responsible party" means the entity responsible for payment of claims for health care services other than (i) the individual to whom the health care services were rendered or (ii) that individual's guardian or legal representative.

(b) Notwithstanding any other provision of law, whenever a managed care company, insurance company, third-party payer, or any entity that represents a responsible party conducts an audit of the records of a pharmacy, the pharmacy has a right to all of the following:

(1) To have at least 14 days' advance notice of the initial on-site audit for each audit cycle.

(2) To have any audit that involves clinical judgment be done with a pharmacist who is licensed, and is employed or working under contract with the auditing entity.

(3) Not to have clerical or record-keeping errors, including typographical errors, scrivener's errors, and computer errors, on a required document or record, in the absence of any other evidence, deemed fraudulent. This subdivision does not prohibit recoupment of fraudulent payments.

(4) If required under the terms of the contract, to have the auditing entity provide a pharmacy, upon request, all records related to the audit in an electronic format or contained in digital media.

(5) To have the properly documented records of a hospital or any person authorized to prescribe controlled substances for the purpose of providing medical or pharmaceutical care for their patients transmitted by any means of communication in order to validate a pharmacy record with respect to a prescription or refill for a controlled substance or narcotic drug.

(6) To have a projection of an overpayment or underpayment based on either the number of patients served with a similar diagnosis or the number of similar prescription orders or refills for similar drugs. This subdivision does not prohibit recoupments of actual overpayments, unless the projection for overpayment or underpayment is part of a settlement by the pharmacy.

(7) Prior to the initiation of an audit, if the audit is conducted for an identified problem, the audit is limited to claims that are identified by prescription number.

(8) If an audit is conducted for a reason other than described in subdivision (6) of this subsection, the audit is limited to 100 selected prescriptions.

(9) If an audit reveals the necessity for a review of additional claims, to have the audit conducted on site.

(10) Except for audits initiated for the reason described in subdivision (6) of this subsection, to be subject to no more than one audit in one calendar year, unless fraud or misrepresentation is reasonably suspected.

(11) Except for cases of Food and Drug Administration regulation or drug manufacturer safety programs, to be free of recoupments based on any of the following unless defined within the billing requirements set forth in the pharmacy provider manual not inconsistent with current North Carolina Board of Pharmacy Regulations:

a. Documentation requirements in addition to or exceeding requirements for creating or maintaining documentation prescribed by the State Board of Pharmacy.

b. A requirement that a pharmacy or pharmacist perform a professional duty in addition to or exceeding professional duties prescribed by the State Board of Pharmacy.

(12) To be subject to recoupment only following the correction of a claim and to have recoupment limited to amounts paid in excess of amounts payable under the corrected claim.

(13) Except for Medicare claims, to be subject to reversals of approval for drug, prescriber, or patient eligibility upon adjudication of a claim only in cases in which the pharmacy obtained the adjudication by fraud or misrepresentation of claim elements.

(14) To be audited under the same standards and parameters as other similarly situated pharmacies audited by the same entity.

(15) To have at least 30 days following receipt of the preliminary audit report to produce documentation to address any discrepancy found during an audit.

(16) To have the period covered by an audit limited to 24 months from the date a claim was submitted to, or adjudicated by, a managed care company, an insurance company, a third-party payer, or any entity that represents responsible parties, unless a longer period is permitted by a federal plan under federal law.

(17) Not to be subject to the initiation or scheduling of audits during the first five calendar days of any month due to the high volume of prescriptions filled during that time, without the express consent of the pharmacy. The pharmacy shall cooperate with the auditor to establish an alternate date should the audit fall within the days excluded.

(18) To have the preliminary audit report delivered to the pharmacy within 120 days after conclusion of the audit.

(19) To have a final audit report delivered to the pharmacy within 90 days after the end of the appeals period, as provided for in G.S. 90-85.51.

(20) Not to have the accounting practice of extrapolation used in calculating recoupments or penalties for audits, unless otherwise required by federal requirements or federal plans.

(21) Not to be subject to recoupment on any portion of the reimbursement for the dispensed product of a prescription, unless otherwise provided in this subdivision:

a. Recoupment of reimbursement, or a portion of reimbursement, for the dispensed product of a prescription may be had in the following cases:

1. Fraud or other intentional and willful misrepresentation evidenced by a review of the claims data, statements, physical review, or other investigative methods.

2. Dispensing in excess of the benefit design, as established by the plan sponsor.

3. Prescriptions not filled in accordance with the prescriber's order.

4. Actual overpayment to the pharmacy.

b. Recoupment of claims in cases set out in sub-subdivision a. of this subdivision shall be based on the actual financial harm to the entity or the actual underpayment or overpayment. Calculations of overpayments shall not include dispensing fees unless one of the following conditions is present:

1. A prescription was not actually dispensed.

2. The prescriber denied authorization.

3. The prescription dispensed was a medication error by the pharmacy. For purposes of this subdivision, a medication error is a dispensing of the wrong drug or dispensing to the wrong patient or dispensing with the wrong directions.

4. The identified overpayment is based solely on an extra dispensing fee.

5. The pharmacy was noncompliant with Risk Evaluation and Mitigation Strategies (REMS) program guidelines.

6. There was insufficient documentation, including electronically stored information, as described in this subsection.

7. Fraud or other intentional and willful misrepresentation by the pharmacy.

(22) To have an audit based only on information obtained by the entity conducting the audit and not based on any audit report or other information gained from an audit conducted by a different auditing entity. This subdivision does not prohibit an auditing entity from using an earlier audit report prepared by that auditing entity for the same pharmacy. Except as required by State or federal law, an entity conducting an audit may have access to a pharmacy's previous audit report only if the previous report was prepared by that entity.

(23) If the audit is conducted by a vendor or subcontractor, that entity is required to identify the responsible party on whose behalf the audit is being conducted without having this information being requested.

(24) To use any prescription that complies with federal or State laws and regulations at the time of dispensing to validate a claim in connection with a prescription, prescription refill, or a change in a prescription. (2011-375, s. 1; 2013-379, s. 3.)

§ 90-85.51. Mandatory appeals process.

(a)   Each entity that conducts an audit of a pharmacy shall establish an appeals process under which a pharmacy may appeal an unfavorable preliminary audit report to the entity.

(b)   If, following the appeal, the entity finds that an unfavorable audit report or any portion of the unfavorable audit report is unsubstantiated, the entity shall dismiss the unsubstantiated portion of the audit report without any further proceedings.

(c)   Each entity conducting an audit shall provide a copy, if required under contractual terms, of the audit findings to the plan sponsor after completion of any appeals process. (2011-375, s. 1.)

§ 90-85.52. Pharmacy audit recoupments.

(a)   The entity conducting an audit shall not recoup any disputed funds, charges, or other penalties from a pharmacy until (i) the deadline for initiating the appeals process established pursuant to G.S. 90-85.51 has elapsed or (ii) after the final internal disposition of an audit, including the appeals process as set forth in G.S. 90-85.51, whichever is later, unless fraud or misrepresentation is reasonably suspected.

(b)   Recoupment on an audit shall be refunded to the responsible party as contractually agreed upon by the parties.

(c)   The entity conducting the audit may charge or assess the responsible party, directly or indirectly, based on amounts recouped if both of the following conditions are met:

(1)   The responsible party and the entity conducting the audit have entered into a contract that explicitly states the percentage charge or assessment to the responsible party.

(2) A commission or other payment to an agent or employee of the entity conducting the audit is not based, directly or indirectly, on amounts recouped. (2011-375, s. 1; 2013-379, s. 4.)

§ 90-85.53. Applicability.

This Article does not apply to any audit, review, or investigation that involves alleged Medicaid fraud, Medicaid abuse, insurance fraud, or other criminal fraud or misrepresentation. (2011-375, s. 1.)

Article 5.

North Carolina Controlled Substances Act.

§ 90-86. Title of Article.

This Article shall be known and may be cited as the "North Carolina Controlled Substances Act." (1971, c. 919, s. 1.)

§ 90-87. Definitions.

As used in this Article:

(1) "Administer" means the direct application of a controlled substance, whether by injection, inhalation, ingestion, or any other means to the body of a patient or research subject by:

a. A practitioner (or, in his presence, by his authorized agent), or

b. The patient or research subject at the direction and in the presence of the practitioner.

(2) "Agent" means an authorized person who acts on behalf of or at the direction of a manufacturer, distributor, or dispenser but does not include a common or contract carrier, public warehouseman, or employee thereof.

(3) "Bureau" means the Bureau of Narcotics and Dangerous Drugs, United States Department of Justice or its successor agency.

(3a) "Commission" means the Commission for Mental Health, Developmental Disabilities, and Substance Abuse Services established under Part 4 of Article 3 of Chapter 143B of the General Statutes.

(4) "Control" means to add, remove, or change the placement of a drug, substance, or immediate precursor included in Schedules I through VI of this Article.

(5) "Controlled substance" means a drug, substance, or immediate precursor included in Schedules I through VI of this Article.

(5a) "Controlled substance analogue" means a substance (i) the chemical structure of which is substantially similar to the chemical structure of a controlled substance in Schedule I or II; (ii) which has a stimulant, depressant, or hallucinogenic effect on the central nervous system that is substantially similar to or greater than the stimulant, depressant, or hallucinogenic effect on the central nervous system of a controlled substance in Schedule I or II; or (iii) with respect to a particular person, which such person represents or intends to have a stimulant, depressant, or hallucinogenic effect on the central nervous system that is substantially similar to or greater than the stimulant, depressant, or hallucinogenic effect on the central nervous system of a controlled substance in Schedule I or II; and does not include (i) a controlled substance; (ii) any substance for which there is an approved new drug application; (iii) with respect to a particular person any substance, if an exemption is in effect for investigational use, for that person, under § 355 of Title 21 of the United States Code to the extent conduct with respect to such substance is pursuant to such exemption; or (iv) any substance to the extent not intended for human consumption before such an exemption takes effect with respect to that substance. The designation of gamma butyrolactone or any other chemical as a listed chemical pursuant to subdivision 802(34) or 802(35) of Title 21 of the United States Code does not preclude a finding pursuant to this subdivision that the chemical is a controlled substance analogue.

(6) "Counterfeit controlled substance" means:

a. A controlled substance which, or the container or labeling of which, without authorization, bears the trademark, trade name, or other identifying mark, imprint, number, or device, or any likeness thereof, of a manufacturer, distributor, or dispenser other than the person or persons who in fact manufactured, distributed, or dispensed such substance and which thereby falsely purports, or is represented to be the product of, or to have been distributed by, such other manufacturer, distributor, or dispenser; or

b. Any substance which is by any means intentionally represented as a controlled substance. It is evidence that the substance has been intentionally misrepresented as a controlled substance if the following factors are established:

1. The substance was packaged or delivered in a manner normally used for the illegal delivery of controlled substances.

2. Money or other valuable property has been exchanged or requested for the substance, and the amount of that consideration was substantially in excess of the reasonable value of the substance.

3. The physical appearance of the tablets, capsules or other finished product containing the substance is substantially identical to a specified controlled substance.

(7) "Deliver" or "delivery" means the actual constructive, or attempted transfer from one person to another of a controlled substance, whether or not there is an agency relationship.

(8) "Dispense" means to deliver a controlled substance to an ultimate user or research subject by or pursuant to the lawful order of a practitioner, including the prescribing, administering, packaging, labeling, or compounding necessary to prepare the substance for that delivery.

(9) "Dispenser" means a practitioner who dispenses.

(10) "Distribute" means to deliver other than by administering or dispensing a controlled substance.

(11) "Distributor" means a person who distributes.

(12) "Drug" means a. substances recognized in the official United States Pharmacopoeia, official Homeopathic Pharmacopoeia of the United States, or official National Formulary, or any supplement to any of them; b. substances intended for use in the diagnosis, cure, mitigation, treatment, or prevention of disease in man or other animals; c. substances (other than food) intended to affect the structure or any function of the body of man or other animals; and d. substances intended for use as a component of any article specified in a, b, or c of this subdivision; but does not include devices or their components, parts, or accessories.

(13) "Drug dependent person" means a person who is using a controlled substance and who is in a state of psychic or physical dependence, or both, arising from use of that controlled substance on a continuous basis. Drug dependence is characterized by behavioral and other responses which include a strong compulsion to take the substance on a continuous basis in order to experience its psychic effects, or to avoid the discomfort of its absence.

(14) "Immediate precursor" means a substance which the Commission has found to be and by regulation designates as being the principal compound commonly used or produced primarily for use, and which is an immediate chemical intermediary used or likely to be used in the manufacture of a controlled substance, the control of which is necessary to prevent, curtail, or limit such manufacture.

(14a) The term "isomer" means, except as used in G.S. 90-87(17)(d), G.S. 90-89(c), G.S. 90-90(1)d., and G.S. 90-95(h)(3), the optical isomer. As used in G.S. 90-89(c) the term "isomer" means the optical, position, or geometric isomer. As used in G.S. 90-87(17)(d), G.S. 90-90(1)d., and G.S. 90-95(h)(3) the term "isomer" means the optical isomer or diastereoisomer.

(15) "Manufacture" means the production, preparation, propagation, compounding, conversion, or processing of a controlled substance by any means, whether directly or indirectly, artificially or naturally, or by extraction from substances of a natural origin, or independently by means of chemical synthesis, or by a combination of extraction and chemical synthesis; and "manufacture" further includes any packaging or repackaging of the substance or labeling or relabeling of its container except that this term does not include the preparation or compounding of a controlled substance by an individual for his own use or the preparation, compounding, packaging, or labeling of a controlled substance:

a. By a practitioner as an incident to his administering or dispensing of a controlled substance in the course of his professional practice, or

b. By a practitioner, or by his authorized agent under his supervision, for the purpose of, or as an incident to research, teaching, or chemical analysis and not for sale.

(16) "Marijuana" means all parts of the plant of the genus Cannabis, whether growing or not; the seeds thereof; the resin extracted from any part of such plant; and every compound, manufacture, salt, derivative, mixture, or preparation of such plant, its seeds or resin, but shall not include the mature stalks of such plant, fiber produced from such stalks, oil, or cake made from the seeds of such plant, any other compound, manufacture, salt, derivative, mixture, or preparation of such mature stalks (except the resin extracted therefrom), fiber, oil, or cake, or the sterilized seed of such plant which is incapable of germination.

(17) "Narcotic drug" means any of the following, whether produced directly or indirectly by extraction from substances of vegetable origin, or independently by means of chemical synthesis, or by a combination of extraction and chemical synthesis:

a. Opium and opiate, and any salt, compound, derivative, or preparation of opium or opiate.

b. Any salt, compound, isomer, derivative, or preparation thereof which is chemically equivalent or identical with any of the substances referred to in clause a, but not including the isoquinoline alkaloids of opium.

c. Opium poppy and poppy straw.

d. Cocaine and any salt, isomer, salts of isomers, compound, derivative, or preparation thereof, or coca leaves and any salt, isomer, salts of isomers, compound, derivative or preparation of coca leaves, or any salt, isomer, salts of isomers, compound, derivative, or preparation thereof which is chemically equivalent or identical with any of these substances, except that the substances shall not include decocanized coca leaves or extraction of coca leaves, which extractions do not contain cocaine or ecgonine.

(18) "Opiate" means any substance having an addiction-forming or addiction-sustaining liability similar to morphine or being capable of conversion into a drug

having addiction-forming or addiction-sustaining liability. It does not include, unless specifically designated as controlled under G.S. 90-88, the dextrorotatory isomer of 3-methoxy-n-methyl-morphinan and its salts (dextromethorphan). It does include its racemic and levorotatory forms.

(19) "Opium poppy" means the plant of the species Papaver somniferum L., except its seeds.

(20) "Person" means individual, corporation, government or governmental subdivision or agency, business trust, estate, trust, partnership or association, or any other legal entity.

(21) "Poppy straw" means all parts, except the seeds, of the opium poppy, after mowing.

(22) "Practitioner" means:

a. A physician, dentist, optometrist, veterinarian, scientific investigator, or other person licensed, registered or otherwise permitted to distribute, dispense, conduct research with respect to or to administer a controlled substance so long as such activity is within the normal course of professional practice or research in this State.

b. A pharmacy, hospital or other institution licensed, registered, or otherwise permitted to distribute, dispense, conduct research with respect to or to administer a controlled substance so long as such activity is within the normal course of professional practice or research in this State.

(23) "Prescription" means:

a. A written order or other order which is promptly reduced to writing for a controlled substance as defined in this Article, or for a preparation, combination, or mixture thereof, issued by a practitioner who is licensed in this State to administer or prescribe drugs in the course of his professional practice; or issued by a practitioner serving on active duty with the Armed Forces of the United States or the United States Veterans Administration who is licensed in this or another state or Puerto Rico, provided the order is written for the benefit of eligible beneficiaries of armed services medical care; a prescription does not include an order entered in a chart or other medical record of a patient by a practitioner for the administration of a drug; or

b. A drug or preparation, or combination, or mixture thereof furnished pursuant to a prescription order.

(24) "Production" includes the manufacture, planting, cultivation, growing, or harvesting of a controlled substance.

(25) "Registrant" means a person registered by the Commission to manufacture, distribute, or dispense any controlled substance as required by this Article.

(26) "State" means the State of North Carolina.

(27) "Ultimate user" means a person who lawfully possesses a controlled substance for his own use, or for the use of a member of his household, or for administration to an animal owned by him or by a member of his household. (1971, c. 919, s. 1; 1973, c. 476, s. 128; c. 540, ss. 2-4; c. 1358, ss. 1, 15; 1977, c. 482, s. 6; 1981, c. 51, ss. 8, 9; c. 75, s. 1; c. 732; 1985, c. 491; 1987, c. 105, ss. 1, 2; 1991 (Reg. Sess., 1992), c. 1030, s. 21; 1997-456, s. 27; 2003-249, s. 2; 2011-183, s. 60.)

§ 90-88. Authority to control.

(a) The Commission may add, delete, or reschedule substances within Schedules I through VI of this Article on the petition of any interested party, or its own motion. In every case the Commission shall give notice of and hold a public hearing pursuant to Chapter 150B of the General Statutes prior to adding, deleting or rescheduling a controlled substance within Schedules I through VI of this Article, except as provided in subsection (d) of this section. A petition by the Commission, the North Carolina Department of Justice, or the North Carolina Board of Pharmacy to add, delete, or reschedule a controlled substance within Schedules I through VI of this Article shall be placed on the agenda, for consideration, at the next regularly scheduled meeting of the Commission, as a matter of right.

(a1) In making a determination regarding a substance, the Commission shall consider the following:

(1) The actual or relative potential for abuse;

(2) The scientific evidence of its pharmacological effect, if known;

(3) The state of current scientific knowledge regarding the substance;

(4) The history and current pattern of abuse;

(5) The scope, duration, and significance of abuse;

(6) The risk to the public health;

(7) The potential of the substance to produce psychic or physiological dependence liability; and

(8) Whether the substance is an immediate precursor of a substance already controlled under this Article.

(b) After considering the required factors, the Commission shall make findings with respect thereto and shall issue an order adding, deleting or rescheduling the substance within Schedules I through VI of this Article.

(c) If the Commission designates a substance as an immediate precursor, substances which are precursors of the controlled precursor shall not be subject to control solely because they are precursors of the controlled precursor.

(d) If any substance is designated, rescheduled or deleted as a controlled substance under federal law, the Commission shall similarly control or cease control of, the substance under this Article unless the Commission objects to such inclusion. The Commission, at its next regularly scheduled meeting that takes place 30 days after publication in the Federal Register of a final order scheduling a substance, shall determine either to adopt a rule to similarly control the substance under this Article or to object to such action. No rule-making notice or hearing as specified by Chapter 150B of the General Statutes is required if the Commission makes a decision to similarly control a substance. However, if the Commission makes a decision to object to adoption of the federal action, it shall initiate rule-making procedures pursuant to Chapter 150B of the General Statutes within 180 days of its decision to object.

(e) The Commission shall exclude any nonnarcotic substance from the provisions of this Article if such substance may, under the federal Food, Drug and Cosmetic Act, lawfully be sold over-the-counter without prescription.

(f) Authority to control under this Article does not include distilled spirits, wine, malt beverages, or tobacco.

(g) The Commission shall similarly exempt from the provisions of this Article any chemical agents and diagnostic reagents not intended for administration to humans or other animals, containing controlled substances which either (i) contain additional adulterant or denaturing agents so that the resulting mixture has no significant abuse potential, or (ii) are packaged in such a form or concentration that the particular form as packaged has no significant abuse potential, where such substance was exempted by the Federal Bureau of Narcotics and Dangerous Drugs.

(h) Repealed by Session Laws 1987, c. 413, s. 4.

(i) The North Carolina Department of Health and Human Services shall maintain a list of all preparations, compounds, or mixtures which are excluded, exempted and excepted from control under any schedule of this Article by the United States Drug Enforcement Administration and/or the Commission. This list and any changes to this list shall be mailed to the North Carolina Board of Pharmacy, the State Bureau of Investigation and each district attorney of this State. (1971, c. 919, s. 1; 1973, c. 476, s. 128; cc. 524, 541; c. 1358, ss. 2, 3, 15; 1977, c. 667, s. 3; 1981, c. 51, s. 9; 1987, c. 413, ss. 1-4; 1989, c. 770, s. 16; 1997-443, s. 11A.118(a); 2000-189, s. 4; 2001-487, s. 22.)

§ 90-89. Schedule I controlled substances.

This schedule includes the controlled substances listed or to be listed by whatever official name, common or usual name, chemical name, or trade name designated. In determining that a substance comes within this schedule, the Commission shall find: a high potential for abuse, no currently accepted medical use in the United States, or a lack of accepted safety for use in treatment under medical supervision. The following controlled substances are included in this schedule:

(1) Any of the following opiates, including the isomers, esters, ethers, salts and salts of isomers, esters, and ethers, unless specifically excepted, or listed in another schedule, whenever the existence of such isomers, esters, ethers, and salts is possible within the specific chemical designation:

a. Acetyl-alpha-methylfentanyl (N[1-(1-methyl-2-phenethyl)-4-piperidinyl]-N-phenylacetamide).

b. Acetylmethadol.

c. Repealed by Session Laws 1987, c. 412, s. 2.

d. Alpha-methylthiofentanyl (N-[1-methyl-2-(2-thienyl)ethyl-4-piperidinyl]-N-phenylpropanamide).

e. Allylprodine.

f. Alphacetylmethadol.

g. Alphameprodine.

h. Alphamethadol.

i. Alpha-methylfentanyl (N-(1-(alpha-methyl-beta-phenyl) ethyl-4-piperidyl) propionalilide; 1(1-methyl-2-phenyl-ethyl)-4-(N-propanilido) piperidine).

j. Benzethidine.

k. Betacetylmethadol.

l. Beta-hydroxfentanyl (N-[1-(2-hydroxy-2-phenethyl)-4-piperidinyl]-N-phenylpropanamide).

m. Beta-hydroxy-3-methylfentanyl (N-[1-(2-hydroxy-2-phenethyl)-3-methyl-4-piperidinyl]-N-phenylpropanamide).

n. Betameprodine.

o. Betamethadol.

p. Betaprodine.

q. Clonitazene.

r. Dextromoramide.

s. Diampromide.

t. Diethylthiambutene.

u. Difenoxin.

v. Dimenoxadol.

w. Dimepheptanol.

x. Dimethylthiambutene.

y. Dioxaphetyl butyrate.

z. Dipipanone.

aa. Ethylmethylthiambutene.

bb. Etonitazene.

cc. Etoxeridine.

dd. Furethidine.

ee. Hydroxypethidine.

ff. Ketobemidone.

gg. Levomoramide.

hh. Levophenacylmorphan.

ii. 1-methyl-4-phenyl-4-propionoxypiperidine (MPPP).

jj. 3-Methylfentanyl (N-[3-methyl-1-(2-Phenylethyl)-4-Piperidyl]-N-Phenylpropanamide).

kk. 3-Methylthiofentanyl (N-[(3-methyl-1-(2-thienyl)ethyl-4-piperidinyl]-N-phenylpropanamide).

ll. Morpheridine.

mm. Noracymethadol.

nn. Norlevorphanol.

oo. Normethadone.

pp. Norpipanone.

qq. Para-fluorofentanyl (N-(4-fluorophenyl)-N-[1-(2-phen-ethyl)-4-piperidinyl]-propanamide.

rr. Phenadoxone.

ss. Phenampromide.

tt. 1-(2-phenethyl)-4-phenyl-4-acetoxypiperidine (PEPAP).

uu. Phenomorphan.

vv. Phenoperidine.

ww. Piritramide.

xx. Proheptazine.

yy. Properidine.

zz. Propiram.

aaa. Racemoramide.

bbb. Thiofentanyl (N-phenyl-N-[1-(2-thienyl)ethyl-4-piperidinyl]-propanamide.

ccc. Tilidine.

ddd. Trimeperidine.

(2) Any of the following opium derivatives, including their salts, isomers, and salts of isomers, unless specifically excepted, or listed in another schedule, whenever the existence of such salts, isomers, and salts of isomers is possible within the specific chemical designation:

a. Acetorphine.

b. Acetyldihydrocodeine.

c. Benzylmorphine.

d. Codeine methylbromide.

e. Codeine-N-Oxide.

f. Cyprenorphine.

g. Desomorphine.

h. Dihydromorphine.

i. Etorphine (except hydrochloride salt).

j. Heroin.

k. Hydromorphinol.

l. Methyldesorphine.

m. Methyldihydromorphine.

n. Morphine methylbromide.

o. Morphine methylsulfonate.

p. Morphine-N-Oxide.

q. Myrophine.

r. Nicocodeine.

s. Nicomorphine.

t. Normorphine.

u. Pholcodine.

v. Thebacon.

w. Drotebanol.

(3) Any material, compound, mixture, or preparation which contains any quantity of the following hallucinogenic substances, including their salts, isomers, and salts of isomers, unless specifically excepted, or listed in another schedule, whenever the existence of such salts, isomers, and salts of isomers is possible within the specific chemical designation:

a. 3, 4-methylenedioxyamphetamine.

b. 5-methoxy-3, 4-methylenedioxyamphetamine.

c. 3, 4-Methylenedioxymethamphetamine (MDMA).

d. 3,4-methylenedioxy-N-ethylamphetamine (also known as N-ethyl-alpha-methyl-3,4-(methylenedioxy)phenethylamine, N-ethyl MDA, MDE, and MDEA).

e. N-hydroxy-3,4-methylenedioxyamphetamine (also known as N-hydroxy-alpha-methyl-3,4-(methylenedioxy)phenethylamine, and N-hydroxy MDA).

f. 3, 4, 5-trimethoxyamphetamine.

g. Alpha-ethyltryptamine. Some trade or other names: etryptamine, Monase, alpha-ethyl-1H-indole-3-ethanamine, 3-(2-aminobutyl) indole, alpha-ET, and AET.

h. Bufotenine.

i. Diethyltryptamine.

j. Dimethyltryptamine.

k. 4-methyl-2, 5-dimethoxyamphetamine.

l. Ibogaine.

m. Lysergic acid diethylamide.

n. Mescaline.

o. Peyote, meaning all parts of the plant presently classified botanically as Lophophora Williamsii Lemaire, whether growing or not; the seeds thereof; any extract from any part of such plant; and every compound, manufacture, salt, derivative, mixture or preparation of such plant, its seed or extracts.

p. N-ethyl-3-piperidyl benzilate.

q. N-methyl-3-piperidyl benzilate.

r. Psilocybin.

s. Psilocin.

t. 2, 5-dimethoxyamphetamine.

u. 2, 5-dimethoxy-4-ethylamphetamine. Some trade or other names: DOET.

v. 4-bromo-2, 5-dimethoxyamphetamine.

w. 4-methoxyamphetamine.

x. Ethylamine analog of phencyclidine. Some trade or other names: N-ethyl-1-phenylcyclohexylamine, (1-phenylcyclohexyl) ethylamine, N-(1-phenylcyclohexyl) ethylamine, cyclohexamine, PCE.

y. Pyrrolidine analog of phencyclidine. Some trade or other names: 1-(1-phenylcyclohexyl)-pyrrolidine, PCPy, PHP.

z. Thiophene analog of phencyclidine. Some trade or other names: 1-[1-(2-thienyl)-cyclohexyl]-piperidine, 2-thienyl analog of phencyclidine, TPCP, TCP.

aa. 1-[1-(2-thienyl)cyclohexyl]pyrrolidine; Some other names: TCPy.

bb. Parahexyl.

cc. 4-Bromo-2, 5-Dimethoxyphenethylamine.

dd. Alpha-Methyltryptamine.

ee. 5-Methoxy-n-diisopropyltryptamine.

(4) Any material compound, mixture, or preparation which contains any quantity of the following substances having a depressant effect on the central nervous system, including its salts, isomers, and salts of isomers whenever the existence of such salts, isomers, and salts of isomers is possible within the specific chemical designation, unless specifically excepted or unless listed in another schedule:

a. Mecloqualone.

b. Methaqualone.

c. Gamma hydroxybutyric acid; Some other names: GHB, gamma-hydroxybutyrate, 4-hydroxybutyrate, 4-hydroxybutanoic acid; sodium oxybate; sodium oxybutyrate.

(5) Stimulants. - Unless specifically excepted or unless listed in another schedule, any material, compound, mixture, or preparation that contains any quantity of the following substances having a stimulant effect on the central nervous system, including its salts, isomers, and salts of isomers:

a. Aminorex. Some trade or other names: aminoxaphen; 2-amino-5-phenyl-2-oxazoline; or 4,5-dihydro-5-phenly-2-oxazolamine.

b. Cathinone. Some trade or other names: 2-amino-1-phenyl-1-propanone, alpha-aminopropiophenone, 2-aminopropiophenone, and norephedrone.

c. Fenethylline.

d. Methcathinone. Some trade or other names: 2-(methylamino)-propiophenone, alpha-(methylamino)propiophenone, 2-(methylamino)-1-phenylpropan-1-one, alpha-N-methylamino- propiophenone, monomethylproprion, ephedrone, N-methylcathinone, methylcathinone, AL-464, AL-422, AL-463, and UR1432.

e. (+-)cis-4-methylaminorex [(+-)cis-4,5-dihydro-4-methyl-5-phenyl-2-oxazolamine] (also known as 2-amino-4-methyl-5-phenyl-2-oxazoline).

f. N,N-dimethylamphetamine. Some other names: N,N,alpha-tri-methylbenzeneethaneamine; N,N,alpha-trimethylphenethylamine.

g. N-ethylamphetamine.

h. 4-methylmethcathinone (also known as mephedrone).

i. 3,4-Methylenedioxypyrovalerone (also known as MDPV).

j. A compound, other than bupropion, that is structurally derived from 2-amino-1-phenyl-1-propanone by modification in any of the following ways: (i) by substitution in the phenyl ring to any extent with alkyl, alkoxy, alkylenedioxy, haloalkyl, or halide substituents, whether or not further substituted in the phenyl ring by one or more other univalent substituents; (ii) by substitution at the 3-position with an alkyl substituent; or (iii) by substitution at the nitrogen atom with alkyl or diakyl groups or by inclusion of the nitrogen atom in a cyclic structure.

k. N-Benzylpiperazine.

l. 2,5-Dimethoxy-4-(n)-propylthiophenethylamine. (1971, c. 919, s. 1; 1973, c. 476, s. 128; c. 844; c. 1358, ss. 4, 5, 15; 1975, c. 443, s. 1; c. 790; 1977, c. 667, s. 3; c. 891, s. 1; 1979, c. 434, s. 1; 1981, c. 51, s. 9; 1983, c. 695, s. 1; 1985, c. 172, ss. 1-3; 1987, c. 412, ss. 1-5; 1989 (Reg. Sess., 1990), c. 1040, s. 1; 1993, c. 319, ss. 1, 2; 1995, c. 186, ss. 1-3; c. 509, s. 135.1(c); 1997-456, ss. 12, 27; 1999-165, s. 1; 2000-140, s. 92.2(a); 2011-12, s. 1; 2011-326, s. 14(a), (b).)

§ 90-89.1. Treatment of controlled substance analogues.

A controlled substance analogue shall, to the extent intended for human consumption, be treated for the purposes of any State law as a controlled substance in Schedule I. (2003-249, s. 1.)

§ 90-90. Schedule II controlled substances.

This schedule includes the controlled substances listed or to be listed by whatever official name, common or usual name, chemical name, or trade name designated. In determining that a substance comes within this schedule, the Commission shall find: a high potential for abuse; currently accepted medical use in the United States, or currently accepted medical use with severe restrictions; and the abuse of the substance may lead to severe psychic or physical dependence. The following controlled substances are included in this schedule:

(1) Any of the following substances whether produced directly or indirectly by extraction from substances of vegetable origin, or independently by means of chemical synthesis, or by a combination of extraction and chemical synthesis, unless specifically excepted or unless listed in another schedule:

a. Opium and opiate, and any salt, compound, derivative, or preparation of opium and opiate, excluding apomorphine, nalbuphine, dextrorphan, naloxone, naltrexone and nalmefene, and their respective salts, but including the following:

1. Raw opium.

2. Opium extracts.

3. Opium fluid extracts.

4. Powdered opium.

5. Granulated opium.

6. Tincture of opium.

7. Codeine.

8. Ethylmorphine.

9. Etorphine hydrochloride.

10. Hydrocodone.

11. Hydromorphone.

12. Metopon.

13. Morphine.

14. Oxycodone.

15. Oxymorphone.

16. Thebaine.

17. Dihydroetorphine.

b. Any salt, compound, derivative, or preparation thereof which is chemically equivalent or identical with any of the substances referred to in paragraph 1 of this subdivision, except that these substances shall not include the isoquinoline alkaloids of opium.

c. Opium poppy and poppy straw.

d. Cocaine and any salt, isomer, salts of isomers, compound, derivative, or preparation thereof, or coca leaves and any salt, isomer, salts of isomers, compound, derivative, or preparation of coca leaves, or any salt, isomer, salts of isomers, compound, derivative, or preparation thereof which is chemically equivalent or identical with any of these substances, except that the substances shall not include decocanized coca leaves or extraction of coca leaves, which extractions do not contain cocaine or ecgonine.

e. Concentrate of poppy straw (the crude extract of poppy straw in either liquid, solid or powder form which contains the phenanthrine alkaloids of the opium poppy).

(2) Any of the following opiates, including their isomers, esters, ethers, salts, and salts of isomers, whenever the existence of such isomers, esters,

ethers, and salts is possible within the specific chemical designation unless specifically exempted or listed in other schedules:

a. Alfentanil.

b. Alphaprodine.

c. Anileridine.

d. Bezitramide.

e. Carfentanil.

f. Dihydrocodeine.

g. Diphenoxylate.

h. Fentanyl.

i. Isomethadone.

j. Levo-alphacetylmethadol. Some trade or other names: levo-alpha-acetylmethadol, levomethadyl acetate, or LAAM.

k. Levomethorphan.

l. Levorphanol.

m. Metazocine.

n. Methadone.

o. Methadone - Intermediate, 4-cyano-2-dimethylamino-4, 4-diphenyl butane.

p. Moramide - Intermediate, 2-methyl-3-morpholino-1, 1-diphenyl-propane-carboxylic acid.

q. Pethidine.

r. Pethidine - Intermediate - A, 4-cyano-1-methyl-4-phenylpiperidine.

s. Pethidine - Intermediate - B, ethyl-4-phenylpiperidine-4-carboxylate.

t. Pethidine - Intermediate - C, 1-methyl-4-phenylpiperidine-4-carboxylic acid.

u. Phenazocine.

v. Piminodine.

w. Racemethorphan.

x. Racemorphan.

y. Remifentanil.

z. Sufentanil.

aa. Tapentadol.

(3) Any material, compound, mixture, or preparation which contains any quantity of the following substances having a potential for abuse associated with a stimulant effect on the central nervous system unless specifically exempted or listed in another schedule:

a. Amphetamine, its salts, optical isomers, and salts of its optical isomers.

b. Phenmetrazine and its salts.

c. Methamphetamine, including its salts, isomers, and salts of isomers.

d. Methylphenidate.

e. Phenylacetone. Some trade or other names: Phenyl-2-propanone; P2P; benzyl methyl ketone; methyl benzyl ketone.

f. Lisdexamfetamine, including its salts, isomers, and salts of isomers.

(4) Any material, compound, mixture, or preparation which contains any quantity of the following substances having a depressant effect on the central nervous system, including its salts, isomers, and salts of isomers whenever the

existence of such salts, isomers, and salts of isomers is possible within the specific chemical designation, unless specifically exempted by the Commission or listed in another schedule:

a. Amobarbital

b. Glutethimide

c. Repealed by Session Laws 1983, c. 695, s. 2.

d. Pentobarbital

e. Phencyclidine

f. Phencyclidine immediate precursors:

1. 1-Phenylcyclohexylamine

2. 1-Piperidinocyclohexanecarbonitrile (PCC)

g. Secobarbital.

(5) Any material, compound, mixture, or preparation which contains any quantity of the following hallucinogenic substances, including their salts, isomers, and salts of isomers, unless specifically excepted, or listed in another schedule, whenever the existence of such salts, isomers, and salts of isomers is possible within the specific chemical designation:

a. Repealed by Session Laws 2001-233, s. 2(a), effective June 21, 2001.

b. Nabilone [Another name for nabilone: (+/-)-trans-3-(1,1-dimethylheptyl)-6,6a,7,8,10,10a-hexahydro-1-hydroxy-6,6-dimethyl-9H-dibenzo[b,d]pyran-9-one]. (1971, c. 919, s. 1; 1973, c. 476, s. 128; c. 540, s. 6; c. 1358, ss. 6, 15; 1975, c. 443, s. 2; 1977, c. 667, s. 3; c. 891, s. 2; 1979, c. 434, s. 2; 1981, c. 51, s. 9; 1983, c. 695, s. 2; 1985, c. 172, ss. 4, 5; 1987, c. 105, s. 3; c. 412, ss. 5A-7; 1989 (Reg. Sess., 1990), c. 1040, s. 2; 1993, c. 319, ss. 3, 4; 1995, c. 186, s. 4; 1997-385, s. 1; 1997-456, s. 27; 1999-165, s. 2; 2001-233, ss. 1, 2(a); 2011-326, s. 14(c), (d).)

§ 90-91. Schedule III controlled substances.

This schedule includes the controlled substances listed or to be listed by whatever official name, common or usual name, chemical name, or trade name designated. In determining that a substance comes within this schedule, the Commission shall find: a potential for abuse less than the substances listed in Schedules I and II; currently accepted medical use in the United States; and abuse may lead to moderate or low physical dependence or high psychological dependence. The following controlled substances are included in this schedule:

(a) Repealed by Session Laws 1973, c. 540, s. 5.

(b) Any material, compound, mixture, or preparation which contains any quantity of the following substances having a depressant effect on the central nervous system unless specifically exempted or listed in another schedule:

1. Any substance which contains any quantity of a derivative of barbituric acid, or any salt of a derivative of barbituric acid.

2. Chlorhexadol.

3. Repealed by Session Laws 1993, c. 319, s. 5.

4. Lysergic acid.

5. Lysergic acid amide.

6. Methyprylon.

7. Sulfondiethylmethane.

8. Sulfonethylmethane.

9. Sulfonmethane.

9a. Tiletamine and zolazepam or any salt thereof. Some trade or other names for tiletamine-zolazepam combination product: Telazol. Some trade or other names for tiletamine:

2-(ethylamino)-2-(2-thienyl)-cyclohexanone. Some trade or other names for zolazepam: 4-(2-fluorophenyl)-6,8-dihydro-1,3,8-trimethylpyrazolo-[3,4-e][1,4]/y-diazepin-7(1H)-one. flupyrazapon.

10. Any compound, mixture or preparation containing

(i) Amobarbital.

(ii) Secobarbital.

(iii) Pentobarbital.

or any salt thereof and one or more active ingredients which are not included in any other schedule.

11. Any suppository dosage form containing

(i) Amobarbital.

(ii) Secobarbital.

(iii) Pentobarbital.

or any salt of any of these drugs and approved by the federal Food and Drug Administration for marketing as a suppository.

12. Ketamine.

(c) Nalorphine.

(d) Any material, compound, mixture, or preparation containing limited quantities of any of the following narcotic drugs, or any salts thereof unless specifically exempted or listed in another schedule:

1. Not more than 1.80 grams of codeine per 100 milliliters or not more than 90 milligrams per dosage unit with an equal or greater quantity of an isoquinoline alkaloid of opium.

2. Not more than 1.80 grams of codeine per 100 milliliters or not more than 90 milligrams per dosage unit, with one or more active, nonnarcotic ingredients in recognized therapeutic amounts.

3. Not more than 300 milligrams of dihydrocodeinone per 100 milliliters or not more than 15 milligrams per dosage unit with a four-fold or greater quantity of an isoquinoline alkaloid of opium.

4. Not more than 300 milligrams of dihydrocodeinone per 100 milliliters or not more than 15 milligrams per dosage unit, with one or more active, nonnarcotic ingredients in recognized therapeutic amounts.

5. Not more than 1.80 grams of dihydrocodeine per 100 milliliters or not more than 90 milligrams per dosage unit, with one or more active, nonnarcotic ingredients in recognized therapeutic amounts.

6. Not more than 300 milligrams of ethylmorphine per 100 milliliters or not more than 15 milligrams per dosage unit, with one or more active, nonnarcotic ingredients in recognized therapeutic amounts.

7. Not more than 500 milligrams of opium per 100 milliliters or per 100 grams, or not more than 25 milligrams per dosage unit, with one or more active, nonnarcotic ingredients in recognized therapeutic amounts.

8. Not more than 50 milligrams of morphine per 100 milliliters or per 100 grams with one or more active, nonnarcotic ingredients in recognized therapeutic amounts.

(e) Any compound, mixture or preparation containing limited quantities of the following narcotic drugs, which shall include one or more active, nonnarcotic, medicinal ingredients in sufficient proportion to confer upon the compound, mixture, or preparation, valuable medicinal qualities other than those possessed by the narcotic drug alone:

1. Paregoric, U.S.P.; provided, that no person shall purchase or receive by any means whatsoever more than one fluid ounce of paregoric within a consecutive 24-hour period, except on prescription issued by a duly licensed physician.

(f) Paregoric, U.S.P., may be dispensed at retail as permitted by federal law or administrative regulation without a prescription only by a registered pharmacist and no other person, agency or employee may dispense paregoric, U.S.P., even if under the direct supervision of a pharmacist.

(g) Notwithstanding the provisions of G.S. 90-91(f), after the pharmacist has fulfilled his professional responsibilities and legal responsibilities required of him in this Article, the actual cash transaction, credit transaction, or delivery of paregoric, U.S.P., may be completed by a nonpharmacist. A pharmacist may refuse to dispense a paregoric, U.S.P., substance until he is satisfied that the product is being obtained for medicinal purposes only.

(h) Paregoric, U.S.P., may only be sold at retail without a prescription to a person at least 18 years of age. A pharmacist must require every retail purchaser of a paregoric, U.S.P., substance to furnish suitable identification, including proof of age when appropriate, in order to purchase paregoric, U.S.P. The name and address obtained from such identification shall be entered in the record of disposition to consumers.

(i) The Commission may by regulation except any compound, mixture, or preparation containing any stimulant or depressant substance listed in paragraphs (a)1 and (a)2 of this schedule from the application of all or any part of this Article if the compound, mixture, or preparation contains one or more active medicinal ingredients not having a stimulant or depressant effect on the central nervous system; and if the ingredients are included therein in such combinations, quantity, proportion, or concentration that vitiate the potential for abuse of the substances which have a stimulant or depressant effect on the central nervous system.

(j) Any material, compound, mixture, or preparation which contains any quantity of the following substances having a stimulant effect on the central nervous system, including its salts, isomers, and salts of said isomers whenever the existence of such salts, isomers, and salts of isomers is possible within the specific chemical designation, unless specifically excluded or listed in some other schedule.

1. Benzphetamine.

2. Chlorphentermine.

3. Clortermine.

4. Repealed by Session Laws 1987, c. 412, s. 10.

5. Phendimetrazine.

(k) Anabolic steroids. The term "anabolic steroid" means any drug or hormonal substance, chemically and pharmacologically related to testosterone (other than estrogens, progestins, and corticosteroids) that promotes muscle growth, including, but not limited to, the following:

1. Methandrostenolone,

2. Stanozolol,

3. Ethylestrenol,

4. Nandrolone phenpropionate,

5. Nandrolone decanoate,

6. Testosterone propionate,

7. Chorionic gonadotropin,

8. Boldenone,

9. Chlorotestosterone (4-chlorotestosterone),

10. Clostebol,

11. Dehydrochlormethyltestosterone,

12. Dibydrostestosterone (4-dihydrotestosterone),

13. Drostanolone,

14. Fluoxymesterone,

15. Formebulone (formebolone),

16. Mesterolene,

17. Methandienone,

18. Methandranone,

19. Methandriol,

20. Methenolene,

21. Methyltestosterone,

22. Mibolerone,

23. Nandrolene,

24. Norethandrolene,

25. Oxandrolone,

26. Oxymesterone,

27. Oxymetholone,

28. Stanolone,

29. Testolactone,

30. Testosterone,

31. Trenbolone, and

32. Any salt, ester, or isomer of a drug or substance described or listed in this subsection, if that salt, ester, or isomer promotes muscle growth. Except such term does not include an anabolic steroid which is expressly intended for administration through implants to cattle or other nonhuman species and which has been approved by the Secretary of Health and Human Services for such administration. If any person prescribes, dispenses, or distributes such steroid for human use, such person shall be considered to have prescribed, dispensed, or distributed an anabolic steroid within the meaning of this subsection.

(l) Repealed by Session Laws 2001-233, s. 3(a), effective June 21, 2001.

(m) Any drug product containing gamma hydroxybutyric acid, including its salts, isomers, and salts of isomers, for which an application is approved under section 505 of the Federal Food, Drug, and Cosmetic Act.

(n) Dronabinol (synthetic) in sesame oil and encapsulated in a soft gelatin capsule in a U.S. Food and Drug Administration approved drug product. [Some other names: (6aR-trans), -6a,7,8,10a-tetrahydro-6,6,9-trimethyl-3-pentyl-6H-dibenzo [b,d]pyran-1-o1 or (-)-delta-9-(trans)-tetrahydrocannabinol]. (1971, c. 919, s. 1; 1973, c. 476, s. 128; c. 540, s. 5; c. 1358, ss. 7, 15; 1975, c. 442; 1977, c. 667, s. 3; 1979, c. 434, s. 3; 1981, c. 51, s. 9; 1987, c. 412, ss. 8-10; 1987 (Reg. Sess., 1988), c. 1055; 1991, c. 413, s. 1; 1993, c. 319, s. 5; 1999-370, s. 3; 2000-140, s. 92.2(b); 2001-233, ss. 2(b), 3(a), 3(b); 2011-326, s. 14(e).)

§ 90-92. Schedule IV controlled substances.

(a) This schedule includes the controlled substances listed or to be listed by whatever official name, common or usual name, chemical name, or trade name designated. In determining that a substance comes within this schedule, the Commission shall find: a low potential for abuse relative to the substances listed in Schedule III of this Article; currently accepted medical use in the United States; and limited physical or pyschological dependence relative to the substances listed in Schedule III of this Article. The following controlled substances are included in this schedule:

(1) Depressants. - Unless specifically excepted or unless listed in another schedule, any material, compound, mixture, or preparation which contains any quantity of the following substances, including its salts, isomers, and salts of isomers whenever the existence of such salts, isomers, and salts of isomers is possible within the specific chemical designation:

a. Alprazolam.

b. Barbital.

c. Bromazepam.

d. Camazepam.

e. Chloral betaine.

f. Chloral hydrate.

g. Chlordiazepoxide.

h. Clobazam.

i. Clonazepam.

j. Clorazepate.

k. Clotiazepam.

l. Cloxazolam.

m. Delorazepam.

n. Diazepam.

o. Estazolam.

p. Ethchlorvynol.

q. Ethinamate.

r. Ethyl loflazepate.

s. Fludiazepam.

t. Flunitrazepam.

u. Flurazepam.

v. Repealed by Session Laws 2000, c. 140, s. 92.2(c).

w. Halazepam.

x. Haloxazolam.

y. Ketazolam.

z. Loprazolam.

aa. Lorazepam.

bb. Lormetazepam.

cc. Mebutamate.

dd. Medazepam.

ee. Meprobamate.

ff. Methohexital.

gg. Methylphenobarbital (mephobarbital).

hh. Midazolam.

ii. Nimetazepam.

jj. Nitrazepam.

kk. Nordiazepam.

ll. Oxazepam.

mm. Oxazolam.

nn. Paraldehyde.

oo. Petrichloral.

pp. Phenobarbital.

qq. Pinazepam.

rr. Prazepam.

ss. Quazepam.

tt. Temazepam.

uu. Tetrazepam.

vv. Triazolam.

ww. Zolpidem.

xx. Zaleplon.

(2) Any material, compound, mixture, or preparation which contains any of the following substances, including its salts, or isomers and salts of such isomers, whenever the existence of such salts, isomers, and salts of isomers is possible:

a. Fenfluramine.

b. Pentazocine.

(3) Stimulants. - Unless specifically excepted or unless listed in another schedule, any material, compound, mixture, or preparation which contains any quantity of the following substances having a stimulant effect on the central nervous system, including its salts, isomers (whether optical, position, or geometric), and salts of such isomers whenever the existence of such salts, isomers, and salts of isomers is possible within the specific chemical designation:

a. Diethylpropion.

b. Mazindol.

c. Pemoline (including organometallic complexes and chelates thereof).

d. Phentermine.

e. Cathine.

f. Fencamfamin.

g. Fenproporex.

h. Mefenorex.

i. Sibutramine.

j. Modafinil.

(4) Other Substances. - Unless specifically excepted or unless listed in another schedule, any material, compound, mixture or preparation which contains any quantity of the following substances, including its salts:

a. Dextropropoxyphene (Alpha-(plus)-4-dimethylamino-1, 2-diphenyl-3-methyl-2-propionoxybutane).

b. Pipradrol.

c. SPA ((-)-1-dimethylamino-1, 2-diphenylethane).

d. Butorphanol.

(5) Narcotic Drugs. - Unless specifically excepted or unless listed in another schedule, any material, compound, mixture, or preparation containing limited quantities of any of the following narcotic drugs, or any salts thereof:

a. Not more than 1 milligram of difenoxin and not less than 25 micrograms of atropine sulfate per dosage unit.

b. Buprenorphine.

(b) The Commission may by regulation except any compound, mixture, or preparation containing any stimulant or depressant substance listed in this schedule from the application of all or any part of this Article if the compound, mixture, or preparation contains one or more active, nonnarcotic, medicinal ingredients not having a stimulant or depressant effect on the central nervous system; provided, that such admixtures shall be included therein in such combinations, quantity, proportion, or concentration as to vitiate the potential for abuse of the substances which do have a stimulant or depressant effect on the central nervous system. (1971, c. 919, s. 1; 1973, c. 476, s. 128; c. 1358, ss. 8, 15; c. 1446, s. 5; 1975, cc. 401, 819; 1977, c. 667, s. 3; c. 891, s. 3; 1979, c. 434, ss. 4-6; 1981, c. 51, s. 9; 1985, c. 172, ss. 6-8; c. 439, s. 1; 1987, c. 412, ss. 11, 12; 1993, c. 319, s. 6; 1995, c. 509, s. 38; 1997-456, s. 27; 1997-501, s. 1; 1999-165, s. 3; 2000-140, s. 92.2(c); 2001-233, s. 4.)

§ 90-93. Schedule V controlled substances.

(a) This schedule includes the controlled substances listed or to be listed by whatever official name, common or usual name, chemical name, or trade name designated. In determining that a substance comes within this schedule, the Commission shall find: a low potential for abuse relative to the substances listed in Schedule IV of this Article; currently accepted medical use in the United States; and limited physical or psychological dependence relative to the substances listed in Schedule IV of this Article. The following controlled substances are included in this schedule:

(1) Any compound, mixture or preparation containing any of the following limited quantities of narcotic drugs or salts thereof, which shall include one or more nonnarcotic active medicinal ingredients in sufficient proportion to confer upon the compound, mixture, or preparation valuable medicinal qualities other than those possessed by the narcotic alone:

a. Not more than 200 milligrams of codeine or any of its salts per 100 milliliters or per 100 grams.

b. Not more than 100 milligrams of dihydrocodeine or any of its salts per 100 milliliters or per 100 grams.

c. Not more than 100 milligrams of ethylmorphine or any of its salts per 100 milliliters or per 100 grams.

d. Not more than 2.5 milligrams of diphenoxylate and not less than 25 micrograms of atropine sulfate per dosage unit.

e. Not more than 100 milligrams of opium per 100 milliliters or per 100 grams.

f. Not more than 0.5 milligram of difenoxin and not less than 25 micrograms of atropine sulfate per dosage unit.

(2) Repealed by Session Laws 1985, c. 172, s. 9.

(3) Stimulants. - Unless specifically exempted or excluded or unless listed in another schedule, any material, compound, mixture, or preparation which contains any quantity of the following substances having a stimulant effect on the central nervous system, including its salts, isomers and salts of isomers:

a. Repealed by Session Laws 1993, c. 319, s. 7.

b. Pyrovalerone.

(b) A Schedule V substance may be sold at retail without a prescription only by a registered pharmacist and no other person, agent or employee may sell a Schedule V substance even if under the direct supervision of a pharmacist.

(c) Notwithstanding the provisions of G.S. 90-93(b), after the pharmacist has fulfilled the responsibilities required of him in this Article, the actual cash transaction, credit transaction, or delivery of a Schedule V substance, may be completed by a nonpharmacist. A pharmacist may refuse to sell a Schedule V substance until he is satisfied that the product is being obtained for medicinal purposes only.

(d) A Schedule V substance may be sold at retail without a prescription only to a person at least 18 years of age. The pharmacist must require every retail purchaser of a Schedule V substance to furnish suitable identification, including proof of age when appropriate, in order to purchase a Schedule V substance. The name and address obtained from such identification shall be entered in the record of disposition to consumers. (1971, c. 919, s. 1; 1973, c. 476, s. 128; c. 1358, ss. 9, 15; 1977, c. 667, s. 3; 1979, c. 434, ss. 7, 8; 1981, c. 51, s. 9; 1985, c. 172, s. 9; 1989 (Reg. Sess., 1990), c. 1040, s. 3; 1993, c. 319, s. 7; 1997-456, s. 27.)

§ 90-94. Schedule VI controlled substances.

This schedule includes the controlled substances listed or to be listed by whatever official name, common or usual name, chemical name, or trade name designated. In determining that such substance comes within this schedule, the Commission shall find: no currently accepted medical use in the United States, or a relatively low potential for abuse in terms of risk to public health and potential to produce psychic or physiological dependence liability based upon present medical knowledge, or a need for further and continuing study to develop scientific evidence of its pharmacological effects.

The following controlled substances are included in this schedule:

(1) Marijuana.

(2) Tetrahydrocannabinols.

(3) Synthetic cannabinoids. - Any quantity of any synthetic chemical compound that (i) is a cannabinoid receptor agonist and mimics the pharmacological effect of naturally occurring substances or (ii) has a stimulant, depressant, or hallucinogenic effect on the central nervous system that is not listed as a controlled substance in Schedule I through V, and is not an FDA-approved drug. Synthetic cannabinoids include, but are not limited to, the substances listed in sub-subdivisions a. through j. of this subdivision and any substance that contains any quantity of their salts, isomers (whether optical, positional, or geometric), homologues, and salts of isomers and homologues, unless specifically excepted, whenever the existence of these salts, isomers, homologues, and salts of isomers and homologues is possible within the specific chemical designation. The following substances are examples of synthetic cannabinoids and are not intended to be inclusive of the substances included in this Schedule:

a. Naphthoylindoles. Any compound containing a 3-(1-naphthoyl)indole structure with substitution at the nitrogen atom of the indole ring by an alkyl, haloalkyl, alkenyl, cycloalkylmethyl, cycloalkylethyl, 1-(N-methyl-2-piperidinyl)methyl, or 2-(4-morpholinyl)ethyl group, whether or not further substituted in the indole ring to any extent and whether or not substituted in the naphthyl ring to any extent. Some trade or other names: JWH-015, JWH-018, JWH-019, JWH-073, JWH-081, JWH-122, JWH-200, JWH-210, JWH-398, AM-2201, WIN 55-212.

b. Naphthylmethylindoles. Any compound containing a 1H-indol-3-yl-(1-naphthyl)methane structure with substitution at the nitrogen atom of the indole ring by an alkyl, haloalkyl, alkenyl, cycloalkylmethyl, cycloalkylethyl, 1-(N-methyl-2-piperidinyl)methyl, or 2-(4-morpholinyl)ethyl group, whether or not further substituted in the indole ring to any extent and whether or not substituted in the naphthyl ring to any extent.

c. Naphthoylpyrroles. Any compound containing a 3-(1-naphthoyl)pyrrole structure with substitution at the nitrogen atom of the pyrrole ring by an alkyl, haloalkyl, alkenyl, cycloalkylmethyl, cycloalkylethyl, 1-(N-methyl-2-piperidinyl)methyl, or 2-(4-morpholinyl)ethyl group, whether or not further substituted in the pyrrole ring to any extent and whether or not substituted in the naphthyl ring to any extent. Another name: JWH-307.

d. Naphthylmethylindenes. Any compound containing a naphthylideneindene structure with substitution at the 3-position of the indene ring by an alkyl, haloalkyl, alkenyl, cycloalkylmethyl, cycloalkylethyl, 1-(N-methyl-2-piperidinyl)methyl, or 2-(4-morpholinyl)ethyl group, whether or not further substituted in the indene ring to any extent and whether or not substituted in the naphthyl ring to any extent.

e. Phenylacetylindoles. Any compound containing a 3-phenylacetylindole structure with substitution at the nitrogen atom of the indole ring by an alkyl, haloalkyl, alkenyl, cycloalkylmethyl, cycloalkylethyl, 1-(N-methyl-2-piperidinyl)methyl, or 2-(4-morpholinyl)ethyl group, whether or not further substituted in the indole ring to any extent and whether or not substituted in the phenyl ring to any extent. Some trade or other names: SR-18, RCS-8, JWH-250, JWH-203.

f. Cyclohexylphenols. Any compound containing a 2-(3-hydroxycyclohexyl)phenol structure with substitution at the 5-position of the phenolic ring by an alkyl, haloalkyl, alkenyl, cycloalkylmethyl, cycloalkylethyl, 1-(N-methyl-2-piperidinyl)methyl, or 2-(4-morpholinyl)ethyl group, whether or not substituted in the cyclohexyl ring to any extent. Some trade or other names: CP 47,497 (and homologues), cannabicyclohexanol.

g. Benzoylindoles. Any compound containing a 3-(benzoyl)indole structure with substitution at the nitrogen atom of the indole ring by an alkyl, haloalkyl, alkenyl, cycloalkylmethyl, cycloalkylethyl, 1-(N-methyl-2-piperidinyl)methyl, or 2-(4-morpholinyl)ethyl group, whether or not further substituted in the indole ring to any extent and whether or not substituted in the phenyl ring to any extent. Some trade or other names: AM-694, Pravadoline (WIN 48,098), RCS-4.

h. 2,3-Dihydro-5-methyl-3-(4-morpholinylmethyl)pyrrolo[1,2,3-de]-1, 4-benzoxazin-6-yl]-1-napthalenylmethanone. Some trade or other names: WIN 55,212-2.

i. (6aR,10aR)-9-(hydroxymethyl)-6, 6-dimethyl-3-(2-methyloctan-2-yl) - 6a,7,10,10a-tetrahydrobenzo[c]chromen-1-ol 7370. Some trade or other names: HU-210.

j. Tetramethylcyclopropanoylindoles. Any compound containing a 3-tetramethylcyclopropanoylindole structure with substitution at the nitrogen atom of the indole ring by an alkyl, haloalkyl, cyanoalkyl, alkenyl, cycloalkylmethyl, cycloalkylethyl, 1-(N-methyl-2-piperidinyl)methyl, 2-(4-morpholinyl)ethyl, 1-(N-methyl-2-pyrrolidinyl)methyl, 1-(N-methyl-3- morpholinyl)methyl, or tetrahydropyranylmethyl group, whether or not further substituted in the indole ring to any extent and whether or not substituted in the tetramethylcyclopropyl ring to any extent. Some trade name or other names: "XLR-11." (1971, c. 919, s. 1; 1973, c. 476, s. 128; c. 1358, s. 15; 1977, c. 667, s. 3; 1981, c. 51, s. 9; 1997-456, s. 27; 2011-12, s. 5; 2013-109, s. 1.)

§ 90-95. Violations; penalties.

(a) Except as authorized by this Article, it is unlawful for any person:

(1) To manufacture, sell or deliver, or possess with intent to manufacture, sell or deliver, a controlled substance;

(2) To create, sell or deliver, or possess with intent to sell or deliver, a counterfeit controlled substance;

(3) To possess a controlled substance.

(b) Except as provided in subsections (h) and (i) of this section, any person who violates G.S. 90-95(a)(1) with respect to:

(1) A controlled substance classified in Schedule I or II shall be punished as a Class H felon, except as follows: (i) the sale of a controlled substance classified in Schedule I or II shall be punished as a Class G felony, and (ii) the manufacture of methamphetamine shall be punished as provided by subdivision (1a) of this subsection.

(1a) The manufacture of methamphetamine shall be punished as a Class C felony unless the offense was one of the following: packaging or repackaging methamphetamine, or labeling or relabeling the methamphetamine container. The offense of packaging or repackaging methamphetamine, or labeling or relabeling the methamphetamine container shall be punished as a Class H felony.

(2) A controlled substance classified in Schedule III, IV, V, or VI shall be punished as a Class I felon, except that the sale of a controlled substance classified in Schedule III, IV, V, or VI shall be punished as a Class H felon. The transfer of less than 5 grams of marijuana or less than 2.5 grams of a synthetic

cannabinoid or any mixture containing such substance for no remuneration shall not constitute a delivery in violation of G.S. 90-95(a)(1).

(c)   Any person who violates G.S. 90-95(a)(2) shall be punished as a Class I felon.

(d)   Except as provided in subsections (h) and (i) of this section, any person who violates G.S. 90-95(a)(3) with respect to:

(1)   A controlled substance classified in Schedule I shall be punished as a Class I felon. However, if the controlled substance is MDPV and the quantity of the MDPV is 1 gram or less, the violation shall be punishable as a Class 1 misdemeanor.

(2)   A controlled substance classified in Schedule II, III, or IV shall be guilty of a Class 1 misdemeanor. If the controlled substance exceeds four tablets, capsules, or other dosage units or equivalent quantity of hydromorphone or if the quantity of the controlled substance, or combination of the controlled substances, exceeds one hundred tablets, capsules or other dosage units, or equivalent quantity, the violation shall be punishable as a Class I felony. If the controlled substance is methamphetamine, amphetamine, phencyclidine, or cocaine and any salt, isomer, salts of isomers, compound, derivative, or preparation thereof, or coca leaves and any salt, isomer, salts of isomers, compound, derivative, or preparation of coca leaves, or any salt, isomer, salts of isomers, compound, derivative or preparation thereof which is chemically equivalent or identical with any of these substances (except decocanized coca leaves or any extraction of coca leaves which does not contain cocaine or ecgonine), the violation shall be punishable as a Class I felony.

(3)   A controlled substance classified in Schedule V shall be guilty of a Class 2 misdemeanor;

(4)   A controlled substance classified in Schedule VI shall be guilty of a Class 3 misdemeanor, but any sentence of imprisonment imposed must be suspended and the judge may not require at the time of sentencing that the defendant serve a period of imprisonment as a special condition of probation. If the quantity of the controlled substance exceeds one-half of an ounce (avoirdupois) of marijuana, 7 grams of a synthetic cannabinoid or any mixture containing such substance, or one-twentieth of an ounce (avoirdupois) of the extracted resin of marijuana, commonly known as hashish, the violation shall be punishable as a Class 1 misdemeanor. If the quantity of the controlled

substance exceeds one and one-half ounces (avoirdupois) of marijuana, 21 grams of a synthetic cannabinoid or any mixture containing such substance, or three-twentieths of an ounce (avoirdupois) of the extracted resin of marijuana, commonly known as hashish, or if the controlled substance consists of any quantity of synthetic tetrahydrocannabinols or tetrahydrocannabinols isolated from the resin of marijuana, the violation shall be punishable as a Class I felony.

(d1) (1) Except as authorized by this Article, it is unlawful for any person to:

a. Possess an immediate precursor chemical with intent to manufacture a controlled substance; or

b. Possess or distribute an immediate precursor chemical knowing, or having reasonable cause to believe, that the immediate precursor chemical will be used to manufacture a controlled substance; [or]

c. Possess a pseudoephedrine product if the person has a prior conviction for the possession or manufacture of methamphetamine.

Any person who violates this subsection shall be punished as a Class H felon, unless the immediate precursor is one that can be used to manufacture methamphetamine.

(2) Except as authorized by this Article, it is unlawful for any person to:

a. Possess an immediate precursor chemical with intent to manufacture methamphetamine; or

b. Possess or distribute an immediate precursor chemical knowing, or having reasonable cause to believe, that the immediate precursor chemical will be used to manufacture methamphetamine.

Any person who violates this subdivision shall be punished as a Class F felon.

(d2) The immediate precursor chemicals to which subsection (d1) and (d1a) of this section applies are those immediate precursor chemicals designated by the Commission pursuant to its authority under G.S. 90-88, and the following (until otherwise specified by the Commission):

(1) Acetic anhydride.

(2) Acetone.

(3) Anhydrous ammonia.

(4) Anthranilic acid.

(5) Benzyl chloride.

(6) Benzyl cyanide.

(7) 2-Butanone (Methyl Ethyl Ketone).

(8) Chloroephedrine.

(9) Chloropseudoephedrine.

(10) D-lysergic acid.

(11) Ephedrine.

(12) Ergonovine maleate.

(13) Ergotamine tartrate.

(14) Ethyl ether.

(15) Ethyl Malonate.

(16) Ethylamine.

(17) Gamma-butyrolactone.

(18) Hydrochloric Acid.

(19) Iodine.

(20) Isosafrole.

(21) Lithium.

(22) Malonic acid.

(23) Methylamine.

(24) Methyl Isobutyl Ketone.

(25) N-acetylanthranilic acid.

(26) N-ethylephedrine.

(27) N-ethylepseudoephedrine.

(28) N-methylephedrine.

(29) N-methylpseudoephedrine.

(30) Norpseudoephedrine.

(31) Phenyl-2-propane.

(32) Phenylacetic acid.

(33) Phenylpropanolamine.

(34) Piperidine.

(35) Piperonal.

(36) Propionic anhydride.

(37) Pseudoephedrine.

(38) Pyrrolidine.

(39) Red phosphorous.

(40) Safrole.

(41) Sodium.

(42) Sulfuric Acid.

(43) Tetrachloroethylene.

(44) Thionylchloride.

(45) Toluene.

(e) The prescribed punishment and degree of any offense under this Article shall be subject to the following conditions, but the punishment for an offense may be increased only by the maximum authorized under any one of the applicable conditions:

(1), (2) Repealed by Session Laws 1979, c. 760, s. 5.

(3) If any person commits a Class 1 misdemeanor under this Article and if he has previously been convicted for one or more offenses under any law of North Carolina or any law of the United States or any other state, which offenses are punishable under any provision of this Article, he shall be punished as a Class I felon. The prior conviction used to raise the current offense to a Class I felony shall not be used to calculate the prior record level.

(4) If any person commits a Class 2 misdemeanor, and if he has previously been convicted for one or more offenses under any law of North Carolina or any law of the United States or any other state, which offenses are punishable under any provision of this Article, he shall be guilty of a Class 1 misdemeanor. The prior conviction used to raise the current offense to a Class 1 misdemeanor shall not be used to calculate the prior conviction level.

(5) Any person 18 years of age or over who violates G.S. 90-95(a)(1) by selling or delivering a controlled substance to a person under 16 years of age but more than 13 years of age or a pregnant female shall be punished as a Class D felon. Any person 18 years of age or over who violates G.S. 90-95(a)(1) by selling or delivering a controlled substance to a person who is 13 years of age or younger shall be punished as a Class C felon. Mistake of age is not a defense to a prosecution under this section. It shall not be a defense that the defendant did not know that the recipient was pregnant.

(6) For the purpose of increasing punishment under G.S. 90-95(e)(3) and (e)(4), previous convictions for offenses shall be counted by the number of separate trials at which final convictions were obtained and not by the number of charges at a single trial.

(7) If any person commits an offense under this Article for which the prescribed punishment requires that any sentence of imprisonment be suspended, and if he has previously been convicted for one or more offenses under any law of North Carolina or any law of the United States or any other state, which offenses are punishable under any provision of this Article, he shall be guilty of a Class 2 misdemeanor.

(8) Any person 21 years of age or older who commits an offense under G.S. 90-95(a)(1) on property used for a child care center, or for an elementary or secondary school or within 1,000 feet of the boundary of real property used for a child care center, or for an elementary or secondary school shall be punished as a Class E felon. For purposes of this subdivision, the transfer of less than five grams of marijuana for no remuneration shall not constitute a delivery in violation of G.S. 90-95(a)(1). For purposes of this subdivision, a child care center is as defined in G.S. 110-86(3)a., and that is licensed by the Secretary of the Department of Health and Human Services.

(9) Any person who violates G.S. 90-95(a)(3) on the premises of a penal institution or local confinement facility shall be guilty of a Class H felony.

(10) Any person 21 years of age or older who commits an offense under G.S. 90-95(a)(1) on property that is a public park or within 1,000 feet of the boundary of real property that is a public park shall be punished as a Class E felon. For purposes of this subdivision, the transfer of less than five grams of marijuana for no remuneration shall not constitute a delivery in violation of G.S. 90-95(a)(1).

(f) Any person convicted of an offense or offenses under this Article who is sentenced to an active term of imprisonment that is less than the maximum active term that could have been imposed may, in addition, be sentenced to a term of special probation. Except as indicated in this subsection, the administration of special probation shall be the same as probation. The conditions of special probation shall be fixed in the same manner as probation, and the conditions may include requirements for rehabilitation treatment. Special probation shall follow the active sentence. No term of special probation shall exceed five years. Special probation may be revoked in the same manner as probation; upon revocation, the original term of imprisonment may be increased by no more than the difference between the active term of imprisonment actually served and the maximum active term that could have been imposed at trial for the offense or offenses for which the person was convicted, and the resulting term of imprisonment need not be diminished by the time spent on special probation.

(g) Whenever matter is submitted to the North Carolina State Crime Laboratory, the Charlotte, North Carolina, Police Department Laboratory or to the Toxicology Laboratory, Reynolds Health Center, Winston-Salem for chemical analysis to determine if the matter is or contains a controlled substance, the report of that analysis certified to upon a form approved by the Attorney General by the person performing the analysis shall be admissible without further authentication and without the testimony of the analyst in all proceedings in the district court and superior court divisions of the General Court of Justice as evidence of the identity, nature, and quantity of the matter analyzed. Provided, however, the provisions of this subsection may be utilized by the State only if:

(1) The State notifies the defendant at least 15 business days before the proceeding at which the report would be used of its intention to introduce the report into evidence under this subsection and provides a copy of the report to the defendant, and

(2) The defendant fails to file a written objection with the court, with a copy to the State, at least five business days before the proceeding that the defendant objects to the introduction of the report into evidence.

If the defendant's attorney of record, or the defendant if that person has no attorney, fails to file a written objection as provided in this subsection, then the report shall be admitted into evidence without the testimony of the analyst. Upon filing a timely objection, the admissibility of the report shall be determined and governed by the appropriate rules of evidence.

Nothing in this subsection precludes the right of any party to call any witness or to introduce any evidence supporting or contradicting the evidence contained in the report.

(g1) Procedure for establishing chain of custody without calling unnecessary witnesses. -

(1) For the purpose of establishing the chain of physical custody or control of evidence consisting of or containing a substance tested or analyzed to determine whether it is a controlled substance, a statement signed by each successive person in the chain of custody that the person delivered it to the

other person indicated on or about the date stated is prima facie evidence that the person had custody and made the delivery as stated, without the necessity of a personal appearance in court by the person signing the statement.

(2) The statement shall contain a sufficient description of the material or its container so as to distinguish it as the particular item in question and shall state that the material was delivered in essentially the same condition as received. The statement may be placed on the same document as the report provided for in subsection (g) of this section.

(3) The provisions of this subsection may be utilized by the State only if:

a. The State notifies the defendant at least 15 days before trial of its intention to introduce the statement into evidence under this subsection and provides the defendant with a copy of the statement, and

b. The defendant fails to notify the State at least five days before trial that the defendant objects to the introduction of the statement into evidence.

If the defendant's attorney of record, or the defendant if that person has no attorney, fails to file a written objection as provided in this subsection, then the statement shall be admitted into evidence without the necessity of a personal appearance by the person signing the statement. Upon filing a timely objection, the admissibility of the report shall be determined and governed by the appropriate rules of evidence.

(4) Nothing in this subsection precludes the right of any party to call any witness or to introduce any evidence supporting or contradicting the evidence contained in the statement.

(h) Notwithstanding any other provision of law, the following provisions apply except as otherwise provided in this Article.

(1) Any person who sells, manufactures, delivers, transports, or possesses in excess of 10 pounds (avoirdupois) of marijuana shall be guilty of a felony which felony shall be known as "trafficking in marijuana" and if the quantity of such substance involved:

a. Is in excess of 10 pounds, but less than 50 pounds, such person shall be punished as a Class H felon and shall be sentenced to a minimum term of 25 months and a maximum term of 39 months in the State's prison and shall be fined not less than five thousand dollars ($5,000);

b.   Is 50 pounds or more, but less than 2,000 pounds, such person shall be punished as a Class G felon and shall be sentenced to a minimum term of 35 months and a maximum term of 51 months in the State's prison and shall be fined not less than twenty-five thousand dollars ($25,000);

c.   Is 2,000 pounds or more, but less than 10,000 pounds, such person shall be punished as a Class F felon and shall be sentenced to a minimum term of 70 months and a maximum term of 93 months in the State's prison and shall be fined not less than fifty thousand dollars ($50,000);

d.   Is 10,000 pounds or more, such person shall be punished as a Class D felon and shall be sentenced to a minimum term of 175 months and a maximum term of 222 months in the State's prison and shall be fined not less than two hundred thousand dollars ($200,000).

(1a)   For the purpose of this subsection, a "dosage unit" shall consist of 3 grams of synthetic cannabinoid or any mixture containing such substance. Any person who sells, manufactures, delivers, transports, or possesses in excess of 50 dosage units of a synthetic cannabinoid or any mixture containing such substance, shall be guilty of a felony, which felony shall be known as "trafficking in synthetic cannabinoids," and if the quantity of such substance involved:

a.   Is in excess of 50 dosage units, but less than 250 dosage units, such person shall be punished as a Class H felon and shall be sentenced to a minimum term of 25 months and a maximum term of 39 months in the State's prison and shall be fined not less than five thousand dollars ($5,000);

b.   Is 250 dosage units or more, but less than 1250 dosage units, such person shall be punished as a Class G felon and shall be sentenced to a minimum term of 35 months and a maximum term of 51 months in the State's prison and shall be fined not less than twenty-five thousand dollars ($25,000);

c.   Is 1250 dosage units or more, but less than 3750 dosage units, such person shall be punished as a Class F felon and shall be sentenced to a minimum term of 70 months and a maximum term of 93 months in the State's prison and shall be fined not less than fifty thousand dollars ($50,000);

d. Is 3750 dosage units or more, such person shall be punished as a Class D felon and shall be sentenced to a minimum term of 175 months and a maximum term of 222 months in the State's prison and shall be fined not less than two hundred thousand dollars ($200,000).

(2) Any person who sells, manufactures, delivers, transports, or possesses 1,000 tablets, capsules or other dosage units, or the equivalent quantity, or more of methaqualone, or any mixture containing such substance, shall be guilty of a felony which felony shall be known as "trafficking in methaqualone" and if the quantity of such substance or mixture involved:

a. Is 1,000 or more dosage units, or equivalent quantity, but less than 5,000 dosage units, or equivalent quantity, such person shall be punished as a Class G felon and shall be sentenced to a minimum term of 35 months and a maximum term of 51 months in the State's prison and shall be fined not less than twenty-five thousand dollars ($25,000);

b. Is 5,000 or more dosage units, or equivalent quantity, but less than 10,000 dosage units, or equivalent quantity, such person shall be punished as a Class F felon and shall be sentenced to a minimum term of 70 months and a maximum term of 93 months in the State's prison and shall be fined not less than fifty thousand dollars ($50,000);

c. Is 10,000 or more dosage units, or equivalent quantity, such person shall be punished as a Class D felon and shall be sentenced to a minimum term of 175 months and a maximum term of 222 months in the State's prison and shall be fined not less than two hundred thousand dollars ($200,000).

(3) Any person who sells, manufactures, delivers, transports, or possesses 28 grams or more of cocaine and any salt, isomer, salts of isomers, compound, derivative, or preparation thereof, or any coca leaves and any salt, isomer, salts of isomers, compound, derivative, or preparation of coca leaves, and any salt, isomer, salts of isomers, compound, derivative or preparation thereof which is chemically equivalent or identical with any of these substances (except decocainized coca leaves or any extraction of coca leaves which does not contain cocaine) or any mixture containing such substances, shall be guilty of a felony, which felony shall be known as "trafficking in cocaine" and if the quantity of such substance or mixture involved:

a. Is 28 grams or more, but less than 200 grams, such person shall be punished as a Class G felon and shall be sentenced to a minimum term of 35 months and a maximum term of 51 months in the State's prison and shall be fined not less than fifty thousand dollars ($50,000);

b.   Is 200 grams or more, but less than 400 grams, such person shall be punished as a Class F felon and shall be sentenced to a minimum term of 70 months and a maximum term of 93 months in the State's prison and shall be fined not less than one hundred thousand dollars ($100,000);

c.   Is 400 grams or more, such person shall be punished as a Class D felon and shall be sentenced to a minimum term of 175 months and a maximum term of 222 months in the State's prison and shall be fined at least two hundred fifty thousand dollars ($250,000).

(3a)   Repealed by Session Laws 1999-370, s. 1, effective December 1, 1999.

(3b)   Any person who sells, manufactures, delivers, transports, or possesses 28 grams or more of methamphetamine or any mixture containing such substance shall be guilty of a felony which felony shall be known as "trafficking in methamphetamine" and if the quantity of such substance or mixture involved:

a.   Is 28 grams or more, but less than 200 grams, such person shall be punished as a Class F felon and shall be sentenced to a minimum term of 70 months and a maximum term of 93 months in the State's prison and shall be fined not less than fifty thousand dollars ($50,000);

b.   Is 200 grams or more, but less than 400 grams, such person shall be punished as a Class E felon and shall be sentenced to a minimum term of 90 months and a maximum term of 120 months in the State's prison and shall be fined not less than one hundred thousand dollars ($100,000);

c.   Is 400 grams or more, such person shall be punished as a Class C felon and shall be sentenced to a minimum term of 225 months and a maximum term of 282 months in the State's prison and shall be fined at least two hundred fifty thousand dollars ($250,000).

(3c)   Any person who sells, manufactures, delivers, transports, or possesses 28 grams or more of amphetamine or any mixture containing such substance shall be guilty of a felony, which felony shall be known as "trafficking in amphetamine", and if the quantity of such substance or mixture involved:

a. Is 28 grams or more, but less than 200 grams, such person shall be punished as a Class H felon and shall be sentenced to a minimum term of 25 months and a maximum term of 39 months in the State's prison and shall be fined not less than five thousand dollars ($5,000);

b. Is 200 grams or more, but less than 400 grams, such person shall be punished as a Class G felon and shall be sentenced to a minimum term of 35 months and a maximum term of 51 months in the State's prison and shall be fined not less than twenty-five thousand dollars ($25,000);

c. Is 400 grams or more, such person shall be punished as a Class E felon and shall be sentenced to a minimum term of 90 months and a maximum term of 120 months in the State's prison and shall be fined at least one hundred thousand dollars ($100,000).

(3d) Any person who sells, manufactures, delivers, transports, or possesses 28 grams or more of MDPV or any mixture containing such substance shall be guilty of a felony, which felony shall be known as "trafficking in MDPV," and if the quantity of such substance or mixture involved:

a. Is 28 grams or more, but less than 200 grams, such person shall be punished as a Class F felon and shall be sentenced to a minimum term of 70 months and a maximum term of 93 months in the State's prison and shall be fined not less than fifty thousand dollars ($50,000);

b. Is 200 grams or more, but less than 400 grams, such person shall be punished as a Class E felon and shall be sentenced to a minimum term of 90 months and a maximum term of 120 months in the State's prison and shall be fined not less than one hundred thousand dollars ($100,000);

c. Is 400 grams or more, such person shall be punished as a Class C felon and shall be sentenced to a minimum term of 225 months and a maximum term of 282 months in the State's prison and shall be fined at least two hundred fifty thousand dollars ($250,000).

(3e) Any person who sells, manufactures, delivers, transports, or possesses 28 grams or more of mephedrone or any mixture containing such substance shall be guilty of a felony, which felony shall be known as "trafficking in mephedrone," and if the quantity of such substance or mixture involved:

a. Is 28 grams or more, but less than 200 grams, such person shall be punished as a Class F felon and shall be sentenced to a minimum term of 70 months and a maximum term of 93 months in the State's prison and shall be fined not less than fifty thousand dollars ($50,000);

b. Is 200 grams or more, but less than 400 grams, such person shall be punished as a Class E felon and shall be sentenced to a minimum term of 90 months and a maximum term of 120 months in the State's prison and shall be fined not less than one hundred thousand dollars ($100,000);

c. Is 400 grams or more, such person shall be punished as a Class C felon and shall be sentenced to a minimum term of 225 months and a maximum term of 282 months in the State's prison and shall be fined at least two hundred fifty thousand dollars ($250,000).

(4) Any person who sells, manufactures, delivers, transports, or possesses four grams or more of opium or opiate, or any salt, compound, derivative, or preparation of opium or opiate (except apomorphine, nalbuphine, analoxone and naltrexone and their respective salts), including heroin, or any mixture containing such substance, shall be guilty of a felony which felony shall be known as "trafficking in opium or heroin" and if the quantity of such controlled substance or mixture involved:

a. Is four grams or more, but less than 14 grams, such person shall be punished as a Class F felon and shall be sentenced to a minimum term of 70 months and a maximum term of 93 months in the State's prison and shall be fined not less than fifty thousand dollars ($50,000);

b. Is 14 grams or more, but less than 28 grams, such person shall be punished as a Class E felon and shall be sentenced to a minimum term of 90 months and a maximum term of 120 months in the State's prison and shall be fined not less than one hundred thousand dollars ($100,000);

c. Is 28 grams or more, such person shall be punished as a Class C felon and shall be sentenced to a minimum term of 225 months and a maximum term of 282 months in the State's prison and shall be fined not less than five hundred thousand dollars ($500,000).

(4a) Any person who sells, manufactures, delivers, transports, or possesses 100 tablets, capsules, or other dosage units, or the equivalent quantity, or more, of Lysergic Acid Diethylamide, or any mixture containing such substance, shall be guilty of a felony, which felony shall be known as "trafficking in Lysergic Acid Diethylamide". If the quantity of such substance or mixture involved:

a. Is 100 or more dosage units, or equivalent quantity, but less than 500 dosage units, or equivalent quantity, such person shall be punished as a Class G felon and shall be sentenced to a minimum term of 35 months and a maximum term of 51 months in the State's prison and shall be fined not less than twenty-five thousand dollars ($25,000);

b. Is 500 or more dosage units, or equivalent quantity, but less than 1,000 dosage units, or equivalent quantity, such person shall be punished as a Class F felon and shall be sentenced to a minimum term of 70 months and a maximum term of 93 months in the State's prison and shall be fined not less than fifty thousand dollars ($50,000);

c. Is 1,000 or more dosage units, or equivalent quantity, such person shall be punished as a Class D felon and shall be sentenced to a minimum term of 175 months and a maximum term of 222 months in the State's prison and shall be fined not less than two hundred thousand dollars ($200,000).

(4b) Any person who sells, manufactures, delivers, transports, or possesses 100 or more tablets, capsules, or other dosage units, or 28 grams or more of 3,4-methylenedioxyamphetamine (MDA), including its salts, isomers, and salts of isomers, or 3,4-methylenedioxymethamphetamine (MDMA), including its salts, isomers, and salts of isomers, or any mixture containing such substances, shall be guilty of a felony, which felony shall be known as "trafficking in MDA/DMA." If the quantity of the substance or mixture involved:

a. Is 100 or more tablets, capsules, or other dosage units, but less than 500 tablets, capsules, or other dosage units, or 28 grams or more, but less than 200 grams, the person shall be punished as a Class G felon and shall be sentenced to a minimum term of 35 months and a maximum term of 51 months in the State's prison and shall be fined not less than twenty-five thousand dollars ($25,000);

b. Is 500 or more tablets, capsules, or other dosage units, but less than 1,000 tablets, capsules, or other dosage units, or 200 grams or more, but less than 400 grams, the person shall be punished as a Class F felon and shall be sentenced to a minimum term of 70 months and a maximum term of 93 months in the State's prison and shall be fined not less than fifty thousand dollars ($50,000);

c. Is 1,000 or more tablets, capsules, or other dosage units, or 400 grams or more, the person shall be punished as a Class D felon and shall be sentenced to a minimum term of 175 months and a maximum term of 222 months in the State's prison and shall be fined not less than two hundred fifty thousand dollars ($250,000).

(5) Except as provided in this subdivision, a person being sentenced under this subsection may not receive a suspended sentence or be placed on probation. The sentencing judge may reduce the fine, or impose a prison term less than the applicable minimum prison term provided by this subsection, or suspend the prison term imposed and place a person on probation when such person has, to the best of his knowledge, provided substantial assistance in the identification, arrest, or conviction of any accomplices, accessories, co-conspirators, or principals if the sentencing judge enters in the record a finding that the person to be sentenced has rendered such substantial assistance.

(6) Sentences imposed pursuant to this subsection shall run consecutively with and shall commence at the expiration of any sentence being served by the person sentenced hereunder.

(i) The penalties provided in subsection (h) of this section shall also apply to any person who is convicted of conspiracy to commit any of the offenses described in subsection (h) of this section. (1971, c. 919, s. 1; 1973, c. 654, s. 1; c. 1078; c. 1358, s. 10; 1975, c. 360, s. 2; 1977, c. 862, ss. 1, 2; 1979, c. 760, s. 5; 1979, 2nd Sess., c. 1251, ss. 4-7; 1983, c. 18; c. 294, s. 6; c. 414; 1985, c. 569, s. 1; c. 675, ss. 1, 2; 1987, c. 90; c. 105, ss. 4, 5; c. 640, ss. 1, 2; c. 783, s. 4; 1989, c. 641; c. 672; c. 690; c. 770, s. 68; 1989 (Reg. Sess., 1990), c. 1024, s. 17; c. 1039, s. 5; c. 1081, s. 2; 1991, c. 484, s. 1; 1993, c. 538, s. 30; c. 539, s. 1358.1; 1994, Ex. Sess., c. 11, s. 1; c. 14, ss. 46, 47; c. 24, s. 14(b); 1996, 2nd Ex. Sess., c. 18, s. 20.13(c); 1997-304, ss. 1, 2; 1997-443, s. 19.25(b), (u), (ii); 1998-212, s. 17.16(e); 1999-165, s. 4; 1999-370, s. 1; 2000-140, s. 92.2(d); 2001-307, s. 1; 2001-332, s. 1; 2004-178, ss. 3, 4, 5, 6; 2007-375, s. 1; 2009-463, ss. 1, 2; 2009-473, s. 7; 2011-12, ss. 2-4, 6-8; 2011-19, s. 5; 2012-188, s. 5; 2013-124, s. 1; 2013-171, ss. 7, 8.)

§ 90-95.1. Continuing criminal enterprise.

(a) Any person who engages in a continuing criminal enterprise shall be punished as a Class C felon and in addition shall be subject to the forfeiture prescribed in subsection (b) of this section.

(b) Any person who is convicted under subsection (a) of engaging in a continuing criminal enterprise shall forfeit to the State of North Carolina:

(1) The profits obtained by him in such enterprise, and

(2) Any of his interest in, claim against, or property or contractual rights of any kind affording a source of influence over, such enterprise.

(c) For purposes of this section, a person is engaged in a continuing criminal enterprise if:

(1) He violates any provision of this Article, the punishment of which is a felony; and

(2) Such violation is a part of a continuing series of violations of this Article;

a. Which are undertaken by such person in concert with five or more other persons with respect to whom such person occupies a position of organizer, a supervisory position, or any other position of management; and

b. From which such person obtains substantial income or resources.

(d) Repealed by Session Laws 1979, c. 760, s. 5. (1971, s. 919, s. 1; 1979, c. 760, s. 5.)

§ 90-95.2. Cooperation between law-enforcement agencies.

(a) The head of any law-enforcement agency may temporarily provide assistance to another agency in enforcing the provisions of this Article if so requested in writing by the head of the other agency. The assistance may comprise allowing officers of the agency to work temporarily with officers of the other agency (including in an undercover capacity) and lending equipment and supplies. While working with another agency under the authority of this section, an officer shall have the same jurisdiction, powers, rights, privileges, and immunities (including those relating to the defense of civil actions and payment of judgments) as the officers of the requesting agency in addition to those he normally possesses. While on duty with the other agency, he shall be subject to the lawful operational commands of his superior officers in the other agency, but he shall for personnel and administrative purposes remain under the control of his own agency, including for purposes of pay. He shall furthermore be entitled to workers' compensation when acting pursuant to this section to the same extent as though he were functioning within the normal scope of his duties.

(b) As used in this section:

(1) "Head" means any director or chief officer of a law-enforcement agency, including the chief of police of a local police department and the sheriff of a county, or an officer of the agency to whom the head of the agency has delegated authority to make or grant requests under this section, but only one officer in the agency shall have this delegated authority at any time.

(2) "Law-enforcement agency" means any State or local agency, force, department, or unit responsible for enforcing criminal laws in this State, including any local police department or sheriff's department.

(c) This section in no way reduces the jurisdiction or authority of State law-enforcement officers. (1975, c. 782, s. 1; 1981, c. 93, s. 1; 1991, c. 636, s. 3.)

§ 90-95.3. Restitution to law-enforcement agencies for undercover purchases; restitution for drug analyses; restitution for seizure and cleanup of clandestine laboratories.

(a) When any person is convicted of an offense under this Article, the court may order him to make restitution to any law-enforcement agency for reasonable expenditures made in purchasing controlled substances from him or his agent as part of an investigation leading to his conviction.

(b) Repealed by Session Laws 2002-126, s. 29A.8(b), effective October 1, 2002. See Editor's Note.

(c) When any person is convicted of an offense under this Article involving the manufacture of controlled substances, the court must order the person to make restitution for the actual cost of cleanup to the law enforcement agency that cleaned up any clandestine laboratory used to manufacture the controlled substances, including personnel overtime, equipment, and supplies. (1975, c. 782, s. 2; 1989 (Reg. Sess., 1990), c. 1039, s. 3; 1999-370, s. 2; 2002-126, s. 29A.8(b).)

§ 90-95.4. Employing or intentionally using minor to commit a drug law violation.

(a) A person who is at least 18 years old but less than 21 years old who hires or intentionally uses a minor to violate G.S. 90-95(a)(1) shall be guilty of a felony. An offense under this subsection shall be punishable as follows:

(1) If the minor was more than 13 years of age, then as a felony that is one class more severe than the violation of G.S. 90-95(a)(1) for which the minor was hired or intentionally used.

(2) If the minor was 13 years of age or younger, then as a felony that is two classes more severe than the violation of G.S. 90-95(a)(1) for which the minor was hired or intentionally used.

(b) A person 21 years of age or older who hires or intentionally uses a minor to violate G.S. 90-95(a)(1) shall be guilty of a felony. An offense under this subsection shall be punishable as follows:

(1) If the minor was more than 13 years of age, then as a felony that is three classes more severe than the violation of G.S. 90-95(a)(1) for which the minor was hired or intentionally used.

(2) If the minor was 13 years of age or younger, then as a felony that is four classes more severe than the violation of G.S. 90-95(a)(1) for which the minor was hired or intentionally used.

(c) Mistake of Age. - Mistake of age is not a defense to a prosecution under this section.

(d) The term "minor" as used in this section is defined as an individual who is less than 18 years of age. (1989 (Reg. Sess., 1990), c. 1081, s. 1; 1998-212, s. 17.16(f).)

§ 90-95.5. Civil liability - employing a minor to commit a drug offense.

A person 21 years of age or older, who hires, employs, or intentionally uses a person under 18 years of age to commit a violation of G.S. 90-95 is liable in a civil action for damages for drug addiction proximately caused by the violation. The doctrines of contributory negligence and assumption of risk are no defense to liability under this section. (1989 (Reg. Sess., 1990), c. 1081, s. 3; 1998-212, s. 17.16(g).)

§ 90-95.6. Promoting drug sales by a minor.

(a) A person who is 21 years of age or older is guilty of promoting drug sales by a minor if the person knowingly:

(1) Entices, forces, encourages, or otherwise facilitates a minor in violating G.S. 90-95(a)(1).

(2) Supervises, supports, advises, or protects the minor in violating G.S. 90-95(a)(1).

(b) Mistake of age is not a defense to a prosecution under this section.

(c) A violation of this section is a Class D felony. (1998-212, s. 17.16(h).)

§ 90-95.7. Participating in a drug violation by a minor.

(a) A person 21 years of age or older who purchases or receives a controlled substance from a minor 13 years of age or younger who possesses, sells, or delivers the controlled substance in violation of G.S. 90-95(a)(1) is guilty of participating in a drug violation of a minor.

(b) Mistake of age is not a defense to a prosecution under this section.

(c) A violation of this section is a Class G felony. (1998-212, s. 17.16(h).)

§ 90-96. Conditional discharge for first offense.

(a) Whenever any person who has not previously been convicted of (i) any felony offense under any state or federal laws; (ii) any offense under this Article; or (iii) an offense under any statute of the United States or any state relating to those substances included in Article 5 or 5A of Chapter 90 or to that paraphernalia included in Article 5B of Chapter 90 of the General Statutes pleads guilty to or is found guilty of (i) a misdemeanor under this Article by possessing a controlled substance included within Schedules I through VI of this Article or by possessing drug paraphernalia as prohibited by G.S. 90-113.22, or (ii) a felony under G.S. 90-95(a)(3), the court shall, without entering a judgment of guilt and with the consent of such person, defer further proceedings and place him on probation upon such reasonable terms and conditions as it may require, unless the court determines with a written finding, and with the agreement of the District Attorney, that the offender is inappropriate for a conditional discharge for factors related to the offense. Notwithstanding the provisions of G.S. 15A-1342(c) or any other statute or law, probation may be imposed under this section for an offense under this Article for which the prescribed punishment includes only a fine. To fulfill the terms and conditions of probation the court may allow the defendant to participate in a drug education program approved for this purpose by the Department of Health and Human Services or in the Treatment for Effective Community Supervision Program under Subpart B of Part 6 of Article 13 of Chapter 143B of the General Statutes. Upon violation of a term or condition, the court may enter an adjudication of guilt and proceed as otherwise provided. Upon fulfillment of the terms and conditions, the court shall discharge such person and dismiss the proceedings against him. Discharge and dismissal under this section shall be without court adjudication of guilt and shall not be deemed a conviction for purposes of this section or for purposes of disqualifications or disabilities imposed by law upon conviction of a crime including the additional penalties imposed for second or subsequent convictions under this Article. Discharge and dismissal under this section or G.S. 90-113.14 may occur only once with respect to any person. Disposition of a case to determine discharge and dismissal under this section at the district court division of the General Court of Justice shall be final for the purpose of appeal. Prior to taking any action to discharge and dismiss under this section the court shall make a finding that the defendant has no record of previous convictions as provided in this subsection.

(a1) Upon the first conviction only of any offense which qualifies under the provisions of subsection (a) of this section, and the provisions of this subsection, the court may place defendant on probation under this section for an offense under this Article including an offense for which the prescribed punishment includes only a fine. The probation, if imposed, shall be for not less than one year and shall contain a minimum condition that the defendant who was found guilty or pleads guilty enroll in and successfully complete, within 150 days of the date of the imposition of said probation, the program of instruction at the drug education school approved by the Department of Health and Human Services pursuant to G.S. 90-96.01. The court may impose probation that does not contain a condition that defendant successfully complete the program of instruction at a drug education school if:

(1)   There is no drug education school within a reasonable distance of the defendant's residence; or

(2)   There are specific, extenuating circumstances which make it likely that defendant will not benefit from the program of instruction.

The court shall enter such specific findings in the record; provided that in the case of subdivision (2) above, such findings shall include the specific, extenuating circumstances which make it likely that the defendant will not benefit from the program of instruction.

Upon fulfillment of the terms and conditions of the probation, the court shall discharge such person and dismiss the proceedings against the person.

For the purposes of determining whether the conviction is a first conviction or whether a person has already had discharge and dismissal, no prior offense occurring more than seven years before the date of the current offense shall be considered. In addition, convictions for violations of a provision of G.S. 90-95(a)(1) or 90-95(a)(2) or 90-95(a)(3), or 90-113.10, or 90-113.11, or 90-113.12, or 90-113.22 shall be considered previous convictions.

Failure to complete successfully an approved program of instruction at a drug education school shall constitute grounds to revoke probation pursuant to this subsection and deny application for expunction of all recordation of defendant's arrest, indictment, or information, trial, finding of guilty, and dismissal and discharge pursuant to G.S. 15A-145.2. For purposes of this subsection, the phrase "failure to complete successfully the prescribed program of instruction at a drug education school" includes failure to attend scheduled classes without a valid excuse, failure to complete the course within 150 days of imposition of probation, willful failure to pay the required fee for the course as provided in

G.S. 90-96.01(b), or any other manner in which the person fails to complete the course successfully. The instructor of the course to which a person is assigned shall report any failure of a person to complete successfully the program of instruction to the court which imposed probation. Upon receipt of the instructor's report that the person failed to complete the program successfully, the court shall revoke probation, shall not discharge such person, shall not dismiss the proceedings against the person, and shall deny application for expunction of all recordation of defendant's arrest, indictment, or information, trial, finding of guilty, and dismissal and discharge pursuant to G.S. 15A-145.2. A person may obtain a hearing before the court of original jurisdiction prior to revocation of probation or denial of application for expunction.

This subsection is supplemental and in addition to existing law and shall not be construed so as to repeal any existing provision contained in the General Statutes of North Carolina.

(b)   Upon the discharge of such person, and dismissal of the proceedings against the person under subsection (a) or (a1) of this section, such person, if he or she was not over 21 years of age at the time of the offense, may be eligible to apply for expunction of certain records relating to the offense pursuant to G.S. 15A-145.2(a).

(c)   Repealed by Session Laws 2009-510, s. 8(b), effective October 1, 2010.

(d)   Whenever any person is charged with a misdemeanor under this Article by possessing a controlled substance included within Schedules I through VI of this Article or a felony under G.S. 90-95(a)(3), upon dismissal by the State of the charges against such person, upon entry of a nolle prosequi, or upon a finding of not guilty or other adjudication of innocence, the person may be eligible to apply for expunction of certain records relating to the offense pursuant to G.S. 15A-145.2(b).

(e)   Whenever any person who has not previously been convicted of (i) any felony offense under any state or federal laws; (ii) any offense under this Article; or (iii) an offense under any statute of the United States or any state relating to controlled substances included in any schedule of this Article or to that paraphernalia included in Article 5B of Chapter 90 of the General Statutes pleads guilty to or has been found guilty of (i) a misdemeanor under this Article by possessing a controlled substance included within Schedules I through VI of this Article, or by possessing drug paraphernalia as prohibited by G.S. 90-113.22 or (ii) a felony under G.S. 90-95(a)(3), the person may be eligible to apply for cancellation of the judgment and expunction of certain records related to the offense pursuant to G.S. 15A-145.2(c).

(f)   Repealed by Session Laws 2009-577, s. 6, effective December 1, 2009, and applicable to petitions for expunctions filed on or after that date. (1971, c. 919, s. 1; 1973, c. 654, s. 2; c. 1066; 1977, 2nd Sess., c. 1147, s. 11B; 1979, c. 431, ss. 3, 4; c. 550; 1981, c. 922, ss. 1-4; 1994, Ex. Sess., c. 11, s. 1.1; 1997-443, s. 11A.118(a); 2002-126, s. 29A.5(d); 2009-510, s. 8(a)-(d); 2009-577, s. 6; 2010-174, ss. 10-12; 2011-192, s. 5(a); 2013-210, s. 1.)

§ 90-96.01. Drug education schools; responsibilities of the Department of Health and Human Services; fees.

(a)   The Commission for Mental Health, Developmental Disabilities, and Substance Abuse Services shall establish standards and guidelines for the curriculum and operation of local drug education programs. The Department of Health and Human Services shall oversee the development of a statewide system of schools and shall insure that schools are available in all localities of the State as soon as is practicable.

(1)   A fee of one hundred fifty dollars ($150.00) shall be paid by all persons enrolling in an accredited drug education school established pursuant to this section. That fee must be paid to an official designated for that purpose and at a time and place specified by the area mental health, developmental disabilities, and substance abuse authority providing the course of instruction in which the person is enrolled. If the clerk of court in the county in which the person is convicted agrees to collect the fees, the clerk shall collect all fees for persons convicted in that county. The clerk shall pay the fees collected to the area mental health, developmental disabilities, and substance abuse authority for the catchment area where the clerk is located regardless of the location where the defendant attends the drug education school and that authority shall distribute the funds in accordance with the rules and regulations of the Department. The fee must be paid in full within two weeks of the date the person is convicted and before he attends any classes, unless the court, upon a showing of reasonable hardship, allows the person additional time to pay the fee or allows him to begin the course of instruction without paying the fee. If the person enrolling in the school demonstrates to the satisfaction of the court that ordered him to enroll in the school that he is unable to pay and his inability to pay is not willful, the court may excuse him from paying the fee. Parents or guardians of persons attending

drug education school shall be allowed to audit the drug education school along with their children or wards at no extra expense.

(2)   The Department of Health and Human Services shall have the authority to approve programs to be implemented by area mental health, developmental disabilities, and substance abuse authorities. Area mental health, developmental disabilities, and substance abuse authorities may subcontract for the delivery of drug education program services. The Department shall have the authority to approve budgets and contracts with public and private governmental and nongovernmental bodies for the operation of such schools.

(3)   Fees collected under this section and retained by the area mental health, developmental disabilities, and substance abuse authority shall be placed in a nonreverting fund. That fund must be used, as necessary, for the operation, evaluation and administration of the drug educational schools; excess funds may only be used to fund other drug or alcohol programs. The area mental health, developmental disabilities, and substance abuse authority shall remit five percent (5%) of each fee collected to the Department of Health and Human Services on a monthly basis. Fees received by the Department as required by this section may only be used in supporting, evaluating, and administering drug education schools, and any excess funds will revert to the General Fund.

(4)   All fees collected by any area mental health, developmental disabilities, and substance abuse authority under the authority of this section may not be used in any manner to match other State funds or be included in any computation for State formula-funded allocations.

(b)   Willful failure to pay the fee is one ground for a finding that a person placed on probation or who may make application for expunction of all recordation of his arrest or conviction has not successfully completed the course. If the court determines the person is unable to pay, he shall not be deemed guilty of a willful failure to pay the fee. (1981, c. 922, s. 8; 1991, c. 636, s. 19(b), (c); 1993, c. 395, s. 1; 1997-443, s. 11A.118(a).)

§ 90-96.1. Immunity from prosecution for minors.

Whenever any person who is not more than 18 years of age, who has not previously been convicted of any offense under this Article or under any statute of the United States of any state relating to controlled substances included in any schedule of this Article, is accused with possessing or distributing a controlled substance in violation of G.S. 90-95(a)(1) or 90-95(a)(2) or 90-95(a)(3), the court may, upon recommendation of the district attorney, grant said person immunity from prosecution for said violation(s) if said person shall disclose the identity of the person or persons from whom he obtained the controlled substance(s) for which said person is being accused of possessing or distributing. (1973, c. 47, s. 2; c. 654, s. 3.)

§ 90-96.2. Drug-related overdose treatment; limited immunity.

(a) As used in this section, "drug-related overdose" means an acute condition, including mania, hysteria, extreme physical illness, coma, or death resulting from the consumption or use of a controlled substance, or another substance with which a controlled substance was combined, and that a layperson would reasonably believe to be a drug overdose that requires medical assistance.

(b) A person acting in good faith who seeks medical assistance for an individual experiencing a drug-related overdose shall not be prosecuted for (i) a misdemeanor violation of G.S. 90-95(a)(3), (ii) a felony violation of G.S. 90-95(a)(3) for possession of less than one gram of cocaine, (iii) a felony violation of G.S. 90-95(a)(3) for possession of less than one gram of heroin, or (iv) a violation of G.S. 90-113.22 if the evidence for prosecution under those sections was obtained as a result of the person seeking medical assistance for the drug-related overdose.

(c) A person who experiences a drug-related overdose and is in need of medical assistance shall not be prosecuted for (i) a misdemeanor violation of G.S. 90-95(a)(3), (ii) a felony violation of G.S. 90-95(a)(3) for possession of less than one gram of cocaine, (iii) a felony violation of G.S. 90-95(a)(3) for possession of less than one gram of heroin, or (iv) a violation of G.S. 90-113.22 if the evidence for prosecution under those sections was obtained as a result of the drug-related overdose and need for medical assistance.

(d) Nothing in this section shall be construed to bar the admissibility of any evidence obtained in connection with the investigation and prosecution of other crimes committed by a person who otherwise qualifies for limited immunity under this section. (2013-23, s. 1.)

§ 90-97. Other penalties.

Any penalty imposed for violation of this Article shall be in addition to, and not in lieu of, any civil or administrative penalty or sanction authorized by law. If a violation of this Article is a violation of a federal law or the law of another state, a conviction or acquittal under federal law or the law of another state for the same act is a bar to prosecution in this State. (1971, c. 919, s. 1.)

§ 90-98. Attempt and conspiracy; penalties.

Except as otherwise provided in this Article, any person who attempts or conspires to commit any offense defined in this Article is guilty of an offense that is the same class as the offense which was the object of the attempt or conspiracy and is punishable as specified for that class of offense and prior record or conviction level in Article 81B of Chapter 15A of the General Statutes. (1971, c. 919, s. 1; 1979, c. 760, s. 5; 1997-80, s. 9.)

§ 90-99. Republishing of schedules.

The North Carolina Department of Health and Human Services shall update and republish the schedules established by this Article on a semiannual basis for two years from January 1, 1972, and thereafter on an annual basis. (1971, c. 919, s. 1; 1977, c. 667, s. 3; 1997-443, s. 11A.118(a).)

§ 90-100. Rules.

The Commission may adopt rules relating to the registration and control of the manufacture, distribution, security, and dispensing of controlled substances within this State. (1971, c. 919, s. 1; 1977, c. 667, s. 3; 1981, c. 51, s. 9; 1991, c. 309, s. 2; 1993, c. 384, s. 1.)

§ 90-101. Annual registration and fee to engage in listed activities with controlled substances; effect of registration; exceptions; waiver; inspection.

(a) Every person who manufactures, distributes, dispenses, or conducts research with any controlled substance within this State or who proposes to engage in any of these activities shall annually register with the North Carolina Department of Health and Human Services, in accordance with rules adopted by the Commission, and shall pay the registration fee set by the Commission for the category to which the applicant belongs. An applicant for registration shall file an application for registration with the Department of Health and Human Services and submit the required fee with the application. The categories of applicants and the maximum fee for each category are as follows:

CATEGORY	MAXIMUM FEE
Clinic	$150.00
Animal Shelter	150.00
Hospital	350.00
Nursing Home	150.00
Teaching Institution	150.00
Researcher	150.00
Analytical Laboratory	150.00
Dog Handler	150.00
Distributor	600.00
Manufacturer	700.00

(a1) Any physician who prescribes or dispenses Buprenorphine for the treatment of opiate dependence shall annually register with the Department, in accordance with rules adopted by the Commission. In the application for registration under this subsection, the applicant shall document plans to ensure that patients are directly engaged or referred to a qualified provider to receive counseling and case management, as appropriate, and shall acknowledge the application of federal confidentiality regulations to patient information. Applicant plans for referral to appropriate services shall be a written document and may include either an executed memorandum of agreement, contractual arrangement, or linkage agreement with qualified providers. The Department shall provide assistance upon request to physicians registered under this subsection to identify and establish linkages with qualified providers of counseling and case management. The Department shall provide the North Carolina Medical Board with any evidence of noncompliance with this subsection by a qualified physician prior to taking action to rescind the physician's registration to prescribe or dispense Buprenorphine for the treatment of opiate dependency.

(a2)   An animal shelter may register under this section for the limited purpose of obtaining, possessing, and using sodium pentobarbital and other drugs approved by the Department in consultation with the North Carolina Veterinary Medical Association for the euthanasia of animals lawfully held by the animal shelter. An animal shelter registered under this section shall also register with the federal Drug Enforcement Agency under the federal Controlled Substances Act. An animal shelter's acquisition of sodium pentobarbital and other approved drugs for use in the euthanizing of animals shall be made only by the shelter's manager or chief operating officer or by a licensed veterinarian.

A person certified by the Department of Agriculture and Consumer Services to administer euthanasia by injection is authorized to possess and administer sodium pentobarbital and other approved euthanasia drugs for the purposes of euthanizing domestic dogs (Canis familiaris) and cats (Felis domestica) lawfully held by an animal shelter. Possession and administration of sodium pentobarbital and other approved drugs for use in the euthanizing of dogs and cats by a certified euthanasia technician shall be limited to the premises of the animal shelter.

For purposes of this section, "animal shelter" means an animal shelter registered under Article 3 of Chapter 19A of the General Statutes and owned, operated, or maintained by a unit of local government or under contract with a unit of local government for the purpose of housing or containing seized, stray, homeless, quarantined, abandoned, or unwanted animals.

(b)   Persons registered by the North Carolina Department of Health and Human Services under this Article (including research facilities) to manufacture, distribute, dispense or conduct research with controlled substances may possess, manufacture, distribute, dispense or conduct research with those substances to the extent authorized by their registration and in conformity with the other provisions of this Article.

(c)   The following persons shall not be required to register and may lawfully possess controlled substances under the provisions of this Article:

(1)   An agent, or an employee thereof, of any registered manufacturer, distributor, or dispenser of any controlled substance if such agent is acting in the usual course of his business or employment;

(2)   The State courier service operated by the Department of Administration, a common or contract carrier, or a public warehouseman, or an employee thereof, whose possession of any controlled substance is in the usual course of his business or employment;

(3)   An ultimate user or a person in possession of any controlled substance pursuant to a lawful order of a practitioner;

(4)   Repealed by Session Laws 1977, c. 891, s. 4.

(5)   Any law-enforcement officer acting within the course and scope of official duties, or any person employed in an official capacity by, or acting as an agent of, any law-enforcement agency or other agency charged with enforcing the provisions of this Article when acting within the course and scope of official duties; and

(6)   A practitioner, as defined in G.S. 90-87(22)a., who is required to be licensed in North Carolina by his respective licensing board.

(d)   The Commission may, by rule, waive the requirement for registration of certain classes of manufacturers, distributors, or dispensers if it finds it consistent with the public health and safety.

(e)   A separate registration shall be required at each principal place of business, research or professional practice where the registrant manufactures, distributes, dispenses or uses controlled substances.

(f)   The North Carolina Department of Health and Human Services is authorized to inspect the establishment of a registrant, applicant for registration, or practitioner in accordance with rules adopted by the Commission.

(g) Practitioners licensed in North Carolina by their respective licensing boards may possess, dispense or administer controlled substances to the extent authorized by law and by their boards.

(h) A physician licensed by the North Carolina Medical Board pursuant to Article 1 of this Chapter may possess, dispense or administer tetrahydrocannabinols in duly constituted pharmaceutical form for human administration for treatment purposes pursuant to rules adopted by the Commission.

(i) A physician licensed by the North Carolina Medical Board pursuant to Article 1 of this Chapter may dispense or administer Dronabinol or Nabilone as scheduled in G.S. 90-90(5) only as an antiemetic agent in cancer chemotherapy. (1971, c. 919, s. 1; 1973, c. 1358, s. 12; 1977, c. 667, s. 3; c. 891, s. 4; 1979, c. 781; 1981, c. 51, s. 9; 1983, c. 375, s. 2; 1985, c. 439, s. 2; 1987, c. 412, s. 13; 1989 (Reg. Sess., 1990), c. 1040, s. 4; 1993, c. 384, s. 2; 1995, c. 94, ss. 26, 27; 1997-443, s. 11A.118(a); 1997-456, s. 27; 2003-335, s. 1; 2003-398, s. 1; 2010-127, s. 1.)

§ 90-102. Additional provisions as to registration.

(a) The North Carolina Department of Health and Human Services shall register an applicant to manufacture or distribute controlled substances included in Schedules I through VI of this Article unless it determines that the issuance of such registration is inconsistent with the public interest. In determining the public interest, the following factors shall be considered:

(1) Maintenance of effective controls against diversion of any controlled substances and any substance compounded therefrom into other than legitimate medical, scientific, or industrial channels;

(2) Compliance with applicable federal, State and local law;

(3) Prior conviction record of applicant, its agents or employees under federal and State laws relating to the manufacture, distribution, or dispensing of such substances;

(4) Past experience in the manufacture of controlled substances, and the existence in the establishment or facility of effective controls against diversion; and

(5) Any factor relating to revocation, suspension, or denial of past registrations, licenses, or applications under this or any other State or federal law;

(6) Such other factors as may be relevant to and consistent with the public health and safety.

(b) Registration granted under subsection (a) of this section shall not entitle a registrant to manufacture and distribute controlled substances included in Schedule I or II other than those specified in the registration.

(c) Individual practitioners licensed to dispense and authorized to conduct research under federal law with Schedules II through V substances must be registered with the North Carolina Department of Health and Human Services to conduct such research.

(d) Manufacturers and distributors registered or licensed under federal law to manufacture or distribute controlled substances included in Schedules I through VI of this Article are entitled to registration under this Article, but this registration is expressly made subject to the provisions of G.S. 90-103.

(e) The North Carolina Department of Health and Human Services shall initially permit persons to register who own or operate any establishment engaged in the manufacture, distribution, or dispensing of any substances prior to January 1, 1972, and who are registered or licensed by the State. (1971, c. 919, s. 1; 1973, c. 1358, s. 14; 1977, c. 667, s. 3; 1985, c. 439, ss. 3, 4; 1997-443, s. 11A.118(a).)

§ 90-102.1. Registration of persons requiring limited use of controlled substances for training purposes in certain businesses.

(a) Definitions. - As used in this Article:

(1) "Commercial detection service" means any person, firm, association, or corporation contracting with another person, firm, association, or corporation for

a fee or other valuable consideration to place, lease, or rent a trained drug detection dog with a dog handler.

(2) "Dog handler" means a person trained in the handling of drug detection dogs, including the care, feeding, and maintenance of drug detection dogs and the procedures necessary to train and control the behavior of drug detection dogs.

(3) "Drug detection dog" means a dog trained to locate controlled substances by scent.

(b) Registration. - A dog handler who is not exempt from registration under G.S. 90-101 who intends to use any controlled substance included in Schedules I through VI for the limited purpose of the initial training and maintenance training of drug detection dogs shall file an application for registration with the Department of Health and Human Services and pay the applicable fee as provided in G.S. 90-101.

(c) Prerequisites for Registration. - Upon receipt of an application, the Department of Health and Human Services shall conduct a background investigation, during the course of which the applicant shall be required to show that the applicant meets all the following requirements and qualifications:

(1) That the applicant is at least 21 years of age.

(2) That the applicant is of good moral character and temperate habits. The following shall be prima facie evidence that the applicant does not have good moral character or temperate habits:

a. Conviction of any crime involving the illegal use, possession, sale, manufacture, distribution, or transportation of a controlled substance, drug, narcotic, or alcoholic beverage;

b. Conviction of a felony or a crime involving an act of violence;

c. Conviction of a crime involving unlawful breaking or entering, burglary, larceny, or any offense involving moral turpitude; or

d. A history of addiction to alcohol or a narcotic drug;

provided that, for purposes of this subsection, conviction means and includes the entry of a plea of guilty or no contest or a verdict rendered in open court by a judge or jury.

(3)   That the applicant has not been convicted of any felony involving the illegal use, possession, sale, manufacture, distribution, or transportation of a controlled substance, drug, narcotic, or alcoholic beverage.

(4)   That the applicant has the necessary training, qualifications, and experience to demonstrate competency and fitness as a dog handler as the Department of Health and Human Services may determine by rule for all registrations to be approved by the Department.

(5)   That the applicant affirms in writing that if the application for registration is approved, the applicant shall report all dog alerts to, or finds of, any controlled substance to a law enforcement agency having jurisdiction in the area where the dog alert occurs or where the controlled substance is found.

(d)   Criminal Record Check. - The Department of Justice may provide a criminal record check to the Department of Health and Human Services for a person who has applied for a new or renewal registration. The Department of Health and Human Services shall provide to the Department of Justice, along with the request, the fingerprints of the applicant, any additional information required by the Department of Justice, and a form signed by the applicant consenting to the check of the criminal record and to the use of the fingerprints and other identifying information required by the State or national repositories. The applicant's fingerprints shall be forwarded to the State Bureau of Investigation for a search of the State's criminal history record file, and the State Bureau of Investigation shall forward a set of the fingerprints to the Federal Bureau of Investigation for a national criminal history check. The Department of Health and Human Services shall keep all information pursuant to this subsection privileged, in accordance with applicable State law and federal guidelines, and the information shall be confidential and shall not be a public record under Chapter 132 of the General Statutes. The Department of Justice may charge each applicant a fee for conducting the checks of criminal history records authorized by this subsection.

(e)   Acquisition of Controlled Substances. - If the application for registration is approved, the registrant may lawfully obtain and possess controlled substances in the manner and to the extent authorized by the registration, in conformity with G.S. 90-105, other provisions of this Article, and rules promulgated by the Commission pursuant to G.S. 90-100.

(f) Record Keeping; Physical Security. - Each registrant shall keep records and maintain inventories in the manner specified in G.S. 90-104. Registrants shall provide effective controls and procedures to guard against theft and diversion of controlled substances. Controlled substances shall be stored in a securely locked, substantially constructed cabinet, and the storage area shall be protected by an alarm system that is continuously monitored by an alarm company central station.

(g) Disclosure of Discovery of Controlled Substances. - A dog handler shall, upon a dog alert or finding of a controlled substance, notify the State or local law enforcement agency having jurisdiction over the area where the dog alert occurs or the controlled substance is found. Before leaving the premises where the dog alert occurs or where the controlled substance is found, the dog handler shall inform law enforcement of the dog alert or the finding of a controlled substance and shall provide all relevant information concerning the dog alert or the discovery of the controlled substance.

(h) Commercial Detection Services; Dog Certification and Client Confidentiality. - Any drug detection dog utilized in a commercial detection service in this State shall first be certified by a canine certification association approved by the Department of Health and Human Services. Any person, including a nonresident, engaged in providing a commercial detection service in this State shall comply with the requirements of subsection (g) of this section regarding disclosure of the discovery of controlled substances. Client records of a dog handler who provides a commercial detection service for controlled substances shall be confidential unless the dog handler is required to report a dog alert or finding of a controlled substance in the course of a search, the records are lawfully subpoenaed, or the records are obtained by a law enforcement officer pursuant to a court order, a search warrant, or an exception to the search warrant requirement.

(i) Notice of Disclosure Requirement. - A dog handler shall provide conspicuous written notice to clients at the dog handler's place of business and in the contract for services stating that the dog handler is required by law to notify law enforcement of any dog alert or finding of a controlled substance.

Any person who contracts with a dog handler to provide commercial drug detection services shall provide conspicuous written notice to any person whose person or property may be subject to search stating that the premises is subject to search and that the dog handler is required by law to notify law enforcement of any dog alert or finding of a controlled substance.

(j) The Department of Health and Human Services shall have the power to investigate or cause to be investigated any complaints, allegations, or suspicions of wrongdoing or violations of this section involving individuals registered or applying to be registered under this section. The Department or the Commission may deny, suspend, or revoke a registration issued under this section if it is determined that the applicant or registrant has:

(1) Made any false statement or given any false information in connection with any application for a registration or for the renewal or reinstatement of a registration.

(2) Violated any provision of this Article.

(3) Violated any rule promulgated by the Department of Health and Human Services or the Commission for Mental Health, Developmental Disabilities, and Substance Abuse Services pursuant to the authority contained in this Article.

(k) This section does not apply to law enforcement agencies, to dog handlers and drug detection dogs that are employed or under contract to law enforcement agencies, or to other persons who are exempt from registration under G.S. 90-101(c)(5). (2003-398, s. 2.)

§ 90-103. Revocation or suspension of registration.

(a) A registration under G.S. 90-102 to manufacture, distribute, or dispense a controlled substance, may be suspended or revoked by the Commission upon a finding that the registrant:

(1) Has furnished false or fraudulent material information in any application filed under this Article;

(2) Has been convicted of a felony under any State or federal law relating to any controlled substance; or

(3) Has had his federal registration suspended or revoked to manufacture, distribute, or dispense controlled substances.

(b) The Commission may limit revocation or suspension of a registration to the particular controlled substance with respect to which grounds for revocation or suspension exist.

(c) Before denying, suspending, or revoking a registration or refusing a renewal of registration, the Commission shall serve upon the applicant or registrant an order to show cause why registration should not be denied, revoked, or suspended, or why the renewal should not be refused. The order to show cause shall contain a statement of the basis therefor and shall call upon the applicant or registrant to appear before the Commission at a time and place not less than 30 days after the date of service of the order, but in the case of a denial or renewal of registration, the show cause order shall be served not later than 30 days before the expiration of the registration. These proceedings shall be conducted in accordance with rules and regulations of the Commission required by Chapter 150B of the General Statutes, and subject to judicial review as provided in Chapter 150B of the General Statutes. Such proceedings shall be independent of, and not in lieu of, criminal prosecutions or other proceedings under this Article or any law of the State.

(d) The Commission may suspend, without an order to show cause, any registration simultaneously with the institutions of proceedings under this section, or where renewal of registration is refused if it finds that there is an imminent danger to the public health or safety which warrants this action. The suspension shall continue in effect until the conclusion of the proceedings, including judicial review thereof, unless sooner withdrawn by the Commission or dissolved by a court of competent jurisdiction.

(e) In the event the Commission suspends or revokes a registration granted under G.S. 90-102, all controlled substances owned or possessed by the registrant pursuant to such registration at the time of suspension or the effective date of the revocation order, as the case may be, may in the discretion of the Commission be placed under seal. No disposition may be made of substances under seal until the time for taking an appeal has elapsed or until all appeals have been concluded unless a court, upon application therefor, orders the sale of perishable substances and the deposit of the proceeds of the sale with the court. Upon a revocation order becoming final, all such controlled substances may be ordered forfeited to the State.

(f)   The Bureau shall promptly be notified of all orders suspending or revoking registration. (1971, c. 919, s. 1; 1973, c. 1331, s. 3; 1977, c. 667, s. 3; 1981, c. 51, s. 9; 1987, c. 827, s. 1.)

§ 90-104. Records of registrants or practitioners.

Each registrant or practitioner manufacturing, distributing, or dispensing controlled substances under this Article shall keep records and maintain inventories in conformance with the record-keeping and the inventory requirements of the federal law and shall conform to such rules and regulations as may be promulgated by the Commission. (1971, c. 919, s. 1; 1977, c. 667, s. 3; 1981, c. 51, s. 9.)

§ 90-105. Order forms.

Controlled substances included in Schedules I and II of this Article shall be distributed only by a registrant or practitioner, pursuant to an order form. Compliance with the provisions of the Federal Controlled Substances Act or its successor respecting order forms shall be deemed compliance with this section. (1971, c. 919, s. 1.)

§ 90-106. Prescriptions and labeling.

(a)   Except when dispensed directly by a practitioner, other than a pharmacist, to an ultimate user, no controlled substance included in Schedule II of this Article may be dispensed without the written prescription of a practitioner. No Schedule II substance shall be dispensed pursuant to a written prescription more than six months after the date it was prescribed.

(b)   In emergency situations, as defined by rule of the Commission, Schedule II drugs may be dispensed upon oral prescription of a practitioner, reduced promptly to writing and filed by the dispensing agent. Prescriptions shall be retained in conformity with the requirements of G.S. 90-104. No prescription for a Schedule II substance may be refilled.

(c)   Except when dispensed directly by a practitioner, other than a pharmacist, to an ultimate user, no controlled substance included in Schedules III or IV, except paregoric, U.S.P., as provided in G.S. 90-91(e)1, may be dispensed without a prescription, and oral prescriptions shall be promptly reduced to writing and filed with the dispensing agent. Such prescription may not be filled or refilled more than six months after the date thereof or be refilled more than five times after the date of the prescription.

(d)   No controlled substance included in Schedule V of this Article or paregoric, U.S.P., may be distributed or dispensed other than for a medical purpose.

(e)   No controlled substance included in Schedule VI of this Article may be distributed or dispensed other than for scientific or research purposes by persons registered under, or permitted by, this Article to engage in scientific or research projects.

(f)   No controlled substance shall be dispensed or distributed in this State unless such substance shall be in a container clearly labeled in accord with regulations lawfully adopted and published by the federal government or the Commission.

(g)   When a copy of a prescription for a controlled substance under this Article is given as required by G.S. 90-70, such copy shall be plainly marked: "Copy - for information only." Copies of prescriptions for controlled substances shall not be filled or refilled.

(h)   A pharmacist dispensing a controlled substance under this Article shall enter the date of dispensing on the prescription order pursuant to which such controlled substance was dispensed.

(i)   A manufacturer's sales representative may distribute a controlled substance as a complimentary sample only upon the written request of a practitioner. Such request must be made on each distribution and must contain the names and addresses of the supplier and the requester and the name and quantity of the specific controlled substance requested. The manufacturer shall maintain a record of each such request for a period of two years. (1971, c. 919, s. 1; 1973, c. 476, s. 128; c. 1358, s. 15; 1975, c. 572; 1977, c. 667, s. 3; 1981, c. 51, s. 9; 2007-248, s. 2; 2013-379, s. 5.)

§ 90-106.1. Photo ID requirement for Schedule II controlled substances.

(a)   Immediately prior to dispensing a Schedule II controlled substance, or any of the Schedule III controlled substances listed in subdivisions 1. through 8. of G.S. 90-91(d), each pharmacy holding a valid permit pursuant to G.S. 90-85.21 shall require the person seeking the dispensation to present one of the following valid, unexpired forms of government-issued photographic identification: (i) a drivers license, (ii) a special identification card issued under G.S. 20-37.7, (iii) a military identification card, or (iv) a passport. Upon presentation of the required photographic identification, the pharmacy shall document the name of the person seeking the dispensation, the type of photographic identification presented by the person seeking the dispensation, and the photographic identification number. The pharmacy shall retain this identifying information on the premises or at a central location apart from the premises as part of its business records for a period of three years following dispensation.

(b)   The pharmacy shall make the identifying information available to any person authorized under G.S. 90-113.74 to receive prescription information data in the controlled substances reporting system within 72 hours after a request for the identifying information. A pharmacy that submits the identifying information required under this section to the controlled substances reporting system established and maintained pursuant to G.S. 90-113.73 is deemed in compliance with this subsection.

(c)   Nothing in this section shall be deemed to require that the person seeking the dispensation and the person to whom the prescription is issued be the same person, and nothing in this section shall apply to the dispensation of controlled substances to employees of "health care facilities", as that term is defined in G.S. 131E-256(b), when the controlled substances are delivered to the health care facilities for the benefit of residents or patients of such health care facilities. (2011-349, s. 1.)

§ 90-106.2. Treatment of overdose with opioid antagonist; immunity.

(a)   As used in this section, "opioid antagonist" means naloxone hydrochloride that is approved by the federal Food and Drug Administration for the treatment of a drug overdose.

(b) A practitioner acting in good faith and exercising reasonable care may directly or by standing order prescribe an opioid antagonist to (i) a person at risk of experiencing an opiate-related overdose or (ii) a family member, friend, or other person in a position to assist a person at risk of experiencing an opiate-related overdose. As an indicator of good faith, the practitioner, prior to prescribing an opioid under this subsection, may require receipt of a written communication that provides a factual basis for a reasonable conclusion as to either of the following:

(1) The person seeking the opioid antagonist is at risk of experiencing an opiate-related overdose.

(2) The person other than the person who is at risk of experiencing an opiate-related overdose, and who is seeking the opioid antagonist, is in relation to the person at risk of experiencing an opiate-related overdose:

a. A family member, friend, or other person.

b. In the position to assist a person at risk of experiencing an opiate-related overdose.

(c) A person who receives an opioid antagonist that was prescribed pursuant to subsection (b) of this section may administer an opioid antagonist to another person if (i) the person has a good faith belief that the other person is experiencing a drug-related overdose and (ii) the person exercises reasonable care in administering the drug to the other person. Evidence of the use of reasonable care in administering the drug shall include the receipt of basic instruction and information on how to administer the opioid antagonist.

(d) All of the following individuals are immune from any civil or criminal liability for actions authorized by this section:

(1) Any practitioner who prescribes an opioid antagonist pursuant to subsection (b) of this section.

(2) Any person who administers an opioid antagonist pursuant to subsection (c) of this section. (2013-23, s. 2.)

§ 90-107. Prescriptions, stocks, etc., open to inspection by officials.

Prescriptions, order forms and records, required by this Article, and stocks of controlled substances included in Schedules I through VI of this Article shall be open for inspection only to federal and State officers, whose duty it is to enforce the laws of this State or of the United States relating to controlled substances included in Schedules I through VI of this Article, and to authorized employees of the North Carolina Department of Health and Human Services. No officer having knowledge by virtue of his office of any such prescription, order, or record shall divulge such knowledge other than to other law-enforcement officials or agencies, except in connection with a prosecution or proceeding in court or before a licensing board or officer to which prosecution or proceeding the person to whom such prescriptions, orders, or records relate is a party. (1971, c. 919, s. 1; 1973, c. 1358, s. 13; 1977, c. 667, s. 3; 1997-443, s. 11A.118(a).)

§ 90-108. Prohibited acts; penalties.

(a)   It shall be unlawful for any person:

(1)   Other than practitioners licensed under Articles 1, 2, 4, 6, 11, 12A of this Chapter to represent to any registrant or practitioner who manufactures, distributes, or dispenses a controlled substance under the provision of this Article that he is a licensed practitioner in order to secure or attempt to secure any controlled substance as defined in this Article or to in any way impersonate a practitioner for the purpose of securing or attempting to secure any drug requiring a prescription from a practitioner as listed above and who is licensed by this State;

(2)   Who is subject to the requirements of G.S. 90-101 or a practitioner to distribute or dispense a controlled substance in violation of G.S. 90-105 or 90-106;

(3)   Who is a registrant to manufacture, distribute, or dispense a controlled substance not authorized by his registration to another registrant or other authorized person;

(4)   To omit, remove, alter, or obliterate a symbol required by the Federal Controlled Substances Act or its successor;

(5) To refuse or fail to make, keep, or furnish any record, notification, order form, statement, invoice or information required under this Article;

(6) To refuse any entry into any premises or inspection authorized by this Article;

(7) To knowingly keep or maintain any store, shop, warehouse, dwelling house, building, vehicle, boat, aircraft, or any place whatever, which is resorted to by persons using controlled substances in violation of this Article for the purpose of using such substances, or which is used for the keeping or selling of the same in violation of this Article;

(8) Who is a registrant or a practitioner to distribute a controlled substance included in Schedule I or II of this Article in the course of his legitimate business, except pursuant to an order form as required by G.S. 90-105;

(9) To use in the course of the manufacture or distribution of a controlled substance a registration number which is fictitious, revoked, suspended, or issued to another person;

(10) To acquire or obtain possession of a controlled substance by misrepresentation, fraud, forgery, deception, or subterfuge;

(11) To furnish false or fraudulent material information in, or omit any material information from, any application, report, or other document required to be kept or filed under this Article, or any record required to be kept by this Article;

(12) To make, distribute, or possess any punch, die, plate, stone, or other thing designed to print, imprint, or reproduce the trademark, trade name, or other identifying mark, imprint, or device of another or any likeness of any of the foregoing upon any drug or container or labeling thereof so as to render such drug a counterfeit controlled substance;

(13) To obtain controlled substances through the use of legal prescriptions which have been obtained by the knowing and willful misrepresentation to or by the intentional withholding of information from one or more practitioners;

(14) Who is an employee of a registrant or practitioner and who is authorized to possess controlled substances or has access to controlled substances by

virtue of his employment, to embezzle or fraudulently or knowingly and willfully misapply or divert to his own use or other unauthorized or illegal use or to take, make away with or secrete, with intent to embezzle or fraudulently or knowingly and willfully misapply or divert to his own use or other unauthorized or illegal use any controlled substance which shall have come into his possession or under his care.

(b) Any person who violates this section shall be guilty of a Class 1 misdemeanor. Provided, that if the criminal pleading alleges that the violation was committed intentionally, and upon trial it is specifically found that the violation was committed intentionally, such violations shall be a Class I felony unless one of the following applies:

(1) A person who violates subdivision (7) of subsection (a) of this section and also fortifies the structure, with the intent to impede law enforcement entry, (by barricading windows and doors) shall be punished as a Class I felon.

(2) A person who violates subdivision (14) of subsection (a) of this section shall be punished as a Class G felon. (1971, c. 919, s. 1; 1973, c. 1358, s. 11; 1979, c. 760, ss. 5, 6; 1979, 2nd Sess., c. 1316, s. 47; 1981, c. 63, s. 1; c. 179, s. 14; 1983, c. 294, s. 7; c. 773; 1991 (Reg. Sess., 1992), c. 1041, s. 1; 1993, c. 539, s. 622; 1994, Ex. Sess., c. 24, s. 14(c); 2013-90, s. 1.)

§ 90-109. Licensing required.

A facility for drug treatment as defined in G.S. 122C-3(14)b. shall obtain the license required by Article 2 of Chapter 122C of the General Statutes permitting operation. Subject to rules governing the operation and licensing of these facilities set by the Commission for Mental Health, Developmental Disabilities, and Substance Abuse Services, the Department of Health and Human Services shall be responsible for issuing licenses. These licensing rules shall be consistent with the licensing rules adopted under Article 2 of Chapter 122C of the General Statutes. (1971, c. 919, s. 1; 1973, c. 1361; 1977, c. 667, s. 3; 1981, c. 51, s. 9; 1983, c. 718, s. 2; 1985, c. 589, s. 32; 1995, c. 509, s. 39; 1997-443, s. 11A.118(a).)

§ 90-109.1. Treatment.

(a) A person may request treatment and rehabilitation for drug dependence from a practitioner, and such practitioner or employees thereof shall not disclose the name of such person to any law-enforcement officer or agency; nor shall such information be admissible as evidence in any court, grand jury, or administrative proceeding unless authorized by the person seeking treatment. A practitioner may undertake the treatment and rehabilitation of such person or refer such person to another practitioner for such purpose and under the same requirement of confidentiality.

(b) An individual who requests treatment or rehabilitation for drug dependence in a program where medical services are to be an integral component of his treatment shall be examined and evaluated by a practitioner before receiving treatment and rehabilitation services. If a practitioner performs an initial examination and evaluation, the practitioner shall prescribe a proper course of treatment and medication, if needed. That practitioner may authorize another practitioner to provide the prescribed treatment and rehabilitation services.

(c) Every practitioner that provides treatment or rehabilitation services to a person dependent upon drugs shall periodically as required by the Secretary of the North Carolina Department of Health and Human Services commencing January 1, 1972, make a statistical report to the Secretary of the North Carolina Department of Health and Human Services in such form and manner as the Secretary shall prescribe for each such person treated or to whom rehabilitation services were provided. The form of the report prescribed shall be furnished by the Secretary of the North Carolina Department of Health and Human Services. Such report shall include the number of persons treated or to whom rehabilitation services were provided; the county of such person's legal residence; the age of such person; the number of such persons treated as inpatients and the number treated as outpatients; the number treated who had received previous treatment or rehabilitation services; and any other data required by the Secretary. If treatment or rehabilitation services are provided to a person by a hospital, public agency, or drug treatment facility, such hospital, public agency, or drug treatment facility shall coordinate with the treating medical practitioner so that statistical reports required in this section shall not duplicate one another. The Secretary shall cause all such reports to be compiled into periodical reports which shall be a public record. (1971, c. 919, s. 1; 1977, c. 667, s. 3; 1985, c. 439, s. 5; 1997-443, s. 11A.118(a).)

§ 90-110. Injunctions.

(a) The superior court of North Carolina shall have jurisdiction in proceedings in accordance with the rules of those courts to enjoin violations of this Article.

(b) In case of an alleged violation of an injunction or restraining order issued under this section, trial shall, upon demand of the accused, be by a jury in accordance with the rules of the superior courts of North Carolina. (1971, c. 919, s. 1.)

§ 90-111. Cooperative arrangements.

The North Carolina Department of Health and Human Services and the Attorney General of North Carolina shall cooperate with federal and other State agencies in discharging their responsibilities concerning traffic in controlled substances and in suppressing the abuse of controlled substances. To this end, they are authorized to:

(1) Arrange for the exchange of information between governmental officials concerning the use and abuse of controlled substances;

(2) Coordinate and cooperate in training programs on controlled substances for law enforcement at the local and State levels;

(3) Cooperate with the Bureau by establishing a centralized unit which will accept, catalogue, file, and collect statistics, including records of drug-dependent persons and other controlled substance law offenders within the State, and make such information available for federal, State, and local law-enforcement purposes. Provided that neither the Attorney General of North Carolina, the North Carolina Department of Health and Human Services nor any other State officer or agency shall be authorized to accept or file, or give out the names or other form of personal identification of drug-dependent persons who voluntarily seek treatment or assistance related to their drug dependency. (1971, c. 919, s. 1; 1977, c. 667, s. 3; 1997-443, s. 11A.118(a).)

§ 90-112. Forfeitures.

(a) The following shall be subject to forfeiture:

(1) All controlled substances which have been manufactured, distributed, dispensed, or acquired in violation of the provisions of this Article;

(2) All money, raw material, products, and equipment of any kind which are acquired, used, or intended for use, in selling, purchasing, manufacturing, compounding, processing, delivering, importing, or exporting a controlled substance in violation of the provisions of this Article;

(3) All property which is used, or intended for use, as a container for property described in subdivisions (1) and (2);

(4) All conveyances, including vehicles, vessels, or aircraft, which are used or intended for use to unlawfully conceal, convey, or transport, or in any manner to facilitate the unlawful concealment, conveyance, or transportation of property described in (1) or (2), except that

a. No conveyance used by any person as a common carrier in the transaction of business as a common carrier shall be forfeited under the provisions of this Article unless it shall appear that the owner or other person in charge of such conveyance was a consenting party or privy to a violation of this Article;

b. No conveyance shall be forfeited under the provisions of this section by reason of any act or omission, committed or omitted while such conveyance was unlawfully in the possession of a person other than the owner in violation of the criminal laws of the United States, or of any state;

c. No conveyance shall be forfeited unless the violation involved is a felony under this Article;

d. A forfeiture of a conveyance encumbered by a bona fide security interest is subject to the interest of the secured party who had no knowledge of or consented to the act or omission.

(5) All books, records, and research, including formulas, microfilm, tapes, and data which are used, or intended for use, in violation of this Article.

(b) Any property subject to forfeiture under this Article may be seized by any law-enforcement officer upon process issued by any district or superior court having jurisdiction over the property except that seizure without such process may be made when:

(1) The seizure is incident to an arrest or a search under a search warrant;

(2) The property subject to seizure has been the subject of a prior judgment in favor of the State in a criminal injunction or forfeiture proceeding under this Article.

(c) Property taken or detained under this section shall not be repleviable, but shall be deemed to be in custody of the law-enforcement agency seizing it, which may:

(1) Place the property under seal; or,

(2) Remove the property to a place designated by it; or,

(3) Request that the North Carolina Department of Justice take custody of the property and remove it to an appropriate location for disposition in accordance with law.

Any property seized by a State, local, or county law enforcement officer shall be held in safekeeping as provided in this subsection until an order of disposition is properly entered by the judge.

(d) Whenever property is forfeited under this Article, the law-enforcement agency having custody of it may:

(1) Retain the property for official use; or

(2) Sell any forfeited property which is not required to be destroyed by law and which is not harmful to the public, provided that the proceeds be disposed of for payment of all proper expenses of the proceedings for forfeiture and sale including expense of seizure, maintenance of custody, advertising, and court costs; or

(3) Transfer any conveyance including vehicles, vessels, or aircraft which are forfeited under the provisions of this Article to the North Carolina Department of Justice when, in the discretion of the presiding judge and upon

application of the North Carolina Department of Justice, said conveyance may be of official use to the North Carolina Department of Justice;

(4) Upon determination by the director of any law-enforcement agency that a vehicle, vessel or aircraft transferred pursuant to the provisions of this Article is of no further use to said agency for use in official investigations, such vehicle, vessel or aircraft may be sold as surplus property in the same manner as other vehicles owned by the law-enforcement agency and the proceeds from such sale after deducting the cost of sale shall be paid to the treasurer or proper officer authorized to receive fines and forfeitures to be used for the school fund of the county in the county in which said vehicle, vessel or aircraft was seized; provided, that any vehicle transferred to any law-enforcement agency under the provisions of this Article which has been modified to increase speed shall be used in the performance of official duties only and not for resale, transfer or disposition other than as junk.

(d1) Notwithstanding the provisions of subsection (d), the law-enforcement agency having custody of money that is forfeited pursuant to this section shall pay it to the treasurer or proper officer authorized to receive fines and forfeitures to be used for the school fund of the county in which the money was seized.

(e) All substances included in Schedules I through VI that are possessed, transferred, sold, or offered for sale in violation of the provisions of this Article shall be deemed contraband and seized and summarily forfeited to the State. All substances included in Schedules I through VI of this Article which are seized or come into the possession of the State, the owners of which are unknown, shall be deemed contraband and summarily forfeited to the State according to rules and regulations of the North Carolina Department of Justice.

All species of plants from which controlled substances included in Schedules I, II and VI of this Article may be derived, which have been planted or cultivated in violation of this Article, or of which the owners or cultivators are unknown, or which are wild growths, may be seized and summarily forfeited to the State.

The failure, upon demand by the Attorney General of North Carolina, or his duly authorized agent, of the person in occupancy or in control of land or premises upon which such species of plants are growing or being stored, to produce an appropriate registration, or proof that he is the holder thereof, shall constitute authority for the seizure and forfeiture.

(f)   All other property subject to forfeiture under the provisions of this Article shall be forfeited as in the case of conveyances used to conceal, convey, or transport intoxicating beverages. (1971, c. 919, s. 1; 1973, cc. 447, 542; c. 1446, s. 6; 1983, c. 528, ss. 1-3; 1989, c. 772, s. 4.)

§ 90-112.1. Remission or mitigation of forfeitures; possession pending trial.

(a)   Whenever, in any proceeding in court for a forfeiture, under G.S. 90-112 of any conveyance seized for a violation of this Article the court shall have exclusive jurisdiction to continue, remit or mitigate the forfeiture.

(b)   In any such proceeding the court shall not allow the claim of any claimant for remission or mitigation unless and until he proves (i) that he has an interest in such conveyance, as owner or otherwise, which he acquired in good faith; (ii) that he had no knowledge, or reason to believe, that it was being or would be used in the violation of laws of this State relating to controlled substances; (iii) that his interest is in an amount in excess or equal to the fair market value of such conveyance.

(c)   If the court, in its discretion, allows the remission or mitigation the conveyance shall be returned to the claimant; and should there be joint request of any two or more claimants, whose claims are allowed, the court shall order the return of the conveyance to such of the joint requesting claimants as have the prior claim on lien. Such return shall be made only upon payment of all expenses incident to the seizure and forfeiture incurred by the State. In all other cases the court shall order disposition of such conveyance as provided in G.S. 90-112, and after satisfaction of the expenses of the sale, and such claims as may be approved by the court, the funds shall be paid to the treasurer or proper officer authorized to receive fines and forfeitures to be used for the school fund of the county in which said vehicle was seized.

(d)   If the court should determine that the conveyance should be held for purposes of evidence, then it may order the vehicle to be held until the case is heard. (1975, c. 601.)

§ 90-113. Repealed by Session Laws 1973, c. 540, s. 7.

§ 90-113.1. Burden of proof; liabilities.

(a) It shall not be necessary for the State to negate any exemption or exception set forth in this Article in any complaint, information, indictment, or other pleading or in any trial, hearing, or other proceeding under this Article, and the burden of proof of any such exemption or exception shall be upon the person claiming its benefit.

(b) In the absence of proof that a person is the duly authorized holder of an appropriate registration or order form issued under this Article, he shall be presumed not to be the holder of such registration or form, and the burden of proof shall be upon him to rebut such presumption.

(c) No liability shall be imposed by virtue of this Article upon any duly authorized officer, engaged in the lawful enforcement of this Article. (1971, c. 919, s. 1.)

§ 90-113.2. Judicial review.

All final determinations, findings, and conclusions of the Commission under this Article shall be final and conclusive decisions of the matters involved, except that any person aggrieved by such decision may obtain review of the decision as provided in Chapter 150B of the General Statutes. Findings of fact by the Commission, if supported by substantial evidence, shall be conclusive. (1971, c. 919, s. 1; 1973, c. 476, s. 128; c. 1331, s. 3; 1977, c. 667, s. 3; c. 891, s. 5; 1981, c. 51, s. 9; 1987, c. 827, s. 1.)

§ 90-113.3. Education and research.

(a) The North Carolina Department of Public Instruction and the Board of Governors of the University of North Carolina are authorized and directed to carry out educational programs designed to prevent and deter misuse and abuse of controlled substances. In connection with such programs, they are authorized to:

(1) Promote better recognition of the problems of misuse and abuse of controlled substances within the regulated industry and among interested groups and organizations;

(2) Assist the regulated industry and interested groups and organizations in contributing to the reduction of misuse and abuse of controlled substances; and

(3) Disseminate the results of research on misuse and abuse of controlled substances to promote a better public understanding of what problems exist and what can be done to combat them.

(b) The North Carolina Department of Public Instruction and the Board of Governors of the University of North Carolina or either of them may enter into contracts for educational activities related to controlled substances.

(c) The North Carolina Department of Health and Human Services is authorized and directed to encourage research on misuse and abuse of controlled substances. In connection with such research and in furtherance of the enforcement of this Article, it is authorized to:

(1) Establish methods to assess accurately the effects of controlled substances and to identify and characterize controlled substances with potential for abuse;

(2) Make studies and undertake programs of research to:

a. Develop new or improved approaches, techniques, systems, equipment, and devices to strengthen the enforcement of this Article;

b. Determine patterns of misuse and abuse of controlled substances and the social effect thereof; and

c. Improve methods for preventing, predicting, understanding, and dealing with the misuse and abuse of controlled substances.

(3) Enter into contracts with other public agencies, any district attorney, institutions of higher education, and private organizations or individuals for the purpose of conducting research, demonstrations, or special projects which bear directly on misuse and abuse of controlled substances.

(d) The North Carolina Department of Health and Human Services may enter into contracts for research activities related to controlled substances, and the North Carolina Department of Public Instruction and the Board of Governors of the University of North Carolina or either of them may enter into contracts for educational activities related to controlled substances, without performance bonds.

(e) The North Carolina Department of Health and Human Services may authorize persons engaged in research on the use and effects of controlled substances to withhold the names and other identifying characteristics of persons who are the subjects of such research. Persons who obtain this authorization may not be compelled in any State civil, criminal, administrative, legislative, or other proceeding to identify the subjects of research for which such authorization was obtained.

(f) The North Carolina Department of Health and Human Services may authorize persons engaged in research to possess and distribute controlled substances in accordance with such restrictions as the authorization may impose. Persons who obtain this authorization shall be exempt from State prosecution for possession and distribution of controlled substances to the extent authorized by the North Carolina Department of Health and Human Services. (1971, c. 919, s. 1; c. 1244, s. 14; 1973, c. 476, s. 128; 1977, c. 667, s. 3; 1981, c. 218; 1997-443, s. 11A.118(a).)

§ 90-113.4. Repealed by Session Laws 1981, c. 500, s. 2, effective October 1, 1981.

§ 90-113.4A: Repealed by Session Laws 1989, c. 784, s. 4.

§ 90-113.5. State Board of Pharmacy, North Carolina Department of Justice and peace officers to enforce Article.

It is hereby made the duty of the State Board of Pharmacy, its officers, agents, inspectors, and representatives, and all peace officers within the State, including agents of the North Carolina Department of Justice, and all State's attorneys, to enforce all provisions of this Article, except those specifically delegated, and to cooperate with all agencies charged with the enforcement of the laws of the United States, of this State, and of all other states, relating to controlled substances. The North Carolina Department of Justice is hereby authorized to make initial investigation of all violations of this Article, and is given original but not exclusive jurisdiction in respect thereto with all other law-enforcement officers of the State. (1971, c. 919, s. 1.)

§ 90-113.6. Payments and advances.

(a) The Attorney General is authorized to pay any person, from funds appropriated for the North Carolina Department of Justice, for information concerning a violation of this Article, such sum or sums of money as he may find appropriate, without reference to any rewards to which such persons may otherwise be entitled by law.

(b) Moneys expended from appropriations of the North Carolina Department of Justice for the purchase of controlled substances or other substances proscribed by this Article which is subsequently recovered shall be reimbursed to the current appropriation for the Department.

(c) The Attorney General is authorized to direct the advance of funds by the State Treasurer in connection with the enforcement of this Article. (1971, c. 919, s. 1.)

§ 90-113.7. Pending proceedings.

(a) Prosecutions for any violation of law occurring prior to January 1, 1972, shall not be affected by these repealers, or amendments, or abated by reason, thereof.

(b) Civil seizures or forfeitures and injunctive proceedings commenced prior to January 1, 1972, shall not be affected by these repealers, or amendments, or abated by reason, thereof.

(c) All administrative proceedings pending on January 1, 1972, shall be continued and brought to final determination in accord with laws and regulations in effect prior to January 1, 1972. Such drugs placed under control prior to January 1, 1972, which are not included within Schedules I through VI of this Article shall automatically be controlled and listed in the appropriate schedule.

(d) The provisions of this Article shall be applicable to violations of law, seizures and forfeiture, injunctive proceedings, administrative proceedings, and investigations which occur following January 1, 1972. (1971, c. 919, s. 1.)

§ 90-113.8. Continuation of regulations.

Any orders, rules, and regulations which have been promulgated under any law affected by this act [c. 919 of the 1971 Session Laws] and which are in effect on the day preceding January 1, 1972, shall continue in effect until modified, superseded, or repealed by proper authority. (1971, c. 919, s. 2.)

Article 5A.

North Carolina Toxic Vapors Act.

§ 90-113.8A. Title.

This Article shall be known and may be cited as the "North Carolina Toxic Vapors Act." (1971, c. 1208, s. 1.)

§ 90-113.9. Definitions.

For purposes of this Article, unless the context requires otherwise,

(1) "Intoxication" means drunkenness, stupefaction, depression, giddiness, paralysis, irrational behavior, or other change, distortion, or disturbance of the auditory, visual, or mental processes.

(2) "Commission" means the Commission for Mental Health, Developmental Disabilities, and Substance Abuse Services, established under Part 4 of Article 3 of Chapter 143B of the General Statutes. (1971, c. 1208, s. 1; 1979, c. 671, s. 1; 1981, c. 51, s. 10; 1995, c. 509, s. 40.)

§ 90-113.10. Inhaling fumes for purpose of causing intoxication.

It is unlawful for any person to knowingly breathe or inhale any compound, liquid, or chemical containing toluol, hexane, trichloroethane, isopropanol, methyl isobutyl ketone, methyl cellosolve acetate, cyclohexanone, ethyl alcohol, or any other substance for the purpose of inducing a condition of intoxication. This section does not apply to any person using as an inhalant any chemical substance pursuant to the direction of a licensed medical provider authorized by law to prescribe the inhalant or chemical substance possessed. (1971, c. 1208, s. 1; 1979, c. 671, s. 2; 2007-134, s. 1.)

§ 90-113.10A. Alcohol vaporizing devices prohibited.

It shall be unlawful for any person to knowingly manufacture, sell, give, deliver, possess, or use an alcohol vaporizing device. As used in this section, "alcohol vaporizing device" or "AVD" means a device, machine, apparatus, or appliance that is designed or marketed for the purpose of mixing ethyl alcohol with pure or diluted oxygen, or another gas, to produce an alcoholic vapor that an individual can inhale or snort. An AVD does not include an inhaler, nebulizer, atomizer, or other device that is designed and intended by the manufacturer to dispense either a substance prescribed by a licensed medical provider authorized by law to prescribe the inhalant or chemical substance possessed, or an over-the-counter medication approved by monograph or new drug application under the Federal Food, Drug, and Cosmetic Act (21 U.S.C. § 301, et seq.), provided the instrument is not used for the purpose of inducing a condition of intoxication through inhalation. Violation of this section is not a lesser included offense of G.S. 90-113.22. (2007-134, s. 2.)

§ 90-113.11. Possession of substances.

It is unlawful for any person to possess any compound, liquid, or chemical containing toluol, hexane, trichloroethane, isopropanol, methyl isobutyl ketone, methyl cellosolve acetate, cyclohexanone, ethyl alcohol, or any other substance which will induce a condition of intoxication through inhalation for the purpose of violating G.S. 90-113.10. (1971, c. 1208, s. 1; 1979, c. 671, s. 3; 2007-134, s. 3.)

§ 90-113.12. Sale of substance.

It is unlawful for any person to sell, offer to sell, deliver, give, or possess with the intent to sell, deliver, or give any other person any compound, liquid, or chemical containing toluol, hexane, trichloroethane, isopropanol, methyl isobutyl ketone, methyl cellosolve acetate, cyclohexanone, ethyl alcohol, or any other substance which will induce a condition of intoxication through inhalation if he has reasonable cause to suspect that the product sold, offered for sale, given, delivered, or possessed with the intent to sell, give, or deliver, will be used for the purpose of violating G.S. 90-113.10. (1971, c. 1208, s. 1; 1979, c. 671, s. 4; 2007-134, s. 4.)

§ 90-113.13. Violation a misdemeanor.

Violation of this Article is a Class 1 misdemeanor. (1979, c. 671, s. 5; 1993, c. 539, s. 623; 1994, Ex. Sess., c. 24, s. 14(c).)

§ 90-113.14. Conditional discharge for first offenses.

(a)   Whenever any person who has not previously been convicted of any offense under this Article or under any statute of the United States or any state relating to those substances included in Article 5 or 5A or 5B of Chapter 90 pleads guilty to or is found guilty of inhaling or possessing any substance having the property of releasing toxic vapors or fumes in violation of Article 5A of Chapter 90, the court may, without entering a judgment of guilt and with the consent of such person, defer further proceedings and place him on probation upon such reasonable terms and conditions as it may require. Notwithstanding the provisions of G.S. 15A-1342(c) or any other statute or law, probation may be imposed under this section for an offense under this Article for which the prescribed punishment includes only a fine. To fulfill the terms and conditions of probation the court may allow the defendant to participate in a drug education program approved for this purpose by the Department of Health and Human Services. Upon violation of a term or condition, the court may enter an adjudication of guilt and proceed as otherwise provided. Upon fulfillment of the terms and conditions, the court shall discharge such person and dismiss the proceedings against him. Discharge and dismissal under this section shall be without court adjudication of guilt and shall not be deemed a conviction for purposes of this section or for purposes of disqualifications or disabilities imposed by law upon conviction of a crime including the additional penalties imposed for second or subsequent convictions. Discharge and dismissal under this section or G.S. 90-96 may occur only once with respect to any person. Disposition of a case to determine discharge and dismissal under this section at the district court division of the General Court of Justice shall be final for the purpose of appeal. Prior to taking any action to discharge or dismiss under this section the court shall make a finding that the defendant has no record of previous convictions under the "North Carolina Toxic Vapors Act", Article 5A, Chapter 90, the "North Carolina Controlled Substances Act", Article 5, Chapter 90, or the "Drug Paraphernalia Act", Article 5B, Chapter 90.

(a1)   Upon the first conviction only of any offense included in G.S. 90-113.10 or 90-113.11 and subject to the provisions of this subsection (a1), the court may place defendant on probation under this section for an offense under this Article including an offense for which the prescribed punishment includes only a fine. The probation, if imposed, shall be for not less than one year and shall contain a minimum condition that the defendant who was found guilty or pleads guilty enroll in and successfully complete, within 150 days of the date of the imposition of said probation, the program of instruction at the drug education school approved by the Department of Health and Human Services pursuant to G.S. 90-96.01. The court may impose probation that does not contain a condition that defendant successfully complete the program of instruction at a drug education school if:

(1)   There is no drug education school within a reasonable distance of the defendant's residence; or

(2)   There are specific, extenuating circumstances which make it likely that defendant will not benefit from the program of instruction.

The court shall enter such specific findings in the record; provided that in the case of subsection (2) above, such findings shall include the specific, extenuating circumstances which make it likely that the defendant will not benefit from the program of instruction.

Upon fulfillment of the terms and conditions of the probation, the court shall discharge such person and dismiss the proceedings against the person.

For the purpose of determining whether the conviction is a first conviction or whether a person has already had discharge and dismissal, no prior offense occurring more than seven years before the date of the current offense shall be considered. In addition, convictions for violations of a provision of G.S. 90-95(a)(1) or 90-95(a)(2) or 90-95(a)(3), or 90-113.10, or 90-113.11, or 90-113.12, or 90-113.22 shall be considered previous convictions.

Failure to complete successfully an approved program of instruction at a drug education school shall constitute grounds to revoke probation pursuant to this subsection and deny application for expunction of all recordation of defendant's arrest, indictment, or information, trial, finding of guilty, and dismissal and discharge pursuant to G.S. 15A-145.3. For purposes of this subsection, the phrase "failure to complete successfully the prescribed program of instruction at a drug education school" includes failure to attend scheduled classes without a valid excuse, failure to complete the course within 150 days of imposition of probation, willful failure to pay the required fee for the course as provided in G.S. 90-96.01(b), or any other manner in which the person fails to complete the course successfully. The instructor of the course to which a person is assigned shall report any failure of a person to complete successfully the program of instruction to the court which imposed probation. Upon receipt of the instructor's report that the person failed to complete the program successfully, the court shall revoke probation, shall not discharge such person, shall not dismiss the proceedings against the person, and shall deny application for expunction of all recordation of defendant's arrest, indictment, or information, trial, finding of guilty, and dismissal and discharge pursuant to G.S. 15A-145.3. A person may obtain a hearing before the court of original jurisdiction prior to revocation of probation or denial of application for expunction.

This subsection is supplemental and in addition to existing law and shall not be construed so as to repeal any existing provision contained in the General Statutes of North Carolina.

(b) Upon the dismissal of such person, and discharge of the proceedings against the person under subsection (a) or (a1) of this section, such person, if he or she was not over 21 years of age at the time of the offense, may be eligible to apply for expunction of certain records relating to the offense pursuant to G.S. 15A-145.3(a).

(c) The clerk of superior court in each county in North Carolina shall, as soon as practicable after each term of court in the clerk's county, file with the Commission, the names of all persons convicted under such Articles, together with the offense or offenses of which such persons were convicted.

(d) Whenever any person is charged with a misdemeanor under this Article or possessing drug paraphernalia as prohibited by G.S. 90-113.22 upon dismissal by the State of the charges against him or her or upon entry of a nolle prosequi or upon a finding of not guilty or other adjudication of innocence, the person may be eligible to apply for expunction of certain records relating to the offense pursuant to G.S. 15A-145.3(b).

(e) Whenever any person who has not previously been convicted of an offense under this Article or under any statute of the United States or any state relating to controlled substances included in any schedule of Article 5 of Chapter 90 of the General Statutes or to that paraphernalia included in Article 5B of Chapter 90 of the General Statutes pleads guilty to or has been found guilty of a misdemeanor under this Article, the person may be eligible to apply for cancellation of the judgment and expunction of certain records related to the offense pursuant to G.S. 15A-145.3(c). (1971, c. 1078; 1975, c. 650, ss. 3, 4; 1977, c. 642, s. 3; 1979, c. 431, ss. 3, 4; 1981, c. 51, s. 11; c. 922, ss. 5-7; 1997-443, s. 11A.118(a); 2009-510, s. 9(a)-(d); 2009-577, s. 7; 2010-174, ss. 13-15.)

§§ 90-113.15 through 90-113.19. Reserved for future codification purposes.

Article 5B.

Drug Paraphernalia.

§ 90-113.20. Title.

This Article shall be known and may be cited as the "North Carolina Drug Paraphernalia Act." (1981, c. 500, s. 1.)

§ 90-113.21. General provisions.

(a) As used in this Article, "drug paraphernalia" means all equipment, products and materials of any kind that are used to facilitate, or intended or designed to facilitate, violations of the Controlled Substances Act, including planting, propagating, cultivating, growing, harvesting, manufacturing, compounding, converting, producing, processing, preparing, testing, analyzing, packaging, repackaging, storing, containing, and concealing controlled substances and injecting, ingesting, inhaling, or otherwise introducing controlled substances into the human body. "Drug paraphernalia" includes, but is not limited to, the following:

(1) Kits for planting, propagating, cultivating, growing, or harvesting any species of plant which is a controlled substance or from which a controlled substance can be derived;

(2) Kits for manufacturing, compounding, converting, producing, processing, or preparing controlled substances;

(3) Isomerization devices for increasing the potency of any species of plant which is a controlled substance;

(4) Testing equipment for identifying, or analyzing the strength, effectiveness, or purity of controlled substances;

(5) Scales and balances for weighing or measuring controlled substances;

(6) Diluents and adulterants, such as quinine, hydrochloride, mannitol, mannite, dextrose, and lactose for mixing with controlled substances;

(7) Separation gins and sifters for removing twigs and seeds from, or otherwise cleaning or refining, marijuana;

(8) Blenders, bowls, containers, spoons, and mixing devices for compounding controlled substances;

(9) Capsules, balloons, envelopes and other containers for packaging small quantities of controlled substances;

(10) Containers and other objects for storing or concealing controlled substances;

(11) Hypodermic syringes, needles, and other objects for parenterally injecting controlled substances into the body;

(12) Objects for ingesting, inhaling, or otherwise introducing marijuana, cocaine, hashish, or hashish oil into the body, such as:

a. Metal, wooden, acrylic, glass, stone, plastic, or ceramic pipes with or without screens, permanent screens, hashish heads, or punctured metal bowls;

b. Water pipes;

c. Carburetion tubes and devices;

d. Smoking and carburetion masks;

e. Objects, commonly called roach clips, for holding burning material, such as a marijuana cigarette, that has become too small or too short to be held in the hand;

f. Miniature cocaine spoons and cocaine vials;

g. Chamber pipes;

h. Carburetor pipes;

i. Electric pipes;

j. Air-driven pipes;

k. Chillums;

l. Bongs;

m. Ice pipes or chillers.

(b) The following, along with all other relevant evidence, may be considered in determining whether an object is drug paraphernalia:

(1) Statements by the owner or anyone in control of the object concerning its use;

(2) Prior convictions of the owner or other person in control of the object for violations of controlled substances law;

(3) The proximity of the object to a violation of the Controlled Substances Act;

(4) The proximity of the object to a controlled substance;

(5) The existence of any residue of a controlled substance on the object;

(6) The proximity of the object to other drug paraphernalia;

(7) Instructions provided with the object concerning its use;

(8) Descriptive materials accompanying the object explaining or depicting its use;

(9) Advertising concerning its use;

(10) The manner in which the object is displayed for sale;

(11) Whether the owner, or anyone in control of the object, is a legitimate supplier of like or related items to the community, such as a seller of tobacco products or agricultural supplies;

(12) Possible legitimate uses of the object in the community;

(13) Expert testimony concerning its use;

(14) The intent of the owner or other person in control of the object to deliver it to persons whom he knows or reasonably should know intend to use the object to facilitate violations of the Controlled Substances Act. (1981, c. 500, s. 1.)

§ 90-113.22. Possession of drug paraphernalia.

(a) It is unlawful for any person to knowingly use, or to possess with intent to use, drug paraphernalia to plant, propagate, cultivate, grow, harvest, manufacture, compound, convert, produce, process, prepare, test, analyze, package, repackage, store, contain, or conceal a controlled substance which it would be unlawful to possess, or to inject, ingest, inhale, or otherwise introduce into the body a controlled substance which it would be unlawful to possess.

(b) Violation of this section is a Class 1 misdemeanor.

(c) Prior to searching a person, a person's premises, or a person's vehicle, an officer may ask the person whether the person is in possession of a hypodermic needle or other sharp object that may cut or puncture the officer or whether such a hypodermic needle or other sharp object is on the premises or in the vehicle to be searched. If there is a hypodermic needle or other sharp object on the person, on the person's premises, or in the person's vehicle and the person alerts the officer of that fact prior to the search, the person shall not be charged with or prosecuted for possession of drug paraphernalia for the needle or sharp object. The exemption under this subsection does not apply to any other drug paraphernalia that may be present and found during the search. For purposes of this subsection, the term "officer" includes "criminal justice officers" as defined in G.S. 17C-2(3) and a "justice officer" as defined in G.S. 17E-2(3). (1981, c. 500, s. 1; 1993, c. 539, s. 624; 1994, Ex. Sess., c. 24, s. 14(c); 2013-147, s. 1.)

§ 90-113.23. Manufacture or delivery of drug paraphernalia.

(a) It is unlawful for any person to deliver, possess with intent to deliver, or manufacture with intent to deliver, drug paraphernalia knowing that it will be used to plant, propagate, cultivate, grow, harvest, manufacture, compound, convert, produce, process, prepare, test, analyze, package, repackage, store, contain, or conceal a controlled substance which it would be unlawful to possess, or that it will be used to inject, ingest, inhale, or otherwise introduce into the body a controlled substance which it would be unlawful to possess.

(b) Delivery, possession with intent to deliver, or manufacture with intent to deliver, of each separate and distinct item of drug paraphernalia is a separate offense.

(c) Violation of this section is a Class 1 misdemeanor. However, delivery of drug paraphernalia by a person over 18 years of age to someone under 18 years of age who is at least three years younger than the defendant shall be punishable as a Class I felony. (1981, c. 500, s. 1; c. 903, s. 1; 1993, c. 539, s. 625; 1994, Ex. Sess., c. 24, s. 14(c).)

§ 90-113.24. Advertisement of drug paraphernalia.

(a) It is unlawful for any person to purchase or otherwise procure an advertisement in any newspaper, magazine, handbill, or other publication, or purchase or otherwise procure an advertisement on a billboard, sign, or other outdoor display, when he knows that the purpose of the advertisement, in whole or in part, is to promote the sale of objects designed or intended for use as drug paraphernalia described in this Article.

(b) Violation of this section is a Class 2 misdemeanor. (1981, c. 500, s. 1; c. 903, s. 1; 1993, c. 539, s. 626; 1994, Ex. Sess., c. 24, s. 14(c).)

§§ 90-113.25 through 90-113.29. Reserved for future codification purposes.

Article 5C.

North Carolina Substance Abuse Professional Practice Act.

§ 90-113.30. Declaration of purpose.

The North Carolina Substance Abuse Professional Practice Board, established by G.S. 90-113.32, is recognized as the registering, certifying, and licensing authority for substance abuse professionals described in this Article in order to safeguard the public health, safety, and welfare, to protect the public from being harmed by unqualified persons, to assure the highest degree of professional care and conduct on the part of credentialed substance abuse professionals, to provide for the establishment of standards for the education of credentialed substance abuse professionals, and to ensure the availability of credentialed substance abuse professional services of high quality to persons in need of these services. It is the purpose of this Article to provide for the regulation of Board-credentialed persons offering substance abuse counseling services, substance abuse prevention services, or any other substance abuse services for which the Board may grant registration, certification, or licensure. (1993 (Reg. Sess., 1994), c. 685, s. 1; 1997-492, s. 1; 2005-431, s. 1.)

§ 90-113.31: Repealed by Session Laws 2005-431, s. 1, effective September 22, 2005.

§ 90-113.31A. Definitions.

The following definitions shall apply in this Article:

(1) Applicant. - A person who has initiated a process to become a substance abuse professional pursuant to this Article.

(2) Applicant supervisor. - A person who provides supervision as required by the Board to persons applying for registration, certification, or licensure as a substance abuse professional pursuant to this Article.

(3) Board. - The North Carolina Substance Abuse Professional Practice Board.

(4) Certified clinical supervisor. - A person certified by the Board to practice as a clinical supervisor in accordance with the provisions of this Article.

(5) Certified criminal justice addictions professional. - A person certified by the Board to practice as a criminal justice addictions professional who, under supervision, provides direct services to clients or offenders exhibiting substance abuse disorders and works in a program determined by the Board to be involved in a criminal justice setting.

(6) Certified substance abuse counselor. - A person certified by the Board to practice under the supervision of a practice supervisor as a substance abuse counselor in accordance with the provisions of this Article.

(7) Certified substance abuse prevention consultant. - A person certified by the Board to practice substance abuse prevention in accordance with the provisions of this Article.

(8) Certified substance abuse residential facility director. - A person certified by the Board to practice as a substance abuse residential facility director in accordance with the provisions of this Article.

(9) Repealed by Session Laws 2008-130, s. 1, effective July 28, 2008.

(10) Clinical supervisor intern. - A person designated by the Board to practice as a clinical supervisor under the supervision of a certified clinical supervisor for a period not to exceed three years without a showing of good cause in accordance with the provisions of this Article.

(11) Counseling. - The utilization of special skills to assist individuals, families, or groups in achieving objectives, including the following:

a. Exploring a problem and its ramifications.

b. Examining attitudes and feelings.

c. Considering alternative solutions.

d. Decision making.

(12) Credential. - Any registration, certification, or license issued by the Board.

(13) Credentialing body. - A board that licenses, certifies, registers, or otherwise regulates a profession or practice.

(14) Criminal history. - A history of conviction of a State crime, whether a misdemeanor or felony, that bears on an applicant's fitness for licensure to practice substance abuse professional services. The crimes include the criminal offenses set forth in any of the following Articles of Chapter 14 of the General Statutes: Article 5, Counterfeiting and Issuing Monetary Substitutes; Article 5A, Endangering Executive and Legislative Officers; Article 6, Homicide; Article 7A, Rape and Other Sex Offenses; Article 8, Assaults; Article 10, Kidnapping and Abduction; Article 13, Malicious Injury or Damage by Use of Explosive or

Incendiary Device or Material; Article 14, Burglary and Other Housebreakings; Article 15, Arson and Other Burnings; Article 16, Larceny; Article 17, Robbery; Article 18, Embezzlement; Article 19, False Pretenses and Cheats; Article 19A, Obtaining Property or Services by False or Fraudulent Use of Credit Device or Other Means; Article 19B, Financial Transaction Card Crime Act; Article 20, Frauds; Article 21, Forgery; Article 26, Offenses Against Public Morality and Decency; Article 26A, Adult Establishments; Article 27, Prostitution; Article 28, Perjury; Article 29, Bribery; Article 31, Misconduct in Public Office; Article 35, Offenses Against the Public Peace; Article 36A, Riots, Civil Disorders, and Emergencies; Article 39, Protection of Minors; Article 40, Protection of the Family; Article 59, Public Intoxication; and Article 60, Computer-Related Crime. The crimes also include possession or sale of drugs in violation of the North Carolina Controlled Substances Act in Article 5 of Chapter 90 of the General Statutes and alcohol-related offenses including sale to underage persons in violation of G.S. 18B-302 or driving while impaired in violation of G.S. 20-138.1 through G.S. 20-138.5.

(15) Deemed status. - Recognition by the Board of the credentials offered by a professional discipline whereby the individuals certified, licensed, or otherwise recognized by the discipline as having met the standards of a clinical addictions specialist may apply individually for licensure as a licensed clinical addictions specialist.

(16) Dual relationship. - A relationship in addition to the professional relationship with a person to whom the substance abuse professional delivers services in the Twelve Core Functions or the performance domains, both as defined in rules adopted by the Board, or as provided in a supervisory capacity. These relationships may result in grounds for disciplinary action.

(17) Human services field. - An area of study that focuses on the biological, psychological, behavioral, and social aspects of human welfare with focus on the direct services designed to improve it.

(18) Independent study. - Any course of study that is not traditional classroom-based that must be preapproved by the Board or any organization that has deemed status with the Board.

(19) Licensed clinical addictions specialist. - A person licensed by the Board to practice as a clinical addictions specialist in accordance with the provisions of this Article.

(19a) Licensed Clinical Addictions Specialist Associate. - A registrant who successfully completes 300 hours of Board-approved supervised practical training in pursuit of licensure as a clinical addictions specialist.

(20) Practice supervisor. - A certified clinical supervisor, clinical supervisor intern, or licensed clinical addictions specialist who provides oversight and responsibility in a face-to-face capacity for each certified substance abuse counselor or criminal justice addictions professional.

(21) Prevention. - The reduction, delay, or avoidance of alcohol and of other drug use behavior. "Prevention" includes the promotion of positive environments and individual strengths that contribute to personal health and well-being over an entire life and the development of strategies that encourage individuals, families, and communities to take part in assessing and changing their lifestyles and environments.

(22) Professional discipline. - A field of study characterized by the technical, educational, and ethical standards of a profession.

(23) Registrant. - A person who completes all requirements to be registered with the Board and is supervised by a certified clinical supervisor or clinical supervisor intern.

(24) Substance abuse counseling. - The assessment, evaluation, and provision of counseling and therapeutic service to persons suffering from substance abuse or dependency.

(25) Substance abuse counselor intern. - A registrant who successfully completes 300 hours of Board-approved supervised practical training in pursuit of credentialing as a substance abuse counselor.

(26) Substance abuse professional. - A registrant, certified substance abuse counselor, substance abuse counselor intern, certified substance abuse prevention consultant, certified clinical supervisor, licensed clinical addictions specialist associate, licensed clinical addictions specialist, certified substance abuse residential facility director, clinical supervisor intern, or certified criminal justice addictions professional. (1993 (Reg. Sess., 1994), c. 685, s. 1; 1997-492, s.2; 1999-164, s. 1; 1999-456, s. 24; 2001-370, s. 1; 2005-431, s. 1; 2008-130, s. 1; 2012-12, s. 2(hh); 2012-72, s. 5.)

§ 90-113.31B. Scope of practice.

The scope of practice is the use by all substance abuse professionals and their ongoing supervisees of principles, methods, and procedures of the Twelve Core Functions or performance domains as prescribed by the International Certification and Reciprocity Consortium/Alcohol and Other Drug Abuse, Incorporated, and as limited by individual credential and supervisory requirements pursuant to this Article. Specifically, the scope of practice for each individual defined as a substance abuse professional under G.S. 90-113.31A is as follows:

(1) The practice of a certified substance abuse counselor consists of the Twelve Core Functions, including screening, intake, orientation, assessment, treatment planning, counseling, case management, crisis intervention, client education, report and record keeping, consultation with other professionals in regard to client treatment and services, and referral to treat addictive disorder or disease and help prevent relapse.

(2) The practice of a certified substance abuse prevention consultant is based on knowledge in the performance domains to prevent or reduce the conditions that place individuals at increased risk of developing addictive disorder or disease and help prevent relapse.

(3) The practice of a certified clinical supervisor is based on knowledge in the performance domains to supervise substance abuse professionals who work to treat, prevent, or reduce the conditions that place individuals at risk of developing addictive disorder or disease and help prevent relapse.

(4) The practice of a licensed clinical addictions specialist may be independent and consists of the Twelve Core Functions, including screening, intake, orientation, assessment, treatment planning, counseling, case management, crisis intervention, client education, report and record keeping, consultation with other professionals in regard to client treatment and services, referral to reduce the conditions that place individuals at risk of developing addictive disorder or disease with co-occurring disorders, and treatment for addictive disorder or disease. The licensed clinical addictions specialist may provide supervision to maintain a professional credential as defined by this Article.

(5) The practice of a certified substance abuse residential facility director is a voluntary credential and consists of the Twelve Core Functions, including screening, intake, orientation, assessment, treatment planning, counseling, case management, crisis intervention, client education, report and record keeping, consultation with professionals in regard to client treatment and services, referral to prevent or reduce the conditions that place individuals at increased risk of developing addictive disorder or disease, treatment for addictive disorder or disease, and the prevention of relapse as well as academic management training.

(6) The practice of a certified criminal justice addictions professional is based on knowledge in the performance domains of dynamics of addiction in criminal behavior; legal, ethical, and professional responsibility; criminal justice system and processes; screening, intake, and assessment; case management; monitoring; and client supervision and counseling to prevent or reduce the conditions that place individuals at increased risk of developing addictive disorder or disease, treat addictive disorder or disease, and help prevent relapse. (2005-431, s. 1.)

§ 90-113.32. Board; composition; voting.

(a) The Board is created as the authority to credential substance abuse professionals in North Carolina.

(b) Repealed by Session Laws 2008-130, s. 2, effective July 28, 2008.

(c) After the initial Board members' terms expire, the Board shall consist of the following members, all of whom shall reside in North Carolina, appointed or elected as follows:

(1) Eleven professionals credentialed pursuant to this Article and elected by the credentialed professionals, at least two of whom shall serve each of the four Division of Mental Health, Developmental Disabilities, and Substance Abuse Services regions of the State. Three members shall serve as members at large.

(2) Three members at large chosen from laypersons or other professional disciplines who have shown a special interest in the field of substance abuse, nominated by the Nominating and Elections Committee established by subsection (d) of this section and elected by the Board.

(3) Two members from the Department of Health and Human Services, appointed by the Chief of Community Policy Management of the Division of Mental Health, Developmental Disabilities, and Substance Abuse Services, at least one of whom administers substance abuse services.

(4) One member of the public at large appointed by the Governor.

(5) One member of the public at large appointed by the General Assembly upon the recommendation of the Speaker of the House of Representatives in accordance with G.S. 120-121 and one member of the public at large appointed by the General Assembly upon the recommendation of the President Pro Tempore of the Senate in accordance with G.S. 120-121.

(6) One member shall represent each of the professional disciplines granted deemed status under G.S. 90-113.41A. The member may be appointed by the professional discipline on or before a date set by the Board. If the professional discipline has at least one association in the State, the member shall be chosen from a list of nominees submitted to the association. The members appointed or elected under this subdivision shall be certified as substance abuse specialists by the professional discipline that the members represent.

No member of the General Assembly shall serve on the Board.

(c1) Every member of the Board shall have the right to vote on all matters before the Board, except for the President who shall vote only in case of a tie or when another member of the Board abstains on the question of whether the professional discipline the member represents shall retain its deemed status.

(d) The Board shall appoint five professionals from the field of substance abuse counseling and substance abuse prevention consulting to serve on the Nominating and Elections Committee. Of these five, at least three shall not be members of the Board. The Board shall appoint a member of the Nominating and Elections Committee to serve as chair. The Committee's purpose is to accept nominations from professionals certified or licensed by the Board to fill vacancies on the Board in membership categories prescribed by subdivisions (1) and (2) of subsection (c) of this section and to conduct the election of Board members. The Committee shall solicit nominations from all professionals it has certified or licensed under this Article when elected members' terms are due to expire. The certified or licensed professionals shall submit to the Committee all nominations beginning 90 days and ending 28 days before the election of new Board members. The Committee shall furnish all certified or licensed professionals with a ballot containing all the nominees for each elected Board member vacancy. In soliciting and making nominations for this process, the Committee shall give consideration to factors that promote representation on the Board by professionals certified or licensed by the Board. The Committee shall serve for a two-year term, its successors to be appointed for the same term by the Board.

(e) Members of the Board shall serve for four-year terms. No Board member shall serve for more than two consecutive terms, but a person who has been a member for two consecutive terms may be reappointed after being off the Board for a period of at least one year. When a vacancy occurs in an unexpired term, the Board shall, as soon as practicable, appoint temporary members to serve until the end of the unexpired terms. Time spent as a temporary member does not count in determining the limitation on consecutive terms.

(f) If a member becomes ineligible to serve on the Board for any reason, except when the member has committed an ethical violation that results in the suspension or revocation of the member's professional credentials, that member may fulfill the remainder of his or her term on the Board. (1993 (Reg. Sess., 1994), c. 685, s. 1; c. 773, s. 15.2(a), (b); 1997-443, s. 11A.118(a); 1997-492, s. 3; 1999-164, ss. 2-4; 2005-431, s. 1; 2008-130, ss. 2, 3.)

§ 90-113.33. Board; powers and duties.

The Board shall:

(1) Examine and determine the qualifications and fitness of applicants for certification and licensure to practice in this State.

(1a) Determine the qualifications and fitness of organizations applying for deemed status.

(2) Issue, renew, deny, suspend, or revoke licensure, certification, or registration to practice in this State or reprimand or otherwise discipline a license, certificate, or registration holder in this State.

(3) Deal with issues concerning reciprocity.

(4) Conduct investigations for the purpose of determining whether violations of this Article or grounds for disciplining exists.

(5) Employ and fix the compensation of personnel and legal counsel that the Board determines is necessary to carry out the provisions of this Article. The Board's employment of legal counsel is subject to the provisions of G.S. 114-2.3. The Board may purchase or rent necessary office space, equipment, and supplies.

(6) Conduct administrative hearings in accordance with Chapter 150B of the General Statutes when a "contested case", as defined in Chapter 150B, arises.

(7) Appoint from its own membership one or more members to act as representatives of the Board at any meeting in which it considers this representation is desirable.

(8) Establish fees for applications for examination, registration, certificates of certification, licensure, and renewal, and other services provided by the Board.

(9) Adopt any rules necessary to carry out the purpose of this Article and its duties and responsibilities pursuant to this Article, including rules related to the approval of a substance abuse specialty curricula developed by a school, college, or university.

(10) Request that the Department of Justice conduct criminal history record checks of applicants for registration, certification, or licensure pursuant to G.S. 114-19.11A.

The powers and duties enumerated in this section are granted for the purposes of enabling the Board to safeguard the public health, safety, and welfare against unqualified or incompetent practitioners and are to be liberally construed to accomplish this objective. When the Board exercises its authority under this Article to discipline a person, it may, as part of the decision imposing the discipline, charge the costs of investigations and the hearing to the person disciplined. (1993 (Reg. Sess., 1994), c. 685, s. 1; 1997-492, s. 4; 1999-164, s. 5; 2001-370, ss. 2, 3; 2005-431, s. 1; 2011-254, s. 3.)

§ 90-113.33A. Officers may administer oaths, and subpoena witnesses, records, and other materials.

The President or other presiding officer of the Board may administer oaths to all persons appearing before it as the Board may deem necessary to perform its duties, and may summon and issue subpoenas for the appearance of any witnesses deemed necessary to testify concerning any matter to be heard before or inquired into by the Board. The Board may order that any client records, documents, or other materials concerning any matter to be heard before or inquired into by the Board shall be produced before the Board or made available for inspection, notwithstanding any other provisions of law providing for the application of any counselor-client or physician-patient privilege with respect to such records, documents, or other materials. All records, documents, or other materials compiled by the Board are subject to the provisions of G.S. 90-113.34, except that in any proceeding before the Board, record of any hearing before the Board, and notice of charges against any person credentialed by the Board, the Board shall withhold from public disclosure the identity of a client, including information relating to dates and places of treatment, or any other information that tends to identify the client unless the client or the client's representative has expressly consented to the disclosure. Upon written request, the Board shall revoke a subpoena if, upon a hearing, it finds that the evidence sought does not relate to a matter in issue, the subpoena does not describe the evidence with sufficient particularity, or the subpoena is invalid. (1999-164, s. 6; 2005-431, s. 1.)

§ 90-113.34. Records to be kept; copies of records.

(a) The Board shall keep a regular record of its proceedings, together with the names of the members of the Board present, the names of the applicants for registration, certification, and licensure as well as other information relevant to its actions. The Board shall cause a record to be kept that shall show the name, last known place of business, last known place of residence, and date and number of the credential assigned to each substance abuse professional meeting the standards set forth in this Article. Any interested person in the State is entitled to obtain a copy of Board records upon application to the Board and payment of a reasonable charge that is based on the costs involved in providing the copy.

(b) The Board may in a closed session receive evidence regarding the provision of substance abuse counseling or other treatment and services provided to a client who has not expressly or through implication consented to the public disclosure of such treatment as may be necessary for the protection of the rights of the client or of the accused registrant or substance abuse professional and the full presentation of relevant evidence. All records, papers, and other documents containing information collected and compiled by the Board, its members, or employees as a result of investigations, inquiries, or interviews conducted in connection with awarding a credential or a disciplinary matter shall not be considered public records within the meaning of Chapter 132 of the General Statutes, except any notice or statement of charges, or notice of hearing shall be a public record notwithstanding that it may contain information collected and compiled as a result of an investigation, inquiry, or interview. If any record, paper, or other document containing information collected and compiled by the Board as provided in this subsection is received and admitted in evidence in any hearing before the Board, it shall thereupon be a public record.

(c) Notwithstanding any provision to the contrary, the Board may, in any proceeding, record of any hearing, and notice of charges, withhold from public disclosure the identity of a client who has not expressly or through implication consented to such disclosure of treatment by the accused substance abuse professional. (1993 (Reg. Sess., 1994), c. 685, s. 1; 1997-492, s. 5; 1999-164, s. 7; 2005-431, s. 1.)

§ 90-113.35. Disposition of funds.

All fees and other moneys collected and received by the Board shall be used to implement this Article. The financial records of the Board shall be subjected to an annual audit and paid for out of the funds of the Board. (1993 (Reg. Sess., 1994), c. 685, s. 1.)

§ 90-113.36. Credentials.

(a) The Board shall furnish a certificate of certification or licensure to each applicant successfully completing the requirements for his or her credential.

(b) The Board may furnish a certificate of certification or licensure to any person in another state or territory if the individual's qualifications were, at the date of registration, certification, or licensure, substantially equal to the requirements under this Article. However, an out-of-state applicant shall first file application and pay any required fees. (1993 (Reg. Sess., 1994), c. 685, s. 1; 2005-431, s. 1.)

§ 90-113.37: Repealed by Session Laws 2005-431, s. 1, effective September 22, 2005.

§ 90-113.37A. Renewal of credential; lapse.

(a) Every person credentialed pursuant to this Article who desires to maintain his or her credentials shall apply to the Board for a renewal of certification or licensure every other year and pay to the treasurer the prescribed fee.

(b) Renewal of licensure is subject to completion of at least 40 hours of the continuing education requirements established by the Board. Renewal of substance abuse counselor or substance abuse prevention consultant certification is subject to completion of at least 60 hours of the continuing education requirements established by the Board. A certified substance abuse counselor shall submit a Board-approved supervision contract signed by the applicant and a practice supervisor documenting ongoing supervision at a ratio of one hour of supervision to every 40 hours of practice after certification is granted by the Board on a form provided by the Board. Any person certified by the Board as a certified alcoholism counselor or certified drug abuse counselor shall become a certified substance abuse counselor.

A clinical supervisor shall complete at least 15 hours of substance abuse clinical supervision training prior to the certificate being renewed. A substance abuse residential facility director shall complete at least 10 hours of substance abuse training for renewal. A certified criminal justice addictions professional shall complete at least 40 hours of continuing education that must be earned in the certified criminal justice addictions professional performance domains. A certified criminal justice addictions professional shall submit a Board-approved supervision contract signed by the criminal justice addictions professional and a practice supervisor documenting ongoing supervision at a ratio of one hour of supervision to every 40 hours of practice after certification is granted by the Board on a form provided by the Board.

(c) Independent study hours shall compose no more than fifty percent (50%) of the total number of hours required for renewal.

(d) A credential that is not renewed automatically lapses, unless the Board approves the late renewal of a credential upon the payment of a late fee.

(e) No late renewal shall be granted more than five years after a certification or licensure expires.

(f) A suspended credential may be renewed as provided in this section. This renewal does not entitle the credentialed person to engage in conduct or activity in violation of the order or judgment by which the credential was suspended, until the credential is reinstated. If a credential revoked on disciplinary grounds is reinstated and requires renewal, the credentialed person shall pay the renewal fee and any applicable late fee.

(g) The Board shall establish the manner in which lapsed certification or licensure may be revived or extended. (1993 (Reg. Sess., 1994), c. 685, s. 1; 1997-492, s. 6; 1999-164, s. 8; 2005-431, s. 1.)

§ 90-113.38. Maximums for certain fees.

(a) The fee to obtain a certificate of certification as a substance abuse counselor, substance abuse prevention consultant, clinical supervisor, substance abuse residential facility director, or certified criminal justice addictions professional may not exceed four hundred seventy-five dollars ($475.00). The fee to renew a certificate may not exceed one hundred fifty dollars ($150.00).

(b) The fee to obtain a certificate of licensure for a clinical addictions specialist pursuant to deemed status shall not exceed one hundred fifty dollars ($150.00). The fee to renew a license for a clinical addictions specialist pursuant to deemed status shall not exceed one hundred dollars ($100.00). The fee to obtain a license for a clinical addictions specialist pursuant to all other procedures authorized by this Article shall not exceed four hundred seventy-five dollars ($475.00). The fee to renew the license shall not exceed one hundred fifty dollars ($150.00).

(b1)   The fee to obtain a registration as a registrant shall not exceed one hundred fifty dollars ($150.00). The fee to renew a registration shall not exceed one hundred fifty dollars ($150.00).

(c)   There shall be a reexamination fee of one hundred fifty dollars ($150.00) which shall be paid for each reexamination in addition to the fees authorized pursuant to subsection (a) of this section. There shall be a fee not to exceed twenty-five dollars ($25.00) for rescheduling any examination.

(d)   There shall be a fee not to exceed twenty-five dollars ($25.00) to obtain a written verification or additional copy of a credential issued by the Board.

(e)   There shall be a late renewal fee not to exceed one hundred twenty-five dollars ($125.00).

(f)   In addition to any other prescribed fees, the Board shall charge a fee not to exceed one hundred fifty dollars ($150.00) for each administration of the test an applicant must pass to be credentialed as a United States Department of Transportation substance abuse professional. (1993 (Reg. Sess., 1994), c. 685, s. 1; 1997-492, s. 7; 1998-217, s. 25(a); 2001-370, s. 4; 2005-431, s. 1.)

§ 90-113.39. Standards for credentials.

The Board shall establish standards to credential substance abuse professionals. The credentialing standards of the International Certification and Reciprocity Consortium/Alcohol and Other Drug Abuse, Incorporated and the standards adopted by professional disciplines granted deemed status or their successor organizations may be used as guidelines for the Board's standards. The Board shall publish these required standards. (1993 (Reg. Sess., 1994), c. 685, s. 1; 1997-492, s. 8; 1999-164, s. 9; 2005-431, s. 1.)

§ 90-113.40. Requirements for certification and licensure.

(a) The Board shall issue a certificate certifying an applicant as a "Certified Substance Abuse Counselor" or as a "Certified Substance Abuse Prevention Consultant" if:

(1) The applicant is of good moral character.

(2) The applicant is not and has not engaged in any practice or conduct that would be grounds for disciplinary action under G.S. 90-113.44.

(3) The applicant is qualified for certification pursuant to the requirements of this Article and any rules adopted pursuant to it.

(4) The applicant has, at a minimum, a high school diploma or a high school equivalency certificate.

(5) The applicant has signed a form attesting to the intention to adhere fully to the ethical standards adopted by the Board.

(5a) The applicant submits to a complete criminal history record check pursuant to G.S. 90-113.46A.

(6) The applicant has completed 270 hours of Board-approved education. The Board may prescribe that a certain number of hours be in a course of study for substance abuse counseling and that a certain number of hours be in a course of study for substance abuse prevention consulting. Independent study hours shall not compose more than fifty percent (50%) of the total number of hours required for initial credentialing.

(7) The applicant has documented completion of a minimum of 300 hours of Supervised Practical Training, has provided a Board-approved supervision contract between the applicant and an applicant supervisor, and has been deemed recommended by the applicant supervisor to advance in the credentialing process.

(8) The applicant for substance abuse counselor has completed a total of 6,000 hours of supervised experience in the field, whether paid or volunteer. The applicant for substance abuse prevention consultant has completed a total of 6,000 hours supervised experience in the field, whether paid or volunteer, or 4,000 hours if the applicant has at least a bachelors degree in a human services field from a regionally accredited college or university.

(9)　The applicant has obtained a passing score on a written examination.

(b)　The Board shall issue a certificate certifying an individual as a "Certified Clinical Supervisor" if the applicant:

(1)　Submits proof of designation by the Board as a clinical supervisor intern.

(2)　Submits proof that the applicant has a minimum of a master's degree in a human services field with a clinical application from a regionally accredited college or university.

(3)　Has 4,000 hours experience as a substance abuse clinical supervisor as documented by his or her certified clinical supervisor.

(4)　Has 30 hours of substance abuse clinical supervision specific education or training. These hours shall be reflective of the Twelve Core Functions in the applicant's clinical application and practice and may also be counted toward the applicant's renewal as a substance abuse counselor or a clinical addictions specialist.

(5)　Submits a letter of reference from a certified clinical supervisor who can attest to the applicant's supervisory competence and two letters of reference from either counselors who have been supervised by the applicant or professionals who can attest to the applicant's competence.

(6)　Obtains a passing score on a written examination administered by the Board.

(b1)　The Board shall designate an applicant as a "Clinical Supervisor Intern" if, in addition to meeting the requirements of subdivisions (a)(1) through (5a) of this section, the applicant meets the following qualifications:

(1)　Submits an application, resume, and official transcript showing that the applicant has obtained a master's degree in a human services field with a clinical application from a regionally accredited college or university.

(2)　Submits verification statements.

(3)　Submits proof of credentialing as a licensed clinical addictions specialist.

(4)   Submits documentation establishing that the applicant has completed at least fifty percent of the required clinical supervision specific training hours as defined by the Board.

(c)   The Board shall issue a license credentialing an applicant as a "Licensed Clinical Addictions Specialist" if, in addition to meeting the requirements of subdivisions (a)(1) through (5a) of this section, the applicant meets one of the following criteria:

(1)   Criteria A. - The applicant:

a.   Has a minimum of a master's degree with a clinical application in a human services field from a regionally accredited college or university.

b.   Has two years postgraduate supervised substance abuse counseling experience.

c.   Submits three letters of reference from licensed clinical addictions specialists or certified substance abuse counselors who have obtained master's degrees.

d.   Has achieved a passing score on a master's level written examination administered by the Board.

e.   Has attained 180 hours of substance abuse specific training from either a regionally accredited college or university, which may include unlimited independent study, or from training events of which no more than fifty percent (50%) shall be in independent study. All hours shall be credited according to the standards set forth in G.S. 90-113.41A.

f.   The applicant has documented completion of a minimum of 300 hours of supervised practical training and has provided a Board-approved supervision contract between the applicant and an applicant supervisor.

(2)   Criteria B. - The applicant:

a.   Has a minimum of a master's degree with a clinical application in a human services field from a regionally accredited college or university.

b.   Has been certified as a substance abuse counselor.

c. Repealed by Session Laws 2008-130, s. 4, effective July 28, 2008.

d. Has achieved a passing score on a master's level written examination administered by the Board.

e. Submits three letters of reference from either licensed clinical addictions specialists or certified substance abuse counselors who have obtained master's degrees.

(3) Criteria C. - The applicant:

a. Has a minimum of a master's degree in a human services field with both a clinical application and a substance abuse specialty from a regionally accredited college or university that includes 180 hours of substance abuse specific education and training pursuant to G.S. 90-113.41A.

b. Has one year of postgraduate supervised substance abuse counseling experience.

c. Has achieved a passing score on a master's level written examination administered by the Board.

d. Submits three letters of reference from licensed clinical addictions specialists or certified substance abuse counselors who have obtained master's degrees.

(4) Criteria D. - The applicant has a substance abuse certification from a professional discipline that has been granted deemed status by the Board.

(d) The Board shall issue a certificate certifying an applicant as a "Substance Abuse Residential Facility Director" if the applicant:

(1) Has been credentialed as a substance abuse counselor or a clinical addictions specialist.

(2) Has 50 hours of Board approved academic or didactic management specific training or a combination thereof. Independent study may compose up to fifty percent (50%) of the total number of hours required for initial credentialing.

(3)   Submits letters of reference from the applicant's current supervisor and a colleague or coworker.

(d1)   The Board shall issue a certificate certifying an applicant as a "Certified Criminal Justice Addictions Professional", with the acronym "CCJP", if in addition to meeting the requirements of subdivisions (a)(1) through (5a) of this section, the applicant:

(1)   Has attained 270 hours of Board-approved education or training, unless the applicant has attained a minimum of a masters degree with a clinical application and a substance abuse specialty from a regionally accredited college or university whereby the applicant must only obtain 180 hours. The hours of education shall be specifically related to the knowledge and skills necessary to perform the tasks within the International Certification and Reciprocity Consortium/Alcohol and Other Drug Abuse, Incorporated, "IC&RC/AODA, Inc.," criminal justice addictions professional performance domains as they relate to both adults and juveniles. Independent study may compose up to fifty percent (50%) of the total number of hours obtained for initial certification or renewal.

(2)   Has documented 300 hours of Board-approved supervised practical training. This supervision shall mean the administrative, clinical, and evaluative process of monitoring, assessing, and enhancing professional performance. A minimum of 10 hours of supervision in each criminal justice domain established by the IC&RC/AODA, Inc., is required.

(3)   Has provided documentation of supervised work experience providing direct service to clients or offenders involved in one of the three branches of the criminal justice system, which include law enforcement, the judiciary, and corrections. The applicant must meet one of the following criteria:

a.   Criteria A. - In addition to having a high school degree or GED, the applicant has a minimum of 6,000 hours of documented work experience in direct services in criminal justice or addictions services or any combination of these services that have been obtained during the past 10 years.

b.   Criteria B. - In addition to having an associate degree, the applicant has a minimum of 5,000 hours of documented work experience in direct services in criminal justice or addictions services or any combination of these services obtained during the past 10 years.

c. Criteria C. - In addition to having at least a bachelors degree, the applicant has a minimum of 4,000 hours of documented work experience in direct services in criminal justice or addictions services, or any combination of these services, and this experience has been obtained during the past 10 years.

d. Criteria D. - In addition to having at least a masters degree in a human services field, the applicant has a minimum of 2,000 hours of documented work experience in direct services in criminal justice or addictions services or any combination of these services that has been obtained during the past 10 years.

e. Criteria E. - In addition to having at least a masters degree in a human services field with a specialty from a regionally accredited college or university that includes 180 hours of substance abuse specific education or training, the applicant has a minimum of 2,000 hours of postgraduate supervised substance abuse counseling experience.

f. Criteria F. - In addition to having obtained the credential of a certified clinical addictions specialist or other advanced credential in a human services field from an organization that has obtained deemed status with the Board, the applicant has a minimum of 1,000 hours of documented work experience in direct services in criminal justice or addictions services that has been obtained during the past 10 years.

(4) Has passed the IC&RC/AODA, Inc., certified criminal justice addictions professional written examination.

(e) The Board shall publish from time to time information in order to provide specifics for potential applicants of an acceptable educational curriculum and the terms of acceptable supervised fieldwork experience.

(f) Effective January 1, 2003, only a person who is certified as a certified clinical supervisor or a clinical supervisor intern shall be qualified to supervise applicants for certified clinical supervisor and certified substance abuse counselor and applicants for licensed clinical addictions specialist who meet the qualifications of their credential other than through deemed status as provided in G.S. 90-113.40(c)(4). (1993 (Reg. Sess., 1994), c. 685, s. 1; 1997-492, s. 9; 1998-217, s. 10; 1999-164, s. 10; 2005-431, s. 1; 2008-130, s. 4.)

§ 90-113.40A. Requirements for registration.

(a) Upon application and payment of the required fee, the Board shall issue a registration designating an applicant as a registrant if the applicant:

(1) Provides documentation that he or she has received a high school diploma, or the equivalent, and evidence of any baccalaureate or advanced degrees the applicant has received.

(2) Completes a registration application on a form provided by the Board.

(3) Provides documentation of three hours of educational training in ethics.

(4) Signs a form attesting to the applicant's commitment to adhere to the ethical standards adopted by the Board.

(4a) Submits to a complete criminal history record check pursuant to G.S. 90-113.46A.

(5) Signs a supervision contract provided by the Board that documents the proposed supervision process by an applicant supervisor.

(b) Registrant status shall be maintained for a period of up to five years while the registrant is in the process of completing his or her requirements for credentials pursuant to this Article. If at the end of a five-year period a registrant has not obtained a credential under this Article, the Board shall renew the registration for up to an additional five-year period after the registrant pays the required fee and complies with all requirements for registration pursuant to G.S. 90-113.40A. The Board shall terminate the registration of any registrant who fails to renew his or her registration.

(c) The registrant shall notify the Board of any criminal conviction imposed during the period of registration. (2001-370, s. 5; 2005-431, s. 1.)

§ 90-113.40B. Applicant supervision.

The Board shall designate a person as an applicant supervisor of individuals applying for registration, certification, or licensure as a substance abuse professional as follows:

(1) A certified clinical supervisor shall supervise a clinical supervisor intern.

(2) A certified clinical supervisor or a clinical supervisor intern shall supervise a substance abuse residential facility director applicant, a clinical addictions specialist applicant, or a substance abuse counselor applicant.

(3) Repealed by Session Laws 2005-431, s. 1, effective September 22, 2005.

(4) A certified substance abuse prevention consultant with a minimum of three years of professional experience, a certified clinical supervisor, or a clinical supervisor intern shall supervise a registrant applying for certification as a prevention consultant.

(5) Pursuant to the deemed status procedure under G.S. 90-113.41A, the supervision requirements described in subdivisions (1) through (4) of this section shall not apply to persons applying for licensure as a licensed clinical addictions specialist.

(6) A criminal justice addictions professional applicant shall be supervised by a certified clinical supervisor or clinical supervisor intern. (2001-370, s. 6; 2005-431, s. 1.)

§ 90-113.41. Examination.

(a) Except for those individuals applying for licensure under G.S. 90-113.41A, applicants for certification or licensure under this Article shall file an application at least 60 days prior to the date of examination and upon the forms and in the manner prescribed by the Board. The application shall be accompanied by the appropriate fee. No portion of this fee is refundable. Applicants who fail an examination may apply for reexamination upon the payment of another examination fee.

(b) Each applicant for certification or licensure under this Article shall be tested in an examination developed by the International Certification and Reciprocity Consortium/Alcohol and Other Drug Abuse, Incorporated and the standards adopted by professional disciplines granted deemed status or their successor organizations.

(c) Applicants for certification or licensure shall be examined at a time and place and under the supervision that the Board determines. Examinations shall be given in this State at least twice each year.

(d) Applicants may obtain their examination scores and may review their examination papers in accordance with rules the Board adopts and agreements between Board-authorized test development companies. (1993 (Reg. Sess., 1994), c. 685, s. 1; 1997-492, s. 10; 1999-164, s. 11; 2005-431, s. 1.)

§ 90-113.41A. Deemed status.

(a) To be granted deemed status by the Board, a credentialing body of a professional discipline or its designee shall demonstrate that its substance abuse credentialing program substantially meets the following:

(1) Each person to whom the credentialing body awards credentials following the effective date of this act meets and maintains minimum requirements in substance abuse specific content areas. Each person also has a minimum of a master's degree with a clinical application in a human services field.

(2) The body requires 180 hours, or the equivalent thereof, of substance abuse specific education and training that covers the following content areas:

a. Basic addiction and cross addiction Physiology and Pharmacology of Psychoactive drugs that are abused.

b. Screening, assessment, and intake of clients.

c. Individual, group, and family counseling.

d. Treatment, planning, reporting, and record keeping.

e. Crisis intervention.

f. Case management and treatment resources.

g. Ethics, legal issues, and confidentiality.

h. Psychological, emotional, personality, and developmental issues.

i. Co-occurring physical and mental disabilities.

j. Special population issues, including age, gender, race, ethnicity, and health status.

k. Traditions and philosophies of recovery treatment models and support groups.

(3) The program requires one year or its equivalent of post-degree supervised clinical substance abuse practice. At least fifty percent (50%) of the practice shall consist of direct substance abuse clinical care.

(b) The professional discipline seeking deemed status shall require its members to adhere to a code of ethical conduct and shall enforce that code with disciplinary action.

(c) The Board may grant deemed status to any professional discipline that substantially meets the standards in this section. Once such status has been granted, an individual within the professional discipline may apply to the Board for the credential of licensed clinical addictions specialist.

(d) The Standards Committee of the Board shall review the standards of each professional discipline every third year from the date it was granted deemed status to determine if the discipline continues to substantially meet the requirements of this section. If the Committee finds that a professional discipline no longer meets the requirements of this section, it shall report its findings to the Board at the Board's next regularly scheduled meeting. The deemed status standing of a professional discipline's credential may be discontinued by a two-thirds vote of the Board. (1997-492, s. 11; 2005-431, s. 1.)

§ 90-113.41B. Change of name or address.

Every person licensed, certified, or registered under the provisions of this Article shall give written notice to the Board of any change in his or her name or address within 60 business days after the change takes place. (2001-370, s. 8; 2005-431, s. 1.)

§ 90-113.42. Violations; exemptions.

(a)   It shall be unlawful for any person not licensed or otherwise credentialed as a substance abuse professional pursuant to this Article to engage in those activities set forth in the scope of practice of a substance abuse professional under G.S. 90-113.31B, unless that person is regulated by another profession or is a registrant or intern as defined by this Article.

(b)   It is not the intent of this Article to regulate members of other regulated professions who provide substance abuse services or consultation in the normal course of the practice of their profession.

(c)   This Article does not apply to any person registered, certified, or licensed by the State or federal government to practice any other occupation or profession while rendering substance abuse services or consultation in the performance of the occupation or profession for which the person is registered, certified, or licensed.

(d)   Only individuals registered, certified, or licensed under this Article may use the title "Certified Substance Abuse Counselor", "Certified Substance Abuse Prevention Consultant", "Certified Clinical Supervisor", "Licensed Clinical Addictions Specialist Associate", "Certified Substance Abuse Residential Facility Director", "Certified Criminal Justice Addictions Professional", "Substance Abuse Counselor Intern", "Provisional Licensed Clinical Addictions Specialist", "Clinical Supervisor Intern", or "Registrant". (1993 (Reg. Sess., 1994), c. 685, s. 1; 1997-492, s. 12; 2005-431, s. 1; 2008-130, s. 5; 2012-72, s. 6.)

§ 90-113.43. Illegal practice; misdemeanor penalty.

(a)   Except as otherwise authorized in this Article, no person shall:

(1)   Offer substance abuse professional services, practice, attempt to practice, or supervise while holding himself or herself out to be a certified substance abuse counselor, certified substance abuse prevention consultant, certified clinical supervisor, licensed clinical addictions specialist, licensed clinical addictions specialist associate, certified substance abuse residential facility director, certified criminal justice addictions professional, clinical

supervisor intern, substance abuse counselor intern, or registrant without first having obtained a notification of registration, certification, or licensure from the Board.

(2)   Use in connection with any name any letters, words, numerical codes, or insignia indicating or implying that this person is a registrant, certified substance abuse counselor, certified substance abuse prevention consultant, certified clinical supervisor, licensed clinical addictions specialist, certified substance abuse residential facility director, substance abuse counselor intern, certified criminal justice addictions professional, or licensed clinical addictions specialist associate, unless this person is registered, certified, or licensed pursuant to this Article.

(3)   Practice or attempt to practice as a certified substance abuse counselor, certified substance abuse prevention consultant, certified clinical supervisor, licensed clinical addictions specialist, certified criminal justice addictions professional, substance abuse counselor intern, licensed clinical addictions specialist associate, clinical supervisor intern, certified substance abuse residential facility director or registrant with a revoked, lapsed, or suspended certification or license.

(4)   Aid, abet, or assist any person to practice as a certified substance abuse counselor, certified substance abuse prevention consultant, certified criminal justice addictions professional, certified clinical supervisor, licensed clinical addictions specialist, certified substance abuse residential facility director, registrant, substance abuse counselor intern, licensed clinical addictions specialist associate, or clinical supervisor intern in violation of this Article.

(5)   Knowingly serve in a position required by State law or rule or federal law or regulation to be filled by a registrant, certified substance abuse counselor, certified substance abuse prevention consultant, certified criminal justice addictions professional, certified clinical supervisor, licensed clinical addictions specialist, certified substance abuse residential facility director, substance abuse counselor intern, licensed clinical addictions specialist associate, or clinical supervisor intern unless that person is registered, certified, or licensed under this Article.

(6)   Repealed by S.L. 1997-492, s. 13.

(7)   Repealed by Session Laws 2008-130, s. 6, effective July 28, 2008.

(b) A person who engages in any of the illegal practices enumerated by this section is guilty of a Class 1 misdemeanor. Each act of unlawful practice constitutes a distinct and separate offense. (1993 (Reg. Sess., 1994), c. 685, s. 1; 1997-492, s. 13; 2005-431, s. 1; 2008-130, s. 6; 2012-72, s. 7.)

§ 90-113.44. Grounds for disciplinary action.

(a) Grounds for disciplinary action for an applicant or credentialed professional include:

(1) The employment of fraud, deceit, or misrepresentation in obtaining or attempting to obtain licensure, certification, or registration or renewal of licensure, certification, or registration.

(2) The use of drugs or alcoholic beverages to the extent that professional competency is affected.

(2a) The use of drugs or alcoholic beverages to the extent that a substance abuse professional suffers impairment.

(3) Conviction of an offense under any municipal, State, or federal law other than traffic laws as prescribed by Chapter 20 of the General Statutes.

(4) Conviction of a felony or other public offense involving moral turpitude. Conviction of a Class A-E felony shall result in an immediate suspension of licensure, certification, or registration for a minimum of one year.

(5) An adjudication of insanity or incompetency, until proof of recovery from this condition can be established by a licensed psychologist or psychiatrist.

(6) Engaging in any act or practice in violation of any of the provisions of this Article or any of the rules adopted pursuant to it, or aiding, abetting, or assisting any other person in such a violation.

(7) The commission of an act of malpractice, gross negligence, or incompetence while serving as a substance abuse professional, intern, or registrant.

(8) Repealed by Session Laws 2005-431, s. 1, effective September 22, 2005.

(9) Engaging in conduct that could result in harm or injury to the public.

(10) Entering into a dual relationship that impairs professional judgment or increases the risk of exploitation with a client or supervisee.

(11) Practicing as a credentialed substance abuse professional outside of his or her scope of practice pursuant to G.S. 90-113.31B.

(b) Denial of an applicant's licensure, certification, or registration or the granting of licensure, certification, or registration on a probationary or other conditional status shall be subject to substantially the same rules and procedures prescribed by the Board for review and disciplinary actions against any person holding a license, certificate, or registration. A suspension of a credential resulting from impairment due to substance use, mental health, or medical disorder shall be imposed for at least six months beginning from the date of successful discharge from a residential substance abuse treatment program or other appropriate treatment modality determined as a result of an assessment by a Board-approved assessor. Disciplinary actions involving a clinical addictions specialist whose licensure is achieved through deemed status shall be initially heard by the specialist's credentialing body. The specialist may appeal the body's decision to the Board. The Board shall, however, have the discretionary authority to hear the initial disciplinary action involving a credentialed professional. (1993 (Reg. Sess., 1994), c. 685, s. 1; 1997-492, s. 14; 2001-370, s. 7; 2005-431, s. 1.)

§ 90-113.45. Enjoining illegal practices.

(a) The Board may, if it finds that any person is violating any of the provisions of this Article or of the rules adopted pursuant to it, apply in its own name to the superior court for a temporary or permanent restraining order or injunction to restrain that person from continuing these illegal practices. The court may grant injunctive relief regardless of whether criminal prosecution or other action has been or may be instituted as a result of the violation. In the court's consideration of the issue of whether to grant or continue an injunction sought by the Board, a showing of conduct in violation of the terms of this Article shall be sufficient to meet any requirement of general North Carolina injunction law for irreparable damage.

(b) The venue for actions brought under this section is the superior court of any county in which the illegal acts are alleged to have been committed or in the county where the defendant resides. (1993 (Reg. Sess., 1994), c. 685, s. 1.)

§ 90-113.46. Application of requirements of Article.

All persons credentialed by the North Carolina Substance Abuse Professional Practice Board, Inc., as of July 1, 1994, shall be credentialed by the Board pursuant to this Article. All these persons are subject to all the other requirements of this Article and of the rules adopted pursuant to it. (1993 (Reg. Sess., 1994), c. 685, s. 1; 1997-492, s. 15; 2005-431, s. 1.)

§ 90-113.46A. Criminal history record checks of applicants for registration, certification, or licensure.

(a) All applicants for registration, certification, or licensure shall consent to a criminal history record check. Refusal to consent to a criminal history record check may constitute grounds for the Board to deny registration, certification, or licensure to an applicant. The Board shall ensure that the State and national criminal history of an applicant is checked. The Board shall be responsible for providing to the North Carolina Department of Justice the fingerprints of the applicant to be checked, a form signed by the applicant consenting to the criminal history record check and the use of fingerprints and other identifying information required by the State or National Repositories, the fee required by the Department of Justice for providing this service, and any additional information required by the Department of Justice. The Board shall keep all information obtained pursuant to this section confidential.

(b) If an applicant's criminal history record check reveals one or more convictions as defined in G.S. 90-113.31A(14), the conviction shall not automatically bar issuance of a credential by the Board to the applicant. The Board shall consider all of the following factors regarding the conviction:

(1) The level of seriousness of the crime.

(2) The date of the crime.

(3) The age of the person at the time of the conviction.

(4) The circumstances surrounding the commission of the crime, if known.

(5) The nexus between the criminal conduct of the person and the job duties of the position to be filled.

(6) The person's prison, jail, probation, parole, rehabilitation, and employment records since the date the crime was committed.

(7) The subsequent commission by the person of a crime as defined in G.S. 90-113.31A(14).

If, after reviewing the factors, the Board determines that the grounds set forth in G.S. 90-113.44 exist, the Board may deny registration, certification, or licensure of the applicant. The Board may disclose to the applicant information contained in the criminal history record check that is relevant to the denial. The Board shall not provide a copy of the criminal history record check to the applicant. The applicant shall have the right to appear before the Board to appeal the Board's decision. However, an appearance before the full Board shall constitute an exhaustion of administrative remedies in accordance with Chapter 150B of the General Statutes.

(c) Limited Immunity. - The Board, its officers and employees, acting in good faith and in compliance with this section, shall be immune from civil liability for denying registration, certification, or licensure to an applicant based on information provided in the applicant's criminal history record check. (2005-431, s. 1.)

§ 90-113.47. Repealed by Session Laws 1999-199, s. 3.1.

§ 90-113.48. Reserved for future codification purposes.

§ 90-113.49. Reserved for future codification purposes.

Article 5D.

Control of Methamphetamine Precursors.

§ 90-113.50. Title.

This Article shall be known and may be cited as the "Methamphetamine Lab Prevention Act of 2005." (2005-434, s. 1.)

§ 90-113.51. Definitions.

(a) For purposes of this Article, "pseudoephedrine product" means a product containing any detectable quantity of pseudoephedrine or ephedrine base, their salts or isomers, or salts of their isomers.

(b) For purposes of this Article, a "retailer" means an individual or entity that is the general owner of an establishment where pseudoephedrine products are available for sale.

(c) For purposes of this Article, the "Commission" means the Commission for Mental Health, Developmental Disabilities, and Substance Abuse Services. (2005-434, s. 1.)

§ 90-113.52. Pseudoephedrine: restrictions on sales.

(a) A pseudoephedrine product in the form of a tablet, caplet, or gel cap shall not be offered for retail sale loose in bottles but shall be sold only in blister packages.

(b) Pseudoephedrine products shall not be offered for retail sale by self-service, but shall be stored and sold in the following manner: Any pseudoephedrine product in the form of a tablet or caplet containing pseudoephedrine as the sole active ingredient or in combination with other active ingredients shall be stored and sold behind a pharmacy counter.

(c) A pseudoephedrine product may be sold at retail without a prescription only to a person at least 18 years of age. The retailer shall require every retail purchaser of a pseudoephedrine product to furnish a valid, unexpired, government-issued photo identification and to provide, in print or orally, a current valid personal residential address. If the retailer has reasonable grounds to believe that the prospective purchaser is under 18 years of age, the retailer shall require the prospective purchaser to furnish photo identification showing the date of birth of the person. The name and address of every purchaser shall be entered in a record of disposition of pseudoephedrine products to the consumer on a form approved by the Commission. The record of disposition shall also identify each pseudoephedrine product purchased, including the number of grams the product contains and the purchase date of the transaction. The retailer shall require that every purchaser sign the form attesting to the validity of the information. The form approved by the Commission shall be constructed so that it allows for entry of information in electronic format, including electronic signature. The form shall also be constructed and maintained so as to minimize disclosure of personal information to unauthorized persons.

(d) A retailer shall maintain a record of disposition of pseudoephedrine products to the consumer for a period of two years from the date of each transaction. A record shall be readily available within 48 hours of the time of the transaction for inspection by an authorized official of a federal, State, or local law enforcement agency. The records maintained by a retailer are privileged information and are not public records but are for the exclusive use of the retailer and law enforcement. The retailer may destroy the information after two years from the date of the transactions.

(e) This section does not apply to any pseudoephedrine product that is in the form of a liquid, liquid capsule, gel capsule, or pediatric product labeled pursuant to federal regulation primarily intended for administration to children under 12 years of age according to label instruction, except as to those specific products for which the Commission issues an order pursuant to G.S. 90-113.58 subjecting the product to requirements under this Article. (2005-434, s. 1; 2006-186, s. 1; 2012-35, s. 2.)

§ 90-113.52A. Electronic record keeping.

(a) A retailer shall, before completing a sale of a product containing a pseudoephedrine product, electronically submit the required information to the National Precursor Log Exchange (NPLEx) administered by the National Association of Drug Diversion Investigators (NADDI), provided that the NPLEx system is available to retailers in the State without a charge for accessing the system and the retailer has Internet access. The seller shall not complete the sale if the system generates a stop alert. Absent negligence, wantoness, recklessness, or deliberate misconduct, any retailer utilizing the electronic sales tracking system in accordance with this subsection shall not be civilly liable as a result of any act or omission in carrying out the duties required by this subsection and shall be immune from liability to any third party unless the retailer has violated any provision of this subsection in relation to a claim brought for such violation.

(b) If a pharmacy selling a product containing a pseudoephedrine product experiences mechanical or electronic failure of the electronic sales tracking system and is unable to comply with the electronic sales tracking requirement, the pharmacy or retail establishment shall record that the sale was made without submission to the NPLEx system in the record of disposition required under G.S. 90-113.52.

(c) The NADDI shall forward North Carolina transaction records in NPLEx to the State Bureau of Investigation weekly and provide real-time access to NPLEx information through the NPLEx online portal to law enforcement in the State as authorized by the SBI, provided that the SBI executes a memorandum of understanding with NADDI governing access.

(d) This system shall be capable of generating a stop sale alert, which shall be a notification that completion of the sale would result in the seller or purchaser violating the quantity limits set forth in G.S. 90-113.52. The system shall contain an override function that may be used by a dispenser of a pseudoephedrine product who has a reasonable fear of imminent bodily harm if the dispenser does not complete a sale. Each instance in which the override function is utilized shall be logged by the system. (2011-240, s. 2.)

§ 90-113.53. Pseudoephedrine transaction limits.

(a) No person shall deliver to any one person, attempt to deliver to any one person, purchase, or attempt to purchase at retail more than 3.6 grams of any pseudoephedrine products per calendar day. This limit does not apply if the product is dispensed under a valid prescription.

(b) No person shall purchase at retail more than 9 grams of pseudoephedrine products within any 30-day period. This limit does not apply if the product is dispensed under a valid prescription.

(c) This section does not apply to any pseudoephedrine products that are in the form of liquids, liquid capsules, gel capsules, or pediatric products labeled pursuant to federal regulation primarily intended for administration to children under 12 years of age according to label instruction, except as to those specific products for which the Commission issues an order pursuant to G.S. 90-113.58 subjecting the product to requirements under this Article. (2005-434, s. 1; 2006-186, s. 2; 2012-35, s. 1.)

§ 90-113.54. Posting of signs.

(a) A retailer shall post a sign or placard in a clear and conspicuous manner in the area of the premises where the pseudoephedrine products are offered for sale substantially similar to the following: "North Carolina law strictly prohibits the purchase of more than 3.6 grams total of certain products containing pseudoephedrine per day, and more than 9 grams total of certain products containing pseudoephedrine within a 30-day period. This store will maintain a record of all sales of these products which may be accessible to law enforcement officers.

(b) This section does not apply to any pseudoephedrine products that are in the form of liquids, liquid capsules, gel capsules, or pediatric products labeled pursuant to federal regulation primarily intended for administration to children under 12 years of age according to label instruction, except as to those specific products for which the Commission issues an order pursuant to G.S. 90-113.58 subjecting the product to requirements under this Article. (2005-434, s. 1; 2006-186, s. 3; 2012-194, s. 60.5.)

§ 90-113.55. Training of employees.

A retailer shall require that employees of the establishment involved in the sale of pseudoephedrine products in the form of tablets or caplets, and any other pseudoephedrine product for which the Commission issues an order pursuant to G.S. 90-113.58 to subject the product to requirements under this Article, be trained in a program conducted by or approved by the Commission pursuant to G.S. 90-113.59. (2005-434, s. 1.)

§ 90-113.56. Penalties.

(a) If a retailer willfully and knowingly violates the provisions of G.S. 90-113.52, 90-113.52A, 90-113.53, or 90-113.54, the retailer shall be guilty of a Class A1 misdemeanor for the first offense and a Class I felony for a second or subsequent offense. A retailer convicted of a third offense occurring on the premises of a single establishment shall be prohibited from making pseudoephedrine products available for sale at that establishment.

(b) Any purchaser or employee who willfully and knowingly violates G.S. 90-113.52A, G.S. 90-113.52(c) or G.S. 90-113.53 shall be guilty of a Class 1 misdemeanor for the first offense, a Class A1 misdemeanor for a second offense, and a Class I felony for a third or subsequent offense. This subsection shall not be construed to apply to bona fide innocent purchasers.

(c) A retailer who fails to train employees in accordance with G.S. 90-113.55, adequately supervise employees in transactions involving pseudoephedrine products, or reasonably discipline employees for violations of this Article shall be fined up to five hundred dollars ($500.00) for the first violation, up to seven hundred fifty dollars ($750.00) for the second violation, and up to one thousand dollars ($1,000) for a third or subsequent violation of this section. (2005-434, s. 1; 2011-240, s. 3.)

§ 90-113.57. Immunity.

A retailer or an employee of the retailer who, reasonably and in good faith, reports to any law enforcement agency any alleged criminal activity related to the sale or purchase of pseudoephedrine products, or who refuses to sell a pseudoephedrine product to a person reasonably believed to be ineligible to purchase a pseudoephedrine product pursuant to this Article, is immune from civil liability for that conduct except in cases of willful misconduct. No retailer shall retaliate in any manner against any employee of the establishment for a report made in good faith to any law enforcement agency concerning alleged criminal activity related to the sale or purchase of pseudoephedrine products. (2005-434, s. 1.)

§ 90-113.58. Commission authority to control pseudoephedrine products.

(a) The Commission may add or delete a specific pseudoephedrine product from requirements of this Article on the petition of any interested party, or its own motion. In addition, the Commission may modify the specific storage, security, transaction limit, and record-keeping requirements applicable to a particular product upon such terms and conditions as they deem appropriate. In every case, the Commission shall give notice of and hold a public hearing pursuant to Chapter 150B of the General Statutes prior to adding or deleting a product. A petition by the Commission or the North Carolina Department of Justice to add or delete a specific product from requirements of this Article shall be placed on the agenda for consideration at the next regularly scheduled meeting of the Commission, as a matter of right. In making a determination regarding a specific product, the Commission shall consider whether or not there is substantial evidence that the specific product would be used to manufacture methamphetamine in the State.

(b) In making a determination, the Commission shall make findings with respect thereto and shall issue an order adding or deleting the specific product from requirements of this Article. The order shall be published in the North Carolina Register at least 60 days prior to the time that the addition or deletion of a specific product from the requirements of this Article becomes effective.

(c) The Commission may adopt temporary and permanent rules in accordance with this section. (2005-434, s. 1.)

§ 90-113.59. Commission development of employee training programs.

The Commission shall develop training and education programs targeted for employees of establishments where pseudoephedrine products are available for sale and shall approve such programs for implementation by retailers. The Commission may also conduct employee training programs for retail establishments. The Commission may adopt temporary and permanent rules in this regard. (2005-434, s. 1.)

§ 90-113.60. Preemption.

This Article shall preempt all local ordinances or regulations governing the sale by a retailer of over-the-counter products containing pseudoephedrine. (2005-434, s. 1.)

§ 90-113.61. Regulation of pseudoephedrine products in the form of liquids, liquid capsules, gel capsules, and pediatric products.

Except as to those specific products for which the Commission issues an order pursuant to G.S. 90-113.58 subjecting the product to requirements under this Article, any pseudoephedrine products that are in the form of liquids, liquid capsules, gel capsules, or pediatric products labeled pursuant to federal regulation primarily intended for administration to children under 12 years of age according to label instruction shall not be subject to requirements under this Article, but such products shall be subject to the requirements of the Combat Methamphetamine Act of 2005, Title VII of the USA PATRIOT Improvement and Reauthorization Act of 2005, P.L. 109-177. (2006-186, s. 4.)

§ 90-113.62: Reserved for future codification purposes.

§ 90-113.63: Reserved for future codification purposes.

§ 90-113.64. SBI annual report.

Beginning with the 2011 calendar year, the State Bureau of Investigation shall determine the number of methamphetamine laboratories discovered in the State each calendar year and report its findings to the Legislative Commission on Methamphetamine Abuse by March 1, 2012, for the 2011 calendar year and each March 1 thereafter for the preceding calendar year. The State Bureau of Investigation shall participate in the High Intensity Drug Trafficking Areas (HIDTA) program, assist in coordinating the drug control efforts between local and State law enforcement agencies, and monitor the implementation and effectiveness of the electronic record-keeping requirements included in G.S. 90-113.52A and G.S. 90-113.56. The SBI shall include its findings in the report to the Commission required by this section. (2011-240, s. 4.)

§ 90-113.65: Reserved for future codification purposes.

§ 90-113.66: Reserved for future codification purposes.

§ 90-113.67: Reserved for future codification purposes.

§ 90-113.68: Reserved for future codification purposes.

§ 90-113.69: Reserved for future codification purposes.

Article 5E.

North Carolina Controlled Substances Reporting System Act.

§ 90-113.70. Short title.

This Article shall be known and may be cited as the "North Carolina Controlled Substances Reporting System Act." (2005-276, s. 10.36(a).)

§ 90-113.71. Legislative findings and purpose.

(a) The General Assembly makes the following findings:

(1) North Carolina is experiencing an epidemic of poisoning deaths from unintentional drug overdoses.

(2) Since 1997, the number of deaths from unintentional drug overdoses has increased threefold, from 228 deaths in 1997 to 690 deaths in 2003.

(3) The number of unintentional deaths from illicit drugs in North Carolina has decreased since 1992 while unintentional deaths from licit drugs, primarily prescriptions, have increased.

(4) Licit drugs are now responsible for over half of the fatal unintentional poisonings in North Carolina.

(5) Over half of the prescription drugs associated with unintentional deaths are narcotics (opioids).

(6) Of these licit drugs, deaths from methadone, usually prescribed as an analgesic for severe pain, have increased sevenfold since 1997.

(7) Methadone from opioid treatment program clinics is a negligible source of the methadone that has contributed to the dramatic increase in unintentional methadone-related deaths in North Carolina.

(8) Review of the experience of the 19 states that have active controlled substances reporting systems clearly documents that implementation of these reporting systems do not create a "chilling" effect on prescribing.

(9) Review of data from controlled substances reporting systems help:

a. Support the legitimate medical use of controlled substances.

b. Identify and prevent diversion of prescribed controlled substances.

c. Reduce morbidity and mortality from unintentional drug overdoses.

d. Reduce the costs associated with the misuse and abuse of controlled substances.

e. Assist clinicians in identifying and referring for treatment patients misusing controlled substances.

f. Reduce the cost for law enforcement of investigating cases of diversion and misuse.

g. Inform the public, including health care professionals, of the use and abuse trends related to prescription drugs.

(b) This Article is intended to improve the State's ability to identify controlled substance abusers or misusers and refer them for treatment, and to identify and stop diversion of prescription drugs in an efficient and cost-effective manner that will not impede the appropriate medical utilization of licit controlled substances. (2005-276, s. 10.36(a).)

§ 90-113.72. Definitions.

The following definitions apply in this Article:

(1) "Commission" means the Commission for Mental Health, Developmental Disabilities, and Substance Abuse Services established under Part 4 of Article 3 of Chapter 143B of the General Statutes.

(2) "Controlled substance" means a controlled substance as defined in G.S. 90-87(5).

(3) "Department" means the Department of Health and Human Services.

(4) "Dispenser" means a person who delivers a Schedule II through V controlled substance to an ultimate user in North Carolina, but does not include any of the following:

a. A licensed hospital or long-term care pharmacy that dispenses such substances for the purpose of inpatient administration.

b. Repealed by Session Laws 2013-152, s. 1, effective January 1, 2014, and applicable to prescriptions delivered on or after that date.

c. A wholesale distributor of a Schedule II through V controlled substance.

d. A person licensed to practice veterinary medicine pursuant to Article 11 of Chapter 90 of the General Statutes.

(5) "Ultimate user" means a person who has lawfully obtained, and who possesses, a Schedule II through V controlled substance for the person's own use, for the use of a member of the person's household, or for the use of an animal owned or controlled by the person or by a member of the person's household. (2005-276, s. 10.36(a); 2013-152, s. 1.)

§ 90-113.73. Requirements for controlled substances reporting system.

(a) The Department shall establish and maintain a reporting system of prescriptions for all Schedule II through V controlled substances. Each dispenser shall submit the information in accordance with transmission methods and frequency established by rule by the Commission. The Department may issue a waiver to a dispenser who is unable to submit prescription information by electronic means. The waiver may permit the dispenser to submit prescription information by paper form or other means, provided all information required of electronically submitted data is submitted. The dispenser shall report the information required under this section no later than the close of business three business days after the day when the prescription was delivered, beginning the next day after the delivery date; however, dispensers are encouraged to report the information no later than 24 hours after the prescription was delivered. The information shall be submitted in a format as determined annually by the Department based on the format used in the majority of the states operating a controlled substances reporting system.

(b) The Commission shall adopt rules requiring dispensers to report the following information. The Commission may modify these requirements as necessary to carry out the purposes of this Article. The dispenser shall report:

(1) The dispenser's DEA number.

(2) The name of the patient for whom the controlled substance is being dispensed, and the patient's:

a. Full address, including city, state, and zip code,

b. Telephone number, and

c. Date of birth.

(3) The date the prescription was written.

(4) The date the prescription was filled.

(5) The prescription number.

(6) Whether the prescription is new or a refill.

(7) Metric quantity of the dispensed drug.

(8) Estimated days of supply of dispensed drug, if provided to the dispenser.

(9) National Drug Code of dispensed drug.

(10) Prescriber's DEA number.

(11) Method of payment for the prescription.

(c) A dispenser shall not be required to report instances in which a controlled substance is provided directly to the ultimate user and the quantity provided does not exceed a 48-hour supply. (2005-276, s. 10.36(a); 2005-345, s. 17; 2009-438, s. 1; 2013-152, s. 2.)

§ 90-113.74. Confidentiality.

(a) Prescription information submitted to the Department is privileged and confidential, is not a public record pursuant to G.S. 132-1, is not subject to subpoena or discovery or any other use in civil proceedings, and except as otherwise provided below may only be used for investigative or evidentiary purposes related to violations of State or federal law and regulatory activities. Except as otherwise provided by this section, prescription information shall not be disclosed or disseminated to any person or entity by any person or entity authorized to review prescription information.

(b) The Department may use prescription information data in the controlled substances reporting system only for purposes of implementing this Article in accordance with its provisions.

(b1) The Department may review the prescription information data in the controlled substances reporting system and upon review may:

(1) Notify practitioners that a patient may have obtained prescriptions for controlled substances in a manner that may represent abuse, diversion of controlled substances, or an increased risk of harm to the patient.

(2) Report information regarding the prescribing practices of a practitioner to the agency responsible for licensing, registering, or certifying the practitioner pursuant to rules adopted by the agency as set forth below in subsection (b2) of this section.

(b2) In order to receive a report pursuant to subdivision (2) of subsection (b1) of this section, an agency responsible for licensing, registering, or certifying a practitioner with prescriptive or dispensing authority shall adopt rules setting the criteria by which the Department may report the information to the agency. The criteria for reporting established by rule shall not establish the standard of care for prescribing or dispensing, and it shall not be a basis for disciplinary action by an agency that the Department reported a practitioner to an agency based on the criteria.

(c) The Department shall release data in the controlled substances reporting system to the following persons only:

(1) Persons authorized to prescribe or dispense controlled substances for the purpose of providing medical or pharmaceutical care for their patients. A

person authorized to receive data pursuant to this paragraph may delegate the authority to receive the data to other persons working under his or her direction and supervision, provided the Department approves the delegation.

(2) An individual who requests the individual's own controlled substances reporting system information.

(3) Special agents of the North Carolina State Bureau of Investigation who are assigned to the Diversion & Environmental Crimes Unit and whose primary duties involve the investigation of diversion and illegal use of prescription medication. SBI agents assigned to the Diversion & Environmental Crimes Unit may then provide this information to other SBI agents who are engaged in a bona fide specific investigation related to enforcement of laws governing licit drugs. The SBI shall notify the Office of the Attorney General of North Carolina of each request for inspection of records maintained by the Department.

(4) Primary monitoring authorities for other states pursuant to a specific ongoing investigation involving a designated person, if information concerns the dispensing of a Schedule II through V controlled substance to an ultimate user who resides in the other state or the dispensing of a Schedule II through V controlled substance prescribed by a licensed health care practitioner whose principal place of business is located in the other state.

(5) To a sheriff or designated deputy sheriff or a police chief or a designated police investigator who is assigned to investigate the diversion and illegal use of prescription medication or pharmaceutical products identified in Article 5 of this Chapter of the General Statutes as Schedule II through V controlled substances and who is engaged in a bona fide specific investigation related to the enforcement of laws governing licit drugs pursuant to a lawful court order specifically issued for that purpose.

(6) The Division of Medical Assistance for purposes of administering the State Medical Assistance Plan.

(7) Licensing boards with jurisdiction over health care disciplines pursuant to an ongoing investigation by the licensing board of a specific individual licensed by the board.

(8) Any county medical examiner appointed by the Chief Medical Examiner pursuant to G.S. 130A-382 and the Chief Medical Examiner, for the purpose of investigating the death of an individual.

(d)   The Department may provide data to public or private entities for statistical, research, or educational purposes only after removing information that could be used to identify individual patients who received prescription medications from dispensers.

(e)   In the event that the Department finds patterns of prescribing medications that are unusual, the Department shall inform the Attorney General's Office of its findings. The Office of the Attorney General shall review the Department's findings to determine if the findings should be reported to the SBI and the appropriate sheriff for investigation of possible violations of State or federal law relating to controlled substances.

(f)   The Department shall purge from the controlled substances reporting system database all information more than six years old.

(g)   Nothing in this Article shall prohibit a person authorized to prescribe or dispense controlled substances pursuant to Article 1 of Chapter 90 of the General Statutes from disclosing or disseminating data regarding a particular patient obtained under subsection (c) of this section to another person (i) authorized to prescribe or dispense controlled substances pursuant to Article 1 of Chapter 90 of the General Statutes and (ii) authorized to receive the same data from the Department under subsection (c) of this section.

(h)   Nothing in this Article shall prevent persons licensed or approved to practice medicine or perform medical acts, tasks, and functions pursuant to Article 1 of Chapter 90 of the General Statutes from retaining data received pursuant to subsection (c) of this section in a patient's confidential health care record. (2005-276, s. 10.36(a); 2009-438, s. 2; 2013-152, s. 3.)

§ 90-113.75. Civil penalties; other remedies; immunity from liability.

(a)   A person who intentionally, knowingly, or negligently releases, obtains, or attempts to obtain information from the system in violation of a provision of this Article or a rule adopted pursuant to this Article shall be assessed a civil penalty by the Department not to exceed ten thousand dollars ($10,000) per violation. The clear proceeds of penalties assessed under this section shall be deposited to the Civil Penalty and Forfeiture Fund in accordance with Article 31A of Chapter 115C of the General Statutes. The Commission shall adopt rules establishing the factors to be considered in determining the amount of the penalty to be assessed.

(b) In addition to any other remedies available at law, an individual whose prescription information has been disclosed in violation of this Article or a rule adopted pursuant to this Article may bring an action against any person or entity who has intentionally, knowingly, or negligently released confidential information or records concerning the individual for either or both of the following:

(1) Nominal damages of one thousand dollars ($1,000). In order to recover damages under this subdivision, it shall not be necessary that the plaintiff suffered or was threatened with actual damages.

(2) The amount of actual damages, if any, sustained by the individual.

(c) A person or entity permitted access to data under this Article that, in good faith, makes a report or transmits data required or allowed by this Article is immune from civil or criminal liability that might otherwise be incurred or imposed as a result of making the report or transmitting the data. (2005-276, s. 10.36(a); 2013-152, s. 4; 2013-410, s. 18.5.)

§ 90-113.76. Commission for Mental Health, Developmental Disabilities, and Substance Abuse Services to adopt rules.

The Commission for Mental Health, Developmental Disabilities, and Substance Abuse Services shall adopt rules necessary to implement this Article. (2005-276, s. 10.36(a).)

§ 90-113.77. Reserved for future codification purposes.

§ 90-113.78. Reserved for future codification purposes.

§ 90-113.79. Reserved for future codification purposes.

Article 5F.

Control of Potential Drug Paraphernalia Products.

§ 90-113.80. Title.

This Article shall be known and may be cited as the "Drug Paraphernalia Control Act of 2009." (2009-205, s. 1.)

§ 90-113.81. Definitions.

For the purposes of this Article:

(a) "Glass tube" means an object which meets all of the following requirements:

(1) A hollow glass cylinder, either open or closed at either end.

(2) No less than two or more than seven inches in length.

(3) No less than one-eighth inch or more than three-fourths inch in diameter.

(4) May be used to facilitate, or intended or designed to facilitate, violations of the Controlled Substances Act, including, but not limited to, processing, preparing, testing, analyzing, packaging, repackaging, storing, containing, and concealing controlled substances and injecting, ingesting, inhaling, or otherwise introducing controlled substances into the human body.

(5) Sold individually, or in connection with another object such as a novelty holder, flower vase, or pen. The foregoing descriptions are intended to be illustrative and not exclusive.

(b) "Retailer" means an individual or entity that is the general owner of an establishment where glass tubes or splitters are available for sale.

(c) "Splitter" means a ring-shaped device that does both of the following:

(1) Allows the insertion of a wrapped tobacco product, such as a cigar, so that it can be pulled through the device.

(2) Cuts or slices the wrapping of the tobacco product along the product's length as it is drawn through the device. (2009-205, s. 1.)

§ 90-113.82. Glass tubes or splitters; restrictions on sales.

(a) Glass tubes or splitters shall not be offered for retail sale by self-service, but shall be stored and sold from behind a counter where the general public cannot access them without the assistance of a retailer's agent or employee.

(b) The retailer shall require any member of the public to whom it transfers a glass tube or splitter, with or without consideration, to do all of the following:

(1) Present identification that includes a photograph that is an accurate depiction of the person and that also includes the person's name and current address.

(2) Enter his or her name and current address on a record that the retailer shall maintain solely for the purposes of this section.

(3) Sign his or her name, verifying by signature the glass tube or splitter will not be used as drug paraphernalia in violation of the criminal laws of the State of North Carolina.

(c) The retailer shall maintain the record described in subsection (b) of this section for a period of two years from the date of each transaction, after which it may be destroyed.

(d) The record shall be readily available within 48 hours of the time of the transaction for inspection by an authorized official of a federal, State, or local law enforcement agency.

(e) The retailer shall train its agents and employees on the requirements of this section. (2009-205, s. 1.)

§ 90-113.83. Penalties.

(a) A retailer, or an employee of the retailer, who willfully and knowingly violates any one of the subsections of G.S. 90-113.82 shall be guilty of a Class 2 misdemeanor.

(b) Any person who knowingly makes a false statement or representation in fulfilling the requirements in G.S. 90-113.82(b) shall be guilty of a Class 1 misdemeanor. (2009-205, s. 1.)

§ 90-113.84. Immunity.

A retailer, or an employee of the retailer, who, reasonably and in good faith, (i) reports to any law enforcement agency any alleged criminal activity related to the sale or purchase of glass tubes or splitters or (ii) refuses to sell a glass tube or splitter to a person reasonably believed to be purchasing it for use as drug paraphernalia is immune from civil liability for that conduct, except in cases of willful misconduct. (2009-205, s. 1.)

Article 6.

Optometry.

§ 90-114. Optometry defined.

Any one or any combination of the following practices shall constitute the practice of optometry:

(1) The examination of the human eye by any method, other than surgery, to diagnose, to treat, or to refer for consultation or treatment any abnormal condition of the human eye and its adnexa; or

(2) The employment of instruments, devices, pharmaceutical agents and procedures, other than surgery, intended for the purposes of investigating, examining, treating, diagnosing or correcting visual defects or abnormal conditions of the human eye or its adnexa; or

(3) The prescribing and application of lenses, devices containing lenses, prisms, contact lenses, orthoptics, vision training, pharmaceutical agents, and prosthetic devices to correct, relieve, or treat defects or abnormal conditions of the human eye or its adnexa. (1909, c. 444, s. 1; C.S., s. 6687; 1923, c. 42, s. 1; 1977, c. 482, s. 1; 1997-75, s. 1.)

§ 90-115. Practice without registration unlawful.

After the passage of this Article it shall be unlawful for any person to practice optometry in the State unless he has first obtained a certificate of registration as hereinafter provided. Within the meaning of this Article, a person shall be deemed as practicing optometry who does, or attempts to, sell, furnish, replace, or duplicate, a lens, frame, or mounting, or furnishes any kind of material or apparatus for ophthalmic use, without a written prescription from a person authorized under the laws of the State of North Carolina to practice optometry, or from a person authorized under the laws of North Carolina to practice medicine: Provided, however, that the provisions of this section shall not prohibit persons or corporations from selling completely assembled spectacles, without advice or aid as to the selection thereof, as merchandise from permanently located or established places of business, nor shall it prohibit persons or corporations from making mechanical repairs to frames for spectacles; nor shall it prohibit any person, firm, or corporation engaged in grinding lenses and filling prescriptions from replacing or duplicating lenses on original prescriptions issued by a duly licensed optometrist, and oculist. (1909, c. 444, s. 2; C.S., s. 6688; 1935, c. 63; 1967, c. 691, s. 43.)

§ 90-115.1. Acts not constituting the unlawful practice of optometry.

In addition to the exemptions from this Article otherwise existing the following acts or practices shall not constitute the unlawful practice of optometry:

(1) The practice of optometry, in the discharge of their official duties, by optometrists in any branch of the Armed Forces of the United States or in the full employ of any agency of the United States.

(2) The teaching of optometry, in optometry schools or colleges operated and conducted in this State and approved by the North Carolina State Board of Examiners in Optometry, by any person or persons licensed to practice optometry anywhere in the United States or in any country, territory or other recognized jurisdiction; provided, however, that such teaching of optometry by any person or persons licensed in any jurisdiction other than a place in the United States must first be approved by the North Carolina State Board of Examiners in Optometry.

(3) The practice of optometry by students enrolled in optometry schools or colleges approved by the North Carolina State Board of Examiners in Optometry when such practice is performed as a part of the student's course of instruction, is under the direct supervision of an optometrist who is either duly licensed in North Carolina or qualified under subdivision (2) above as a teacher, and is conducted in accordance with such rules as may be established for such practice by the North Carolina State Board of Examiners in Optometry. Additionally, the practice of optometry by such students at any location upon patients or inmates of institutions wholly owned or operated by the State of North Carolina or any political subdivision or subdivisions thereof when, in the opinion of the dean of such optometry school or college or his designee, the student's optometric education and experience is adequate therefor, subject to review and approval by the said Board of Examiners in Optometry, and such practice is a part of the course of instruction of such students, is performed under the supervision of a duly licensed optometrist acting as a teacher or instructor and is without remuneration except for expenses and subsistence as defined and permitted by the rules and regulations of said Board of Examiners in Optometry.

(4) The temporary practice of optometry by licensed optometrists of another state or of any territory or country when the same is performed, as clinicians, at meetings or organized optometric societies, associations, colleges or similar optometric organizations, or when such optometrists appear in emergency cases upon the specific call of and in consultation with an optometrist duly licensed to practice in this State.

(5) The practice of optometry by a person who is a graduate of an optometric school or college approved by the North Carolina State Board of

Examiners in Optometry and who is not licensed to practice optometry in this State, when such person is the holder of a valid intern permit, or provisional license, issued to him by the North Carolina State Board of Examiners in Optometry pursuant to the terms and provisions of this Article, and when such practice of optometry complies with the conditions of said intern permit, or provisional license.

(6) Any act or acts performed by an optometric assistant or technician to an optometrist licensed to practice in this State when said act or acts are authorized and permitted by and performed in accordance with rules and regulations promulgated by the Board.

(7) Optometric assisting and related functions as a part of their instructions by optometric assistant students enrolled in a course conducted in this State and approved by the Board, when such functions are performed under the supervision of an optometrist acting as a teacher or instructor who is either duly licensed in North Carolina or qualified for the teaching of optometry pursuant to the provisions of subdivision (2) above. (1975, c. 733; 1989, c. 321; 2011-183, s. 61.)

§ 90-116. Board of Examiners in Optometry.

In order to properly regulate the practice of optometry, there is established a North Carolina State Board of Examiners in Optometry, which shall consist of five regularly graduated optometrists who have been engaged in the practice of optometry in this State for at least five years and two members to represent the public at large.

No public member shall at any time be a health care provider, be related to or be the spouse of a health care provider, or have any pecuniary interest in the profitability of a health care provider. For purposes of this section, the term "health care provider" shall have the same meaning as provided in G.S. 58-47-5(4). The Governor shall appoint the two public members not later than July 1, 1981.

The optometric members of the Board shall be appointed by the Governor from a list provided by the North Carolina State Optometric Society. For each vacancy, the society must submit at least three names to the Governor. The society shall establish procedures for the nomination and election of optometrist members of the Board. These procedures shall be adopted under the rule-making procedures described in Article 2A, Chapter 150B of the General Statutes, and notice of the proposed procedures shall be given to all licensed optometrists residing in North Carolina. Such procedures shall not conflict with the provisions of this section. Every optometrist with a current North Carolina license residing in the State shall be eligible to vote in all such elections, and the list of licensed optometrists shall constitute the registration list for elections. Any decision of the society relative to the conduct of such elections may be challenged by civil action in the Wake County Superior Court. A challenge must be filed not later than 30 days after the society has rendered the decision in controversy, and all such cases shall be heard de novo.

All Board members serving on June 30, 1981, shall be eligible to complete their respective terms. No member appointed to a term on or after July 1, 1981, shall serve more than two complete consecutive five-year terms, except that each member shall serve until his successor is chosen and qualifies.

The Governor may remove any member for good cause shown. Any vacancy in the optometrist membership of the Board shall be filled for the period of the unexpired term by the Governor from a list of at least three names submitted by the North Carolina State Optometric Society Executive Council. Any vacancy in the public membership of the Board shall be filled by the Governor for the unexpired term. (1909, c. 444, s. 3; 1915, c. 21, s. 1; C.S., s. 6689; 1935, c. 63; 1981, c. 496, s. 1; 1987, c. 827, s. 1; 2000-189, s. 5.)

§ 90-117. Officers; common seal.

The North Carolina State Board of Examiners in Optometry shall, at each annual meeting thereof, elect one of its members president and one secretary-treasurer. The common seal which has already been adopted by said Board, pursuant to law, shall be continued as the seal of said Board. (1909, c. 444, s. 4; C.S., s. 6690; 1935, c. 63; 1953, c. 1041, s. 11; 1973, c. 800, s. 1.)

§ 90-117.1. Quorum; adjourned meetings.

A majority of the members of said Board shall constitute a quorum for the transaction of business. If a majority of members are not present at the time and the place appointed for a Board meeting, those members of the Board in attendance may adjourn from day to day until a quorum is present, and the action of the Board taken at any adjourned meeting thus had shall have the same force and effect as if had upon the day and at the hour of the meeting called and adjourned from day to day. (1973, c. 800, s. 2; 1981, c. 496, s. 2.)

§ 90-117.2. Records and transcripts.

The said Board shall keep a record of its transactions at all annual or special meetings and shall provide a record book in which shall be entered the names and proficiency of all persons to whom licenses may be granted under the provisions of law. The said book shall show, also, the license number and the date upon which such license was issued and shall show such other matters as in the opinion of the Board may be necessary or proper. Said book shall be deemed a book of record of said Board and a transcript of any entry therein or a certification that there is not entered therein the name, proficiency and license number or date of granting such license, certified under the hand of the secretary-treasurer, attested by the seal of the North Carolina State Board of Examiners in Optometry, shall be admitted as evidence in any court of this State when the same shall otherwise be competent. (1973, c. 800, s. 3.)

§ 90-117.3. Annual and special meetings.

The North Carolina State Board of Examiners in Optometry shall meet annually in June of each year at such place as may be determined by the Board, and at such other times and places as may be determined by action of the Board or by a majority of the members thereof. Notice of the place of the annual meeting and of the time and place of any special or called meeting shall be given in writing, by registered or certified mail or personally, to each member of the Board at least 10 days prior to said meeting; provided the requirements of notice may be waived by any member of the Board. At the annual meeting or at any special or called meeting, the said Board shall have the power to conduct examination of applicants and to transact such other business as may come before it, provided that in case of a special meeting, the purpose for which said meeting is called shall be stated in the notice. (1973, c. 800, s. 4; 1981, c. 496, s. 3.)

§ 90-117.4. Judicial powers; additional data for records.

The president of the North Carolina State Board of Examiners in Optometry, and/or the secretary-treasurer of said Board, shall have the power to administer oaths, issue subpoenas requiring the attendance of persons and the production of papers and records before said Board in any hearing, investigation or proceeding conducted by it. The sheriff or other proper official of any county of the State shall serve the process issued by said president or secretary-treasurer of said Board pursuant to its requirements and in the same manner as process issued by any court of record. The said Board shall pay for the service of all process, such fees as are provided by law for the service of like process in other cases.

Any person who shall neglect or refuse to obey any subpoena requiring him to attend and testify before said Board or to produce books, records or documents shall be guilty of a Class 1 misdemeanor.

The Board shall have the power, upon the production of any papers, records or data, to authorize certified copies thereof to be substituted in the permanent record of the matter in which such books, records or data shall have been introduced in evidence. (1973, c. 800, s. 5; 1993, c. 539, s. 627; 1994, Ex. Sess., c. 24, s. 14(c).)

§ 90-117.5. Bylaws and regulations.

The North Carolina State Board of Examiners in Optometry shall have the power to make necessary bylaws and regulations, not inconsistent with the provisions of this Article, regarding any matter referred to in this Article and for the purpose of facilitating the transaction of business by the said Board. (1973, c. 800, s. 6.)

§ 90-118. Examination and licensing of applicants; qualifications; causes for refusal to grant license; void licenses; educational requirements for prescription and use of pharmaceutical agents.

(a) The North Carolina State Board of Examiners in Optometry shall grant licenses to practice optometry to such applicants who are graduates of an accredited optometric institution, who, in the opinion of a majority of the Board, shall undergo a satisfactory examination of proficiency in the knowledge and practice of optometry, subject, however, to the further provisions of this section and to the provisions of this Article.

(b) The applicant shall be of good moral character and at least 18 years of age at the time the application for examination is filed. The application shall be made to the said Board in writing and shall be accompanied by evidence satisfactory to said Board that the applicant is a person of good moral character; has an academic education, the standard of which shall be determined by the said Board; and that he is a graduate of and has a diploma from an accredited optometric college or the optometric department of an accredited university or college recognized and approved as such by the said Board.

(c) The North Carolina State Board of Examiners in Optometry is authorized to conduct both written or oral and clinical examinations of such character as to thoroughly test the qualifications of the applicant, and may refuse to grant a license to any person who, in its discretion, is found deficient in said examination, or to any person guilty of cheating, deception, or fraud during such examination, or whose examination discloses, to the satisfaction of the Board, a deficiency in academic education. The Board may employ such optometrists found qualified therefor by the Board in examining applicants for licenses as it deems appropriate.

(d) Any license obtained through fraud or by any false representation shall be void ab initio and of no effect.

(e) The Board shall not license any person to practice optometry in the State of North Carolina beyond the scope of the person's educational training as determined by the Board. No optometrist presently licensed in this State shall prescribe and use pharmaceutical agents in the practice of optometry unless and until he (i) has submitted to the Board evidence of satisfactory completion of all educational requirements established by the Board to prescribe and use pharmaceutical agents in the practice of optometry and (ii) has been certified by the Board as educationally qualified to prescribe and use pharmaceutical agents.

Provided, however, that no course or courses in pharmacology shall be approved by the Board unless (i) taught by an institution having facilities for both the didactic and clinical instruction in pharmacology and which is accredited by a regional or professional accrediting organization that is recognized and approved by the Council on Postsecondary Accreditation or the United States Office of Education and (ii) transcript credit for the course or courses is certified to the Board by the institution as being equivalent in both hours and content to those courses in pharmacology required by the other licensing boards in this Chapter whose licensees or registrants are permitted the use of pharmaceutical agents in the course of their professional practice. (1909, c. 444, s. 5; 1915, c. 21, ss. 2, 3, 4; C.S., s. 6691; 1923, c. 42, ss. 2, 3; 1935, c. 63; 1949, c. 357; 1959, c. 464; 1973, c. 800, s. 7; 1975, c. 19, s. 23; 1977, c. 482, s. 2; 1981, c. 496, ss. 4, 5; 1997-75, s. 4.1.)

§ 90-118.1. Contents of original license.

The original license granted by the North Carolina State Board of Examiners in Optometry shall bear a serial number, the full name of the applicant, the date of issuance and shall be signed by the president and a majority of the members of the said Board and attested by the seal of said Board and the secretary thereof. The certificate of renewal of license shall bear a serial number which need not be the serial number of the original license issued, the full name of the applicant and the date of issuance. (1973, c. 800, s. 8.)

§ 90-118.2. Displaying license and current certificate of renewal.

The license and the current certificate of renewal of license to practice optometry issued, as herein provided, shall at all times be displayed in a conspicuous place in the office of the holder thereof and whenever requested the license and the current certificate of renewal shall be exhibited to or produced before the North Carolina State Board of Examiners in Optometry or to its authorized agents.

A licensee who practices in more than one office location shall make application to the Board for a duplicate license for each branch office for display as required by this section. In issuing a duplicate license, the address of the branch office location and the original certificate number shall be included. At the time of the annual renewal of licenses, those optometrists who have been issued a duplicate license for a branch office, shall make application to the North

Carolina Board of Examiners in Optometry on a form provided by the Board for the renewal of the license in the same manner as provided for in G.S. 90-118.10 for the renewal of his license. The holder of a certificate for a branch office may cancel it by returning the certificate to the Secretary of the Board. (1973, c. 800, s. 9; 1981, c. 811, s. 1.)

§ 90-118.3. Refusal to grant renewal of license.

For nonpayment of fee or fees required by this Article, or for violation of any of the terms or provisions of G.S. 90-121.2, the North Carolina State Board of Examiners in Optometry may refuse to issue a certificate of renewal of license. (1973, c. 800, s. 10; 1981, c. 811, s. 2.)

§ 90-118.4. Duplicate licenses.

When a person is a holder of a license to practice optometry in North Carolina or the holder of a certificate of renewal of license, he may make application to the North Carolina State Board of Examiners in Optometry for the issuance of a copy or a duplicate thereof accompanied by a reasonable fee set by the Board. Upon the filing of the application and the payment of the fee, the said Board shall issue a copy or duplicate. (1973, c. 800, s. 11.)

§ 90-118.5. Licensing practitioners of other states.

(a)   If an applicant for licensure is already licensed in another state in optometry, the North Carolina State Board of Examiners in Optometry shall issue a license to practice optometry to the applicant without examination other than a clinical practicum examination upon evidence that:

(1)   The applicant is currently an active, competent practitioner in good standing, and

(2)   The applicant has practiced at least three out of the five years immediately preceding his or her application, and

(3) The applicant currently holds a valid license in another state, and

(4) No disciplinary proceeding or unresolved complaint is pending anywhere at the time a license is to be issued by this State, and

(5) The licensure requirements in the other state are equivalent to or higher than those required by this State.

(b) Application for license to be issued under the provisions of this section shall be accompanied by a certificate from the optometry board or like board of the state from which said applicant removed, certifying that the applicant is the legal holder of a license to practice optometry in that state, and for a period of at least three out of five years immediately preceding the application has engaged in the practice of optometry; is of good moral character and that during the period of his practice no charges have been filed with said board against the applicant for the violation of the criminal laws of the state or the United States, or for the violation of the ethics of the profession of optometry.

(c) Application for a license under this section shall be made to the North Carolina State Board of Examiners in Optometry within six months of the date of the issuance of the certificate hereinbefore required, and said certificate shall be accompanied by the diploma or other evidence of the graduation from an accredited, recognized and approved optometry college, school or optometry department of a college or university.

(d) Any license issued upon the application of any optometrist from any other state or territory shall be subject to all of the provisions of this Article with reference to the license issued by the North Carolina State Board of Examiners in Optometry upon examination of applicants and the rights and privileges to practice the profession of optometry under any license so issued shall be subject to the same duties, obligations, restrictions and the conditions as imposed by this Article on optometrists originally examined by the North Carolina State Board of Examiners in Optometry. (1973, c. 800, s. 12; 1981, c. 496, ss. 6, 7.)

§ 90-118.6. Certificate issued to optometrist moving out of State.

Any optometrist duly licensed by the North Carolina State Board of Examiners in Optometry, desiring to move from North Carolina to another state, territory or foreign country, if a holder of a certificate of renewal of license from said Board, upon application to said Board and the payment to it of the fee in this Article provided, shall be issued a certificate showing his full name and address, the date of license originally issued to him, the date and number of his renewal of license, and whether any charges have been filed with the Board against him. The Board may provide forms for such certificate, requiring such additional information as it may determine proper. (1973, c. 800, s. 13.)

§ 90-118.7. Licensing former optometrists who have moved back into State or resumed practice.

Any person who shall have been licensed by the North Carolina State Board of Examiners in Optometry to practice optometry in this State who shall have retired from practice or who shall have moved from the State and shall have returned to the State, may, upon a satisfactory showing to said Board of his proficiency in the profession of optometry and his good moral character during the period of his retirement, or absence from the State, be granted by said Board a license to resume the practice of optometry upon making application to the said Board in such form as it may require. The license to resume practice, after issuance thereof, shall be subject to all the provisions of this Article. (1973, c. 800, s. 14.)

§§ 90-118.8 through 90-118.9. Repealed by Session Laws 1981, c. 811, ss. 4, 5.

§ 90-118.10. Annual renewal of licenses.

Since the laws of North Carolina now in force provided for the annual renewal of any license issued by the North Carolina State Board of Examiners in Optometry, it is hereby declared to be the policy of this State that all licenses heretofore issued by the North Carolina State Board of Examiners in Optometry, or hereafter issued by said Board are subject to annual renewal and the exercise of any privilege granted by any license heretofore issued or hereafter issued by the North Carolina State Board of Examiners in Optometry is subject to the issuance on or before the first day of January of each year of a certificate of renewal of license.

On or before the first day of January of each year, each optometrist engaged in the practice of optometry in North Carolina shall make application to the North Carolina State Board of Examiners in Optometry and receive from said Board, subject to the further provisions of this section and of this Article, a certificate of renewal of said license.

The application shall show the serial number of the applicant's license, his full name, address and the county in which he has practiced during the preceding year, the date of the original issuance of license to said applicant and such other information as the said Board from time to time may prescribe by regulation.

If the application for such renewal certificate, accompanied by the fee required by this Article, is not received by the Board before January 31 of each year, an additional fee of fifty dollars ($50.00) shall be charged for renewal certificate. If such application accompanied by the renewal fee is not received by the Board before March 31 of each year, every person thereafter continuing to practice optometry without having applied for a certificate of renewal shall be guilty of the unauthorized practice of optometry and shall be subject to the penalties prescribed by G.S. 90-118.11.

In issuing a certificate of renewal, the Board shall expressly state whether such person, otherwise licensed in the practice of optometry, has been certified to prescribe and use pharmaceutical agents. (1973, c. 800, s. 17; c. 1092, s. 1; 1977, c. 482, s. 3; 1987, c. 645, s. 3.)

§ 90-118.11. Unauthorized practice; penalty for violation of Article.

If any person shall practice or attempt to practice optometry in this State without first having passed the examination and obtained a license from the North Carolina State Board of Examiners in Optometry; or without having obtained a provisional license from said Board; or if he shall practice optometry after March 31 of each year without applying for a certificate of renewal of license, as provided in G.S. 90-118.10; or shall practice or attempt to practice optometry while his license is revoked, or suspended, or when a certificate of renewal of license has been refused; or shall practice or attempt to practice optometry by means or methods that the Board has determined is beyond the scope of the person's educational training; or shall violate any of the provisions of this Article for which no specific penalty has been provided; or shall practice, or attempt to practice, optometry in violation of the provisions of this Article; or shall practice optometry under any name other than his own name, said person shall be guilty of a Class 1 misdemeanor. Each day's violation of this Article shall constitute a separate offense. (1973, c. 800, s. 18; 1977, c. 482, s. 4; 1981, c. 496, s. 10; 1993, c. 539, s. 628; 1994, Ex. Sess., c. 24, s. 14(c).)

§ 90-119. Persons in practice before passage of statute.

Every person who had been engaged in the practice of optometry in the State for two years prior to the date of the passage of this Article shall hereafter file an affidavit as proof thereof with the Board. The secretary shall keep a record of such persons who shall be exempt from the provisions of the preceding section [G.S. 90-118]. Upon payment of three dollars ($3.00) he shall issue to each of them certificates of registration without the necessity of an examination. Failure on the part of a person so entitled within six months of the enactment of this Article to make written application to the Board for the certificate of registration accompanied by a written statement, signed by him and duly verified before an officer authorized to administer oaths within this State, fully setting forth the grounds upon which he claims such certificate, shall be deemed a waiver of his right to a certificate under the provisions of this section. A person who has thus waived his right may obtain a certificate thereafter by successfully passing examination and paying a fee as provided herein. (1909, c. 444, ss. 6, 7, 9; C.S., s. 6692.)

§§ 90-120 through 90-121. Repealed by Session Laws 1973, c. 800, ss. 19, 20.

§ 90-121.1. Board may enjoin illegal practices.

In view of the fact that the illegal practice of optometry imminently endangers the public health and welfare, and is a public nuisance, the North Carolina State Board of Examiners in Optometry may, if it shall find that any person is violating any of the provisions of this Article, apply to the superior court for a temporary or permanent restraining order or injunction to restrain such person from continuing such illegal practices. If upon such application, it shall appear to the court that such person has violated, or is violating, the provisions of this Article, the court shall issue an order restraining any further violating thereof. All such actions by the Board for injunctive relief shall be governed by the provisions of Article 37 of Chapter 1 of the General Statutes: provided, such injunctive relief may be granted regardless of whether criminal prosecution has been or may be instituted under the provisions of G.S. 90-124. Actions under this section shall be commenced in the superior court district or set of districts as defined in G.S. 7A-41.1 in which the respondent resides or has his principal place of business. (1973, c. 800, s. 19; 1981, c. 496, s. 11; 1987 (Reg. Sess., 1988), c. 1037, s. 101.)

§ 90-121.2. Rules and regulations; discipline, suspension, revocation and regrant of certificate.

(a)   The Board shall have the power to make, adopt, and promulgate such rules and regulations, including rules of ethics, as may be necessary and proper for the regulation of the practice of the profession of optometry and for the performance of its duties. The Board shall have jurisdiction and power to hear and determine all complaints, allegations, charges of malpractice, corrupt or unprofessional conduct, and of the violation of the rules and regulations, including rules of ethics, made against any optometrist licensed to practice in North Carolina. The Board shall also have the power and authority to: (i) refuse to issue a license to practice optometry; (ii) refuse to issue a certificate of renewal of a license to practice optometry; (iii) revoke or suspend a license to practice optometry; and (iv) invoke such other disciplinary measures, censure, or probative terms against a licensee as it deems fit and proper; in any instance or instances in which the Board is satisfied that such applicant or licensee:

(1)   Has engaged in any act or acts of fraud, deceit or misrepresentation in obtaining or attempting to obtain a license or the renewal thereof;

(2)   Is a chronic or persistent user of intoxicants, drugs or narcotics to the extent that the same impairs his ability to practice optometry;

(3)   Has been convicted of any of the criminal provisions of this Article or has entered a plea of guilty or nolo contendere to any charge or charges arising therefrom;

(4)   Has been convicted of or entered a plea of guilty or nolo contendere to any felony charge or to any misdemeanor charge involving moral turpitude;

(5) Has been convicted of or entered a plea of guilty or nolo contendere to any charge of violation of any State or federal narcotic or barbiturate law;

(6) Has engaged in any act or practice violative of any of the provisions of this Article or violative of any of the rules and regulations promulgated and adopted by the Board, or has aided, abetted or assisted any other person or entity in the violation of the same;

(7) Is mentally, emotionally, or physically unfit to practice optometry or is afflicted with such a physical or mental disability as to be deemed dangerous to the health and welfare of his patients. An adjudication of mental incompetency in a court of competent jurisdiction or a determination thereof by other lawful means shall be conclusive proof of unfitness to practice optometry unless or until such person shall have been subsequently lawfully declared to be mentally competent;

(8) Repealed by Session Laws 1981, c. 496, s. 12.

(9) Has permitted the use of his name, diploma or license by another person either in the illegal practice of optometry or in attempting to fraudulently obtain a license to practice optometry;

(10) Has engaged in such immoral conduct as to discredit the optometry profession;

(11) Has obtained or collected or attempted to obtain or collect any fee through fraud, misrepresentation, or deceit;

(12) Has been negligent in the practice of optometry;

(13) Has employed a person not licensed in this State to do or perform any act of service, or has aided, abetted or assisted any such unlicensed person to do or perform any act or service which under this Article can lawfully be done or performed only by an optometrist licensed in this State;

(14) Is incompetent in the practice of optometry;

(15) Has practiced any fraud, deceit or misrepresentation upon the public or upon any individual in an effort to acquire or retain any patient or patients, including false or misleading advertising;

(16) Has made fraudulent or misleading statements pertaining to his skill, knowledge, or method of treatment or practice;

(17) Has committed any fraudulent or misleading acts in the practice of optometry;

(18) Repealed by Session Laws 1981, c. 496, s. 12.

(19) Has, in the practice of optometry, committed an act or acts constituting malpractice;

(20) Repealed by Session Laws 1981, c. 496, s. 12.

(21) Has permitted an optometric assistant in his employ or under his supervision to do or perform any act or acts violative to this Article or of the rules and regulations promulgated by the Board;

(22) Has wrongfully or fraudulently or falsely held himself out to be or represented himself to be qualified as a specialist in any branch of optometry;

(23) Has persistently maintained, in the practice of optometry, unsanitary offices, practices, or techniques;

(24) Is a menace to the public health by reason of having a serious communicable disease;

(25) Has engaged in any unprofessional conduct as the same may be from time to time defined by the rules and regulations of the Board.

In addition to and in conjunction with the actions described above, the Board may make a finding adverse to a licensee or applicant but withhold imposition of judgment and penalty or it may impose judgment and penalty but suspend enforcement thereof and place the licensee on probation, which probation may be vacated upon noncompliance with such reasonable terms as the Board may impose. The Board may administer a public or private reprimand or a private letter of concern, and the private reprimand and private letter of concern shall not require a hearing in accordance with G.S. 90-121.3 and shall not be disclosed to any person except the licensee. The Board may require a licensee to: (i) make specific redress or monetary redress; (ii) provide free public or charity service; (iii) complete educational, remedial training, or treatment programs; (iv) pay a fine; and (v) reimburse the Board for disciplinary costs.

(b) If any person engages in or attempts to engage in the practice of optometry while his license is suspended, his license to practice optometry in the State of North Carolina may be permanently revoked.

(c) The Board may, on its own motion, initiate the appropriate legal proceedings against any person, firm or corporation when it is made to appear to the Board that such person, firm or corporation has violated any of the provisions of this Article.

(d) The Board may appoint, employ or retain an investigator or investigators for the purpose of examining or inquiring into any practices committed in this State that might violate any of the provisions of this Article or any of the rules and regulations promulgated by the Board.

(e) The Board may employ or retain legal counsel for such matters and purposes as may seem fit and proper to said Board.

(f) As used in this section the term "licensee" includes licensees, provisional licensees and holders of intern permits, and the term "license" includes license, provisional license and intern permit.

(g) A person, partnership, firm, corporation, association, authority, or other entity acting in good faith without fraud or malice shall be immune from civil liability for (i) reporting or investigating the acts or omissions of a licensee or applicant that violate the provisions of subsection (a) of this section or any other provision of law relating to the fitness of a licensee or applicant to practice optometry and (ii) initiating or conducting proceedings against a licensee or applicant if a complaint is made or action is taken in good faith without fraud or malice. A person shall not be held liable in any civil proceeding for testifying before the Board in good faith and without fraud or malice in any proceeding involving a violation of subsection (a) of this section or any other law relating to the fitness of an applicant or licensee to practice optometry, or for making a recommendation to the Board in the nature of peer review, in good faith and without fraud and malice. (1973, c. 800, s. 20; 1981, c. 496, ss. 12, 13; 2000-184, s. 6.)

§ 90-121.3. Hearings.

(a) The Board shall grant any person whose license is affected the right to be heard before the Board, before any of the following action is finally taken, the effect of which would be:

(1) To deny permission to take an examination for licensing for which application has been duly made; or

(2) To deny a license after examination for any cause other than failure to pass an examination; or

(3) To withhold the renewal of a license for any cause other than failure to pay a statutory renewal fee; or

(4) To suspend a license; or

(5) To revoke a license; or

(6) To revoke or suspend a provisional license or an intern permit; or

(7) To invoke any other disciplinary measures, censure, or probative terms against a licensee, a provisional licensee, or an intern.

(b) Proceedings under this section shall be conducted in accordance with the provisions of Chapter 150B of the General Statutes of North Carolina.

(c) In lieu of or as a part of such hearings and subsequent proceedings the Board is authorized and empowered to enter any consent order relative to the discipline, censure, or probation of a licensee, an intern, or an applicant for a license, or relative to the revocation or suspension of a license, provisional license, or intern permit.

(d) Following the service of the notice of hearing as required by Chapter 150B of the General Statutes, the Board and the person upon whom such notice is served shall have the right to conduct adverse examinations, take depositions, and engage in such further discovery proceedings as are permitted by the laws of this State in civil matters. The Board is hereby authorized and empowered to issue such orders, commissions, notices, subpoenas, or other process as might be necessary or proper to effect the purposes of this subsection; provided, however, that no member of the Board shall be subject to examination hereunder. (1973, c. 800, s. 21; c. 1331, s. 3; 1987, c. 827, s. 1.)

§ 90-121.4. Restoration of revoked license.

Whenever any optometrist has been deprived of his license, the North Carolina State Board of Examiners in Optometry in its discretion may restore said license upon due notice being given and hearing had, and satisfactory evidence produced or proper reformation of the licentiate, before restoration. (1973, c. 800, s. 22.)

§ 90-121.5. Confidentiality of investigative information; cooperation with law enforcement; self-reporting requirements.

(a) The Board may, in a closed session, receive information or evidence involving or concerning the treatment of a patient who has not expressly or impliedly consented to the public disclosure of the treatment when necessary for the protection of the rights of the patient or the accused licensee and the full presentation of relevant evidence.

(b) All records, papers, investigative files, investigative notes, reports, other investigative information, and other documents containing information in the possession of or received, gathered, or completed by the Board, its members, staff, employees, attorneys, or consultants as a result of investigations, inquiries, assessments, or interviews conducted in connection with a license, complaint, assessment, potential impairment, disciplinary matter, or report of professional liability insurance awards or settlements shall not be considered public records within the meaning of Chapter 132 of the General Statutes. Such documents are privileged, confidential, and not subject to discovery, subpoena, or other means of legal compulsion for release to any person other than the Board or its employees or consultants involved in the application for licensure, impairment assessment, or discipline of a licensee, except as provided in this section. However, any notice or statement of charges against any licensee or applicant, any notice to any licensee or applicant of a hearing in any proceeding, or any decision rendered in connection with a hearing in any proceeding shall be a public record within the meaning of Chapter 132 of the General Statutes, notwithstanding that the documentation may contain information collected and compiled as a result of the investigation, inquiry, or hearing. Identifying information concerning the treatment of or delivery of services to a patient or client who has not consented to the public disclosure of the treatment or services may be deleted. If any record, paper, or other document containing information collected and compiled by or on behalf of the Board is received and admitted in evidence in any hearing before the Board, the documents shall be a public record within the meaning of Chapter 132 of the General Statutes, subject to any deletions of identifying information concerning the treatment of or delivery of professional services to a patient who has not consented to the public disclosure of the treatment or services.

For purposes of this subsection, "investigative information" includes (i) formal or informal complaints received or information relating to the identity of, or a report made by, another licensee or other person performing an expert review or similar analysis for the Board or (ii) transcripts of any deposition taken or affidavit or statement obtained by Board counsel in preparation for or anticipation of a hearing held pursuant to this Article but not admitted into evidence at the hearing.

(c) When the Board receives a complaint regarding a licensee's care of a patient, the Board shall determine whether there is reasonable cause to believe that a licensee has violated a statute or rule governing the practice of optometry. In making such determination, the Board shall provide the licensee with a copy of the complaint and ask for a response. If providing a copy of the complaint identifies an anonymous complainant or compromises the integrity of an investigation, the Board shall provide the licensee with a summary of all substantial elements of the complaint. Upon written request of a patient, the Board may provide the patient a licensee's written response to a complaint filed by the patient with the Board regarding the patient's care. Upon written request of a complainant, who is not the patient but is authorized by State and federal law to receive protected health information about the patient, the Board may provide the complainant a licensee's written response to a complaint filed with the Board regarding the patient's care.

(d) If information in the possession of the Board, its employees, or agents indicates that a crime may have been committed, the Board may report the information to the appropriate law enforcement agency or district attorney of the district in which the offense was committed.

(e) The Board shall cooperate with and assist a law enforcement agency or district attorney conducting a criminal investigation or prosecution of a licensee by providing information that is relevant to the criminal investigation or prosecution to the investigating agency or district attorney. Information disclosed by the Board to an investigative agency or district attorney remains confidential and may not be disclosed by the investigating agency except as necessary to further the investigation.

(f) All persons licensed under this Article shall self-report to the Board within 30 days of arrest or indictment any of the following:

(1) Any felony arrest or indictment.

(2) Any arrest for driving while impaired or driving under the influence.

(3) Any arrest or indictment for the possession, use, or sale of any controlled substance.

(g) The Board, its members, attorneys, and staff may release confidential or nonpublic information to any health care licensure board in this State or another state or authorized Department of Health and Human Services personnel with enforcement or investigative responsibilities about (i) the issuance, denial, annulment, suspension, revocation, or other public disciplinary action taken concerning a license, (ii) the voluntary surrender to the Board of a license by a licensee, including the reasons for the action, or (iii) any disciplinary action taken by the Board. The Board shall notify the licensee in writing within 60 days after the information is transmitted. A summary of the information that is being transmitted shall be furnished to the licensee. If the licensee requests in writing within 30 days after being notified that the information has been transmitted, the licensee shall be furnished a copy of all information transmitted but shall be liable for the reasonable expense of the copies. The notice or copies of the information shall not be provided if the information relates to an ongoing criminal investigation by any law enforcement agency or authorized Department of Health and Human Services personnel with enforcement or investigative responsibilities. (2011-336, s. 1.)

§ 90-121.6. Reporting and publication of judgments, awards, payments, and settlements.

(a) All optometrists licensed or applying for licensure by the Board shall report to the Board:

(1) All medical malpractice judgments or awards affecting or involving the optometrist.

(2) All settlements in the amount of seventy-five thousand dollars ($75,000) or more related to an incident of alleged medical malpractice affecting or involving the optometrist where the settlement occurred on or after May 1, 2008.

(3) All settlements in the aggregate amount of seventy-five thousand dollars ($75,000) or more related to any one incident of alleged medical malpractice affecting or involving the optometrist not already reported pursuant to subdivision (2) of this subsection where, instead of a single payment of seventy-five thousand dollars ($75,000) or more occurring on or after May 1, 2008, there is a series of payments made to the same claimant which, in the aggregate, equal or exceed seventy-five thousand dollars ($75,000).

(b) The report required under subsection (a) of this section shall contain the following information:

(1) The date of the judgment, award, payment, or settlement.

(2) The city, state, and country in which the incident occurred that resulted in the judgment, award, payment, or settlement.

(3) The date the incident occurred that resulted in the judgment, award, payment, or settlement.

(c) The Board shall publish on the Board's Web site or other publication information collected under this section. The Board shall publish this information for seven years from the date of the judgment, award, payment, or settlement. The Board shall not release or publish individually identifiable numeric values of the reported judgment, award, payment, or settlement. The Board shall not release or publish the identity of the patient associated with the judgment, award, payment, or settlement. The Board shall allow the optometrist to publish a statement explaining the circumstances that led to the judgment, award, payment, or settlement, and whether the case is under appeal. The Board shall ensure these statements:

(1) Conform to the ethics of optometry.

(2) Not contain individually identifiable numeric values of the judgment, award, payment, or settlement.

(3) Not contain information that would disclose the patient's identity.

(d) The term "settlement" for the purpose of this section includes a payment made from personal funds, a payment by a third party on behalf of the optometrist, or a payment from any other source of funds.

(e) Nothing in this section shall limit the Board from collecting information needed to administer this Article. (2011-336, s. 2.)

§ 90-122. Compensation and expenses of Board.

Notwithstanding G.S. 93B-5(a), each member of the North Carolina State Board of Examiners in Optometry shall receive as compensation for his services in the performance of his duties under this Article two hundred dollars ($200.00) for each day actually engaged in the performance of the duties of his office, and all legitimate and necessary expenses incurred in attending meetings of the said Board.

All per diem allowances and all expenses paid as provided in this section shall be paid upon vouchers drawn by the Executive Director of the Board in accordance with Board policy.

The Board is authorized and empowered to expend from funds collected such sum or sums as it may determine necessary in the administration and enforcement of this Article, and employ such personnel as it may deem requisite to assist in carrying out the administrative functions required by this Article and by the Board. (1909, c. 444, s. 11; C.S., s. 6695; 1923, c. 42, s. 4; 1935, c. 63; 1959, c. 574; 1973, c. 800, s. 23; 1979, c. 771, s. 3; 1987, c. 645, s. 2; 2001-493, s. 1.)

§ 90-123. Fees.

In order to provide the means of carrying out and enforcing the provisions of this Article and the duties of devolving upon the North Carolina State Board of Examiners in Optometry, the Board is authorized to charge and collect the following fees:

(1)....... Each application for general optometry examination............................ $800.00

(2)   Each general optometry license renewal, which fee shall be annually fixed by the Board, and not later than December 15 of each year written notice of the amount of the renewal fee shall be given to each optometrist licensed to practice in this State by mailing the notice to the last address of record with the Board of each such optometrist.. 300.00

(3)   Each certificate of license to a resident optometrist desiring to change to another state or territory... 300.00

(4)   Each license issued to a practitioner of another state or territory to practice in this State... 350.00

(5)   Each license to resume practice issued to an optometrist who has retired from the practice of optometry or who has removed from and returned to this State.. 350.00

(6)   Each application for registration as an optometric assistant or renewal thereof.. 100.00

(7)   Each application for registration as an optometric technician or renewal thereof.. 100.00

(8)   Each duplicate license or renewal thereof for each branch office... 100.00.

(1909, c. 444, s. 12; C.S., s. 6696; 1923, c. 42, s. 5; 1933, c. 492; 1937, c. 362, s. 1; 1959, c. 477; 1969, c. 624; 1973, c. 1092, s. 2; 1979, c. 771, ss. 1, 2; 1981, c. 909; 1987, c. 645, s. 1; 2001-493, s. 2.)

§ 90-123.1. Continuing education courses required.

All registered optometrists now or hereafter licensed in the State of North Carolina are and shall be required to take annual courses of study in subjects relating to the practice of the profession of optometry to the end that the utilization and application of new techniques, scientific and clinical advances, and the achievements of research will assure expansive and comprehensive care to the public. The length of study shall be prescribed by the Board but shall not exceed 25 hours in any calendar year. Attendance must be at a course or courses approved by the Board. Attendance at any course or courses of study are to be certified to the Board upon a form approved by the Board and shall be submitted by each registered optometrist at the time he makes application to the Board for the renewal of his license and payment of his renewal fee. The Board is authorized to use up to one half of its annual renewal fees for the purposes of contracting with institutions of higher learning, professional organizations, or qualified individuals for the providing of educational programs that meet this requirement. The Board is further authorized to treat funds set aside for the purpose of continuing education as State funds for the purpose of accepting any funds made available under federal law on a matching basis for the promulgation and maintenance of programs of continuing education. In no instance may the Board require a greater number of hours of study than are available at approved courses held within the State, and shall be allowed to waive this requirement in cases of certified illness or undue hardship. (1969, c. 354; 1981, c. 811, s. 3.)

§ 90-124. Rules and regulations of Board; violation a misdemeanor.

Rules and regulations adopted by the Board shall become effective 30 days after passage, and the same may be proven, as evidence, by the president and/or the secretary-treasurer of the Board, and/or by certified copy under the hand and seal of the secretary-treasurer. A certified copy of any rule or regulation shall be receivable in all courts as prima facie evidence thereof if otherwise competent, and any person, firm, or corporation violating any such rule or regulation shall be guilty of a Class 2 misdemeanor, and each day that this section is violated shall be considered a separate offense.

The Board shall issue every two years to each licensed optometrist a compilation or supplement of the Optometric Practice Act and the Board Rules and Regulations, and upon written request by such licensed optometrist, a directory of optometrists. (1909, c. 444, s. 13; C.S., s. 6697; 1935, c. 63; 1953, c. 189; c. 1041, s. 12; 1955, c. 996; 1973, c. 800, s. 24; 1993, c. 539, s. 629; 1994, Ex. Sess., c. 24, s. 14(c).)

§ 90-125. Practicing under other than own name or as a salaried or commissioned employee.

Except as provided for in Chapter 55B of the General Statutes of North Carolina, it shall be unlawful for any person licensed to practice optometry under the provisions of this Article to advertise, practice, or attempt to practice under a name other than his own, except as an associate of or assistant to an optometrist licensed under the laws of the State of North Carolina; and it shall be likewise unlawful for any corporation, lay body, organization, group, or lay individuals to engage, or undertake to engage, in the practice of optometry through means of engaging the services, upon a salary or commission basis, of one licensed to practice optometry or medicine in any of its branches in this State. Likewise, it shall be unlawful for any optometrist licensed under the provisions of this Article to undertake to engage in the practice of optometry as a salaried or commissioned employee of any corporation, lay body, organization, group, or lay individual. (1935, c. 63; 1937, c. 362, s. 2; 1969, c. 718, s. 16.)

§§ 90-126 through 90-126.1. Repealed by Session Laws 1973, c. 800, s. 26.

§ 90-127. Application of Article.

Nothing in this Article shall be construed to apply to physicians and surgeons authorized to practice under the laws of North Carolina, except the provisions contained in G.S. 90-125, or prohibit persons to sell spectacles, eyeglasses, or lenses as merchandise from permanently located and established places of business. (1909, c. 444, s. 15; C.S., s. 6699; 1937, c. 362, s. 3.)

§ 90-127.1. Free choice by patient guaranteed.

No agency of the State, county or municipality, nor any commission or clinic, nor any board administering relief, social security, health insurance or health service under the laws of the State of North Carolina shall deny to the recipients or beneficiaries of their aid or services the freedom to choose a duly licensed optometrist or duly licensed physician as the provider of care or services which are within the scope of practice of the profession of optometry as defined in this Chapter. (1965, c. 396, s. 3; 1973, c. 800, s. 25.)

§ 90-127.2. Filling prescriptions.

Legally licensed druggists of this State may fill prescriptions of optometrists duly licensed by the North Carolina State Board of Examiners in Optometry to prescribe, apply or use pharmaceutical agents. (1977, c. 482, s. 5.)

§ 90-127.3. Copy of prescription furnished on request.

All persons licensed or registered under this Chapter shall upon request give each patient having received an eye examination a copy of his spectacle prescription. No person, firm or corporation licensed or registered under Article 17 of this Chapter shall fill a prescription or dispense lenses, other than spectacle lenses, unless the prescription specifically states on its face that the prescriber intends it to be for contact lenses and includes the type and specifications of the contact lenses being prescribed. The prescriber shall state the expiration date on the face of every prescription, and the expiration date shall be no earlier than 365 days after the examination date.

Any person, firm or corporation that dispenses contact lenses on the prescription of a practitioner licensed under Articles 1 or 6 of this Chapter shall, at the time of delivery of the lenses, inform the recipient both orally and in writing that he return to the prescriber for insertion of the lens, instruction on lens insertion and care, and to ascertain the accuracy and suitability of the prescribed lens. The statement shall also state that if the recipient does not return to the prescriber after delivery of the lens for the purposes stated above, the prescriber shall not be responsible for any damages or injury resulting from the prescribed lens, except that this sentence does not apply if the dispenser and the prescriber are the same person.

Prescriptions filled pursuant to this section shall be kept on file by the prescriber and the person filling the prescription for at least 24 months after the prescription is filled. (1981, c. 496, s. 14.)

§ 90-128: Repealed by Session Laws 1973, c. 800, s. 26.

Article 6A.

Optometry Peer Review.

§ 90-128.1. Peer review agreements.

(a) The North Carolina State Board of Examiners in Optometry may, under rules adopted by the Board in compliance with Chapter 150B of the General Statutes, enter into agreements with the North Carolina State Optometric Society (Society), for the purpose of conducting peer review activities. Peer review activities to be covered by such agreements shall be limited in peer review proceedings to review of clinical outcomes as they relate to the quality of health care delivered by optometrists licensed by the Board.

(b) Peer review agreements shall include provisions for the Society to receive relevant information from the Board and other sources, provide assurance of confidentiality of nonpublic information and of the review process, and make reports to the Board. Peer review agreements shall include provisions assuring due process.

(c) Any confidential patient information and other nonpublic information acquired, created, or used in good faith by the Society pursuant to this section shall remain confidential and shall not be subject to discovery or subpoena in a civil case.

(d) Peer review activities conducted in good faith pursuant to any agreement under this section are deemed to be State directed and sanctioned and shall constitute State action for the purposes of application of antitrust laws. The Board shall be responsible for legal fees arising from peer review activities. (1997-75, s. 3.)

§§ 90-128.2 through 90-128.6. Reserved for future codification purposes.

Article 7.

Osteopathy.

§ 90-129: Repealed by Session Laws 2009-447, s. 2, effective August 7, 2009.

§ 90-130: Repealed by Session Laws 2009-447, s. 2, effective August 7, 2009.

§ 90-131: Repealed by Session Laws 2009-447, s. 2, effective August 7, 2009.

§ 90-132: Repealed by Session Laws 2009-447, s. 2, effective August 7, 2009.

§ 90-133: Repealed by Session Laws 2009-447, s. 2, effective August 7, 2009.

§ 90-134: Repealed by Session Laws 2009-447, s. 2, effective August 7, 2009.

§ 90-135: Repealed by Session Laws 2009-447, s. 2, effective August 7, 2009.

§ 90-136: Repealed by Session Laws 2009-447, s. 2, effective August 7, 2009.

§ 90-137: Repealed by Session Laws 2009-447, s. 2, effective August 7, 2009.

§ 90-138: Repealed by Session Laws 2009-447, s. 2, effective August 7, 2009.

Article 8.

Chiropractic.

§ 90-139. Creation and membership of Board of Examiners.

(a)   The State Board of Chiropractic Examiners is created to consist of eight members appointed by the Governor and General Assembly. Six of the members shall be practicing doctors of chiropractic, who are residents of this State and who have actively practiced chiropractic in the State for at least eight consecutive years immediately preceding their appointments; four of these six members shall be appointed by the Governor, and two by the General Assembly in accordance with G.S. 120-121, one each upon the recommendation of the President Pro Tempore of the Senate and the Speaker of the House of Representatives. No more than three members of the Board may be graduates of the same college or school of chiropractic. The other two members shall be persons chosen by the Governor to represent the public at large. The public members shall not be health care providers nor the spouses of health care providers. For purposes of Board membership, "health care provider" means any licensed health care professional and any agent or employee of any health care institution, health care insurer, health care professional school, or a member of any allied health profession. For purposes of this section, a person enrolled in a program to prepare him to be a licensed health care professional or an allied health professional shall be deemed a health care provider. For purposes of this section, any person with significant financial interest in a health service or profession is not a public member.

(b) All Board members serving on June 30, 1981, shall be eligible to complete their respective terms. No member appointed to the Board on or after July 1, 1981, shall serve more than two complete consecutive terms, except that each member shall serve until his successor is chosen and qualifies. The initial appointment of the General Assembly upon the recommendation of the President of the Senate shall be for a term to expire June 30, 1986, and the initial appointment of the General Assembly upon the recommendation of the Speaker of the House of Representatives shall be for a term to expire June 30, 1985, subsequent appointments upon the recommendation of the President Pro Tempore of the Senate shall be for terms of three years, subsequent appointments upon the recommendation of the Speaker of the House of Representatives shall be for terms of two years.

(c) The Governor and General Assembly, respectively, may remove any member appointed by them for good cause shown. In addition, upon the request of the Speaker of the House of Representatives or the President Pro Tempore of the Senate concerning a person appointed by the General Assembly upon the recommendation of the Speaker of the House of Representatives or the President Pro Tempore of the Senate, respectively, the Governor may remove such appointee for good cause shown, if the request is made and removal occurs either (i) when the General Assembly has adjourned to a date certain, which date is more than 10 days after the date of adjournment, or (ii) after sine die adjournment of the regular session. The Governor may appoint persons to fill vacancies of persons appointed by him to fill unexpired terms. Vacancies in appointments made by the General Assembly shall be in accordance with G.S. 120-122. (1917, c. 73, s. 1; C.S., s. 6710; 1979, c. 108, s. 1; 1981, c. 766, s. 1; 1983, c. 717, ss. 100-104; 1995, c. 490, s. 11; 1999-405, s. 3; 1999-431, s. 3.9; 2000-181, s. 2.7(a); 2005-421, s. 2.7(b).)

§ 90-140. Selection of chiropractic members of Board.

The Governor and the General Assembly upon the recommendation of the President Pro Tempore of the Senate shall appoint chiropractic members of the Board for terms of three years from a list provided by the Board, and the General Assembly upon the recommendation of the Speaker of the House of Representatives shall appoint a chiropractic member of the Board for a term of two years from a list provided by the Board. For each vacancy, the Board must submit at least three names to the Governor, President Pro Tempore of the Senate and Speaker of the House.

The Board shall establish procedures for the nomination and election of chiropractic members. These procedures shall be adopted under Article 2A of Chapter 150B of the General Statutes, and notice of the proposed procedures shall be given to all licensed chiropractors residing in North Carolina. These procedures shall not conflict with the provisions of this section. Every chiropractor with a current North Carolina license residing in this State shall be eligible to vote in all such elections, and the list of licensed chiropractors shall constitute the registration list for elections. Any decision of the Board relative to the conduct of such elections may be challenged by civil action in the Wake County Superior Court. A challenge must be filed not later than 30 days after the Board has rendered the decision in controversy, and all such cases shall be heard de novo. (1917, c. 73, s. 2; C.S., s. 6711; 1933, c. 442, s. 1; 1963, c. 646, s. 1; 1979, c. 108, s. 2; 1981, c. 766, s. 2; 1983, c. 717, s. 106; 1987, c. 827, s. 1; 1995, c. 490, s. 11.1; 2000-189, s. 6.)

§ 90-141. Organization; quorum.

The Board of Chiropractic Examiners shall elect such officers as they may deem necessary. Four members of the Board shall constitute a quorum for the transaction of business. (1917, c. 73, s. 4; C.S., s. 6713; 1933, c. 442, s. 1; 1981, c. 766, s. 3.)

§ 90-142. Rules and regulations.

The State Board of Chiropractic Examiners may adopt suitable rules and regulations for the performance of their duties and the enforcement of the provisions of this Article. (1919, c. 148, s. 4; C.S., s. 6714; 1967, c. 263, s. 2.)

§ 90-143. Definitions of chiropractic; examinations; educational requirements.

(a) "Chiropractic" is herein defined to be the science of adjusting the cause of disease by realigning the spine, releasing pressure on nerves radiating from the spine to all parts of the body, and allowing the nerves to carry their full quota of health current (nerve energy) from the brain to all parts of the body.

(b) It shall be the duty of the North Carolina State Board of Chiropractic Examiners (hereinafter referred to as "Board") to examine for licensure to practice chiropractic in this State any applicant who is or will become, within 60 days of examination, a graduate of a four-year chiropractic college that is either accredited by the Council on Chiropractic Education or deemed by the Board to be the equivalent of such a college and who furnishes to the Board, in the manner prescribed by the Board, all of the following:

(1) Satisfactory evidence of good moral character.

(2) Proof that the applicant has received a baccalaureate degree from a college or university accredited by a regional accreditation body recognized by the United States Department of Education.

(3) A transcript confirming that the applicant has received at least 4,200 hours of accredited chiropractic education. The Board shall not count any hours earned at an institution that was not accredited by the Council on Chiropractic Education or was not, as determined by the Board, the equivalent of such an institution at the time the hours were earned.

The examination shall include the following studies: neurology, chemistry, pathology, anatomy, histology, physiology, embryology, dermatology, diagnosis, microscopy, gynecology, hygiene, eye, ear, nose and throat, orthopody, diagnostic radiology, North Carolina jurisprudence, palpation, nerve tracing, chiropractic philosophy, theory, teaching and practice of chiropractic, and any other related studies as the Board may consider necessary to determine an applicant's fitness to practice. The Board may include as part of the examination any examination developed and administered by the National Board of Chiropractic Examiners or its successor organization that the Board considers appropriate, and the examination may be administered by a national testing service. The Board shall set the passing scores for all parts of the examination.

(c) The Board shall not issue a license to any applicant until the applicant exhibits a diploma or other proof that the Doctor of Chiropractic degree has been conferred.

(d) The Board may grant a license to an applicant if the applicant's scores on all parts of the examination required by the Board equal or exceed passing scores set by the Board and the applicant satisfies all other requirements for licensure as provided in this Article. (1917, c. 73, s. 5; 1919, c. 148, ss. 1, 2, 5; C.S., s. 6715; 1933, c. 442, s. 1; 1937, c. 293, s. 1; 1963, c. 646, s. 2; 1967, c. 263, s. 3; 1977, c. 1109, s. 1; 1981, c. 766, s. 4; 1987, c. 304; 1989, c. 555, ss. 2, 3, 4; 1997-230, s. 1; 2003-155, s. 1.)

§ 90-143.1. Applicants licensed in other states.

If an applicant for licensure is already licensed in another state to practice chiropractic, the Board shall issue a license to practice chiropractic to the applicant upon evidence that:

(1) The applicant is currently an active, competent practitioner and is in good standing; and

(2) The applicant has practiced at least one year out of the three years immediately preceding his or her application; and

(3) The applicant currently holds a valid license in another state; and

(4) No disciplinary proceeding or unresolved complaint is pending anywhere at the time a license is to be issued by this State; and

(5) The licensure requirements in the other state are equivalent to or higher than those required by this State.

Any license issued upon the application of any chiropractor from any other state shall be subject to all of the provisions of this Article with reference to the license issued by the State Board of Chiropractic Examiners upon examination, and the rights and privileges to practice the profession of chiropractic under any license so issued shall be subject to the same duties, obligations, restrictions, and conditions as imposed by this Article on chiropractors originally examined by the State Board of Chiropractic Examiners. (1981, c. 766, s. 5.)

§ 90-143.2. Certification of diagnostic imaging technicians.

(a) The State Board of Chiropractic Examiners shall certify the competence of any person employed by a licensed chiropractor practicing in the State if the employee's duties include the production of diagnostic images, whether by X ray or other imaging technology. Applicants for certification must demonstrate proficiency in the following subjects:

(1) Physics and equipment of radiographic imaging;

(2) Principles of radiographic exposure;

(3) Radiographic protection;

(4) Anatomy and physiology;

(5) Radiographic positioning and procedure.

The State Board of Chiropractic Examiners may adopt rules pertaining to initial educational requirements, examination of applicants, and continuing education requirements as are reasonably required to enforce this provision.

(b) Any person seeking to renew a certification of competence previously issued by the Board shall pay to the secretary of the Board a fee as prescribed and set by the Board which fee shall not be more than fifty dollars ($50.00). (1991, c. 633, s. 1; 2002-59, s. 1.)

§ 90-143.3. Criminal record checks of applicants for licensure.

(a) Any person applying for licensure as a chiropractic physician in this State shall provide to the Board a fingerprint card in a format acceptable to the Board and a form signed by the applicant consenting to a criminal record check and the use of the applicant's fingerprints and such other identifying information as may be required by the State or national data banks. The Board shall submit these documents to the Department of Justice, along with a request for a criminal record check of the applicant.

(b) Upon receipt of the Board's submission, the Department of Justice shall commence the requested criminal record check. The Department of Justice shall forward a set of the applicant's fingerprints to the State Bureau of

Investigation for a search of the State's criminal records, and the State Bureau of Investigation shall forward a set of the applicant's fingerprints to the Federal Bureau of Investigation for a search of national criminal records. The Department of Justice may charge the licensure applicant a fee for performing the criminal record check.

(c) The Board shall keep all information obtained from criminal record checks privileged and confidential, in accordance with applicable State law and federal guidelines, and the information shall not be a public record under Chapter 132 of the General Statutes. If the Board refuses to issue a license based in whole or part on information obtained from a criminal record check, the Board may disclose the relevant information to the applicant but shall not provide a copy of the record check to the applicant.

(d) When acting in good faith and in conformity with this section, the Board, its officers, and employees shall be immune from civil liability for initially refusing licensure based on information contained in a criminal record check supplied by the Department of Justice, even if the information relied upon is later shown to be erroneous. (2007-525, s. 1.)

§ 90-143.4. (Effective July 1, 2014) Chiropractic clinical assistants; certification of competency.

(a) "Chiropractic clinical assistant" means a nonlicensed employee of a chiropractic physician whose duties include (i) collecting general health data, such as the taking of an oral history or vital sign measurements, (ii) applying therapeutic procedures, such as thermal, sound, light and electrical modalities, and hydrotherapy, and (iii) monitoring prescribed rehabilitative activities. Nothing in this section shall be construed to allow a chiropractic clinical assistant to provide a chiropractic adjustment, manual therapy, nutritional instruction, counseling, or any other therapeutic service that requires individual licensure.

(b) Any person employed as a chiropractic clinical assistant shall obtain a certificate of competency from the State Board of Chiropractic Examiners (Board) within 120 days after the person begins employment. Certification shall not be required for employees whose duties are limited to administrative activities of a nonclinical nature. Except as otherwise provided in this section, it shall be unlawful for any person to practice as a chiropractic clinical assistant unless duly certified by the Board.

(c)   An applicant for certification under this section shall be (i) at least 18 years of age, (ii) a high school graduate or the equivalent, (iii) of good moral character, and (iv) able to demonstrate proficiency in the following subjects:

(1)   Basic anatomy.

(2)   Chiropractic philosophy and terminology.

(3)   Utilization of standard therapeutic modalities.

(4)   Contraindications and response to emergencies.

(5)   Jurisprudence and patient privacy protection.

(d)   If an applicant for certification is already certified or registered as a chiropractic clinical assistant in another state, the Board shall issue a certificate of competency upon evidence that the applicant is in good standing in the other state, provided the requirements for certification or registration in the other state are substantially similar to or more stringent than the requirements for certification in this State.

(e)   Any certificate issued under this section shall expire at the end of the calendar year unless renewed in a time and manner established by the Board. Applicants for initial certification or renewal of certification shall pay to the secretary of the Board a fee as prescribed and set by the Board, which fee shall not exceed fifty dollars ($50.00).

(f)   The Board may adopt rules pertaining to initial educational requirements, course approval, instructor credentials, examination of applicants, grandfathering, reciprocity, continuing education requirements, and the submission and processing of applications as are reasonably necessary to enforce this section. (2013-290, s. 1.)

§ 90-144. Meetings of Board of Examiners.

The North Carolina Board of Chiropractic Examiners shall meet at least once a year at such time and place as said Board shall determine at which meetings applicants for license shall be examined. (1917, c. 73, s. 6; C.S., s. 6716; 1933, c. 442, s. 1; 1949, c. 785, s. 1; 1985, c. 760, s. 1.)

§ 90-145. Grant of license.

The Board of Chiropractic Examiners shall grant to each applicant who is found to be competent, upon examination, a license authorizing him or her to practice chiropractic in North Carolina. (1917, c. 73, s. 7; C.S., s. 6717; 1949, c. 785, s. 2; 1981, c. 766, s. 6.)

§ 90-146. Graduates from other states.

A graduate of a regular chiropractic school who comes into this State from another state may be granted a license by the Board of Examiners as required in this Article. (1917, c. 73, s. 8; C.S., s. 6718.)

§ 90-147. Practice without license a misdemeanor; injunctions.

Any person practicing chiropractic in this State without possessing a license as provided in this Article shall be guilty of a Class 1 misdemeanor.

The Board of Chiropractic Examiners may appear in its own name in the superior court in an action for injunctive relief to prevent violation of this section, and the superior court shall have the power to grant such injunction regardless of whether criminal prosecution has been or may be instituted. An action under this section shall be commenced in the superior court district in which the respondent resides or has his principal place of business or in which the alleged violation occurred. (1917, c. 73, s. 9; C.S., s. 6719; 1993, c. 539, s. 631; 1994, Ex. Sess., c. 24, s. 14(c); 2001-281, s. 4.)

§ 90-148. Records of Board.

The secretary of the Board of Chiropractic Examiners shall keep a record of the proceedings of the Board, giving the name of each applicant for license, and the name of each applicant licensed and the date of such license. (1917, c. 73, s. 10; C.S., s. 6720.)

§ 90-149. Application fee.

Each applicant shall pay the secretary of the Board a fee as prescribed and set by the Board which fee shall not be more than three hundred dollars ($300.00). (1917, c. 73, s. 11; C.S., s. 6721; 1977, c. 922, s. 1; 2001-493, s. 6.)

§ 90-150. Repealed by Session Laws 1967, c. 218, s. 4.

§ 90-151. Extent and limitation of license.

Any person obtaining a license from the Board of Chiropractic Examiners shall have the right to practice the science known as chiropractic, in accordance with the method, thought, and practice of chiropractors, as taught in recognized chiropractic schools and colleges, but shall not prescribe for or administer to any person any medicine or drugs, nor practice osteopathy or surgery. (1917, c. 73, s. 12; C.S., s. 6722; 1933, c. 442, s. 3.)

§ 90-151.1. Selling nutritional supplements to patients.

A chiropractic physician may sell nutritional supplements at a chiropractic office to a patient as part of the patient's plan of treatment but may not otherwise sell nutritional supplements at a chiropractic office. A chiropractic physician who sells nutritional supplements to a patient must keep a record of the sale that complies with G.S. 105-164.24, except that the record may not disclose the name of the patient. (1997-369, s. 1.)

§ 90-152. Repealed by Session Laws 1967, c. 691, s. 59.

§ 90-153. Licensed chiropractors may practice in public hospitals.

A licensed chiropractor in this State may have access to and practice chiropractic in any hospital or sanitarium in this State that receives aid or support from the public, and shall have access to diagnostic X-ray records and laboratory records relating to the chiropractor's patient. (1919, c. 148, s. 3; C.S., s. 6724; 1977, c. 1109, s. 2.)

§ 90-154. Grounds for professional discipline.

(a) The Board of Chiropractic Examiners may impose any of the following sanctions, singly or in combination, when it finds that a practitioner or applicant is guilty of any offense described in subsection (b):

(1) Permanently revoke a license to practice chiropractic;

(2) Suspend a license to practice chiropractic;

(3) Refuse to grant a license;

(4) Censure a practitioner;

(5) Issue a letter of reprimand;

(6) Place a practitioner on probationary status and require him to report regularly to the Board upon the matters which are the basis of probation.

(b) Any one of the following is grounds for disciplinary action by the Board under subsection (a):

(1) Advertising services in a false or misleading manner.

(2) Conviction of a felony or of a crime involving moral turpitude.

(3) Addiction to or severe dependency upon alcohol or any other drug that impairs the ability to practice safely.

(4) Unethical conduct as defined in G.S. 90-154.2.

(5) Negligence, incompetence, or malpractice in the practice of chiropractic.

(6) Repealed by Session Laws 1995, c. 188, s. 1.

(7) Not rendering acceptable care in the practice of the profession as defined in G.S. 90-154.3.

(8) Lewd or immoral conduct toward a patient.

(9) Committing or attempting to commit fraud, deception, or misrepresentation.

(10) Offering to waive a patient's obligation to pay any deductible or copayment required by the patient's insurer.

(11) Failing to honor promptly a patient's request for a copy of any claim form submitted to the patient's insurer.

(12) Rebating or offering to rebate to a patient any portion of the funds received from the patient's insurer, unless the sum rebated constitutes the refund of an overpayment to which the patient is lawfully entitled.

(13) Advertising any free or reduced rate service without prominently stating in the advertisement the usual fee for that service.

(14) Charging an insurer or other third-party payor a fee greater than a patient would be charged for the same service if the patient were paying directly.

(15) Charging an insurer or other third-party payor a fee greater than the advertised fee for the same service.

(16) Violating the provisions of G.S. 90-154.1.

(17) Physical, mental, or emotional infirmity of such severity as to impair the ability to practice safely.

(18) Violating the provisions of G.S. 90-151 regarding the extent and limitation of license.

(19) Concealing information from the Board or failing to respond truthfully and completely to an inquiry from the Board concerning any matter affecting licensure.

(20) Failing to comply with a decision of the Board that is final.

(21) Committing an act on or after October 1, 2007, which demonstrates a lack of good moral character which would have been a basis for denying a license under G.S. 90-143(b)(1), had it been committed before application for a license.

(c) If a licensee is found guilty in a contested case arising under subsection (b) of this section, the Board may assess the licensee the reasonable cost of the hearing held to make such a determination if the Board finds that the licensee's defense at the hearing was dilatory or not asserted in good faith. (1917, c. 73, s. 14; C.S., s. 6725; 1949, c. 785, s. 3; 1963, c. 646, s. 3; 1981, c. 766, s. 7; 1983 (Reg. Sess., 1984), c. 1067, s. 1; 1985, c. 367, ss. 1, 2; c. 760, ss. 2, 3; 1995, c. 188, s. 1; 1999-430, s. 1; 2007-525, s. 4.)

§ 90-154.1. Collection of certain fees prohibited.

(a) Any patient or any other person responsible for payment has the right to refuse to pay, cancel payment, or be reimbursed for payment for any service, examination, or treatment other than the advertised reduced rate service, examination or treatment which is performed as a result of and within 72 hours of responding to any advertisement for a free or reduced rate service, free or reduced rate examination, or free or reduced rate treatment. Any further treatment shall be agreed upon in writing and signed by both parties.

(b) Any chiropractic advertisement that offers a free or reduced rate service, examination or treatment shall contain the following notice to prospective patients: "If you decide to purchase additional treatment, you have the legal right to change your mind within three days and receive a refund." If the advertisement is published in print, the foregoing notice shall appear in capital letters clearly distinguishable from the rest of the text. If the advertisement is broadcast on radio or television, the foregoing notice shall be recited at the end of the advertisement.

(c) Repealed by Session Laws 1995, c. 188, s. 2.

(d) Any bill sent to a patient or any other person responsible for payment as a result of the patient responding to a chiropractic advertisement shall clearly contain the language of the first sentence of subsection (a) and have distinguished on its face the charge for the reduced rate services, including an itemization of free services, and the separate charge for any services, examinations or treatments other than the advertised free or reduced rate services, examinations, or treatments. The reduced rate charges shall be labeled "Free or Reduced Rate Charges" and any other charges shall be labeled "Non-advertised Services, Examinations, or Treatments". (1985, c. 367, s. 3; 1987, c. 733; 1995, c. 188, s. 2.)

§ 90-154.2. Unethical conduct.

Unethical conduct is defined as:

(1) The over-utilization or improper use, in the providing of treatment, physiological therapeutics, radiographics, or any other service not commensurate with the stated diagnosis and clinical findings. This determination shall be based upon the collective findings and experience of the Board utilizing the best available, relative information and advice. There must be a rationale for the services provided the patient.

(2) The billing or otherwise charging of a fee to a third party payor for a service offered by the doctor as a free service, which service is accepted as a free service by any patient when, in fact, the doctor of chiropractic is transmitting any charge to a third-party payor for payment.

(3) The over-utilization of ionizing radiation in the re-X-ray of a patient. The acceptable guidelines for re-X-ray are:

a. When fractures are evident;

b. When bone pathologies are under evaluation;

c. When soft tissue pathologies are under evaluation;

d. When there is reinjury;

e. When the original X-ray findings have revealed limitations of ranges and motion, re-X-ray may be done after clinical progress has revealed objective improvement, but not within 12 days and only limited views would be indicated.

(4) Any licensee's failure to use the words Chiropractic Physician, Chiropractor or the initials D.C. in conjunction with the use of his name in his capacity as a Chiropractor on all reports, statements of claim for services rendered and on all signs, letterheads, business cards, advertising, and any other items of identification.

(5) Violation of the Rules of Ethics of Advertising and Publicity.

(6) The allowance of any unlicensed person to practice chiropractic in the office of a licensed chiropractic. (1985, c. 760, s. 4.)

§ 90-154.3. Acceptable care in the practice of chiropractic.

(a) It shall be unlawful for a doctor of chiropractic to examine, treat, or render any professional service to a patient that does not conform to the standards of acceptable care.

(b) For purposes of disciplinary action, the Board of Chiropractic Examiners may adopt rules that establish and define standards of acceptable care with respect to:

(1) Examination and diagnosis;

(2) The use of chiropractic adjustive procedures;

(3) Physiological therapeutic agents;

(4) Diagnostic radiology;

(5) The maintenance of patient records; and

(6) Sanitation, safety, and the adequacy of clinical equipment.

(c) If the Board has not defined a standard of acceptable care by rule, then the standard of acceptable care shall be the usual and customary method as taught in the majority of recognized chiropractic colleges.

(d) Nothing in this section shall alter the lawful scope of practice of chiropractic as defined in G.S. 90-143 or the limitation of license as defined in G.S. 90-151. (1985, c. 760, s. 5; 1995, c. 188, s. 3.)

§ 90-154.4. Enticements prohibited.

(a) For purposes of this section, an enticement is anything of monetary value offered by a chiropractor to a prospective patient as an incentive to enter treatment. Except as permitted in subsection (b) of this section, it shall be an unlawful rebate, in violation of G.S. 90-154(b)(12), for a chiropractor to offer an enticement to a prospective patient if, at the time the offer is made, the chiropractor knows or has reason to believe that the prospective patient's treatment expenses will be paid in whole or part by an insurer or other third-party payor.

(b) Unless prohibited by other State or federal law, the following marketing practices shall not be construed as violations of subsection (a) of this section:

(1) Free or reduced rates, services, examinations, or treatments advertised and delivered in conformity with G.S. 90-154.1.

(2) Cash or point-of-service discounts not more than 30 percentage points lower than the charges customarily billed to third-party payors.

(3) Prepaid wellness plans covering only services that can be performed entirely by the offering chiropractor or the chiropractor's staff within the confines of the chiropractor's office.

(4) Merchandise with a value of not more than ten dollars ($10.00) given to a prospective patient for promotional purposes. (2007-525, s. 3.)

§ 90-155. Annual fee for renewal of license.

Any person practicing chiropractic in this State, in order to renew his license, shall, on or before the first Tuesday after the first Monday in January in each year after a license is issued to him as herein provided, pay to the secretary of the Board of Chiropractic Examiners a renewal license fee as prescribed and set by the said Board which fee shall not be more than one hundred fifty dollars ($150.00), and shall furnish the Board evidence that he has attended two days of educational sessions or programs approved by the Board during the preceding 12 months, provided the Board may waive this educational requirement due to sickness or other hardship of applicant.

Any license or certificate granted by the Board under this Article shall automatically be canceled if the holder thereof fails to secure a renewal within 30 days from the time herein provided; but any license thus canceled may, upon evidence of good moral character and proper proficiency, be restored upon the payment of the renewal fee and an additional twenty-five dollars ($25.00) reinstatement fee.

If any licensee of the Board retires from active practice, the licensee may renew his license annually by paying the license fee and shall not be required to furnish the Board proof of continuing education; however, if at a later time the licensee desires to resume active practice, the licensee shall first appear before the Board and the Board shall determine his competency to practice. (1917, c. 73, s. 15; C.S., s. 6726; 1933, c. 442, s. 4; 1937, c. 293, s. 2; 1963, c. 646, s. 4; 1971, c. 715; 1977, c. 922, ss. 2, 3; 1985, c. 760, s. 6; 2001-493, s. 4.)

§ 90-156. Pay of Board and authorized expenditures.

Notwithstanding G.S. 93B-5(a), the members of the Board of Chiropractic Examiners shall receive as compensation for their services a sum not to exceed two hundred dollars ($200.00) for each day during which they are engaged in the official business of the Board and their actual expenses, including transportation and lodging, when meeting for the purpose of holding examinations, and performing any other duties placed upon them by this Article, to be paid by the treasurer of the Board out of the moneys received by him as license fees, or from renewal fees. The Board shall also expend out of such fund so much as may be necessary for preparing licenses, securing seal, providing for programs for licensed doctors of chiropractic in North Carolina, and all other necessary expenses in connection with the duties of the Board. (1917, c. 73, s. 16; C.S., s. 6727; 1949, c. 785, s. 4; 1981, c. 766, s. 8; 2001-493, s. 5.)

§ 90-157. Chiropractors subject to State and municipal regulations.

Chiropractors shall observe and be subject to all State and municipal regulations relating to the control of contagious and infectious diseases. (1917, c. 73, s. 17; C.S., s. 6728.)

§ 90-157.1. Free choice by patient guaranteed.

No agency of the State, county or municipality, nor any commission or clinic, nor any board administering relief, social security, health insurance or health service under the laws of the State of North Carolina shall deny to the recipients or beneficiaries of their aid or services the freedom to choose a duly licensed chiropractor as the provider of care or services which are within the scope of practice of the profession of chiropractic as defined in this Chapter. (1977, c. 1109, s. 3.)

§ 90-157.2. Chiropractor as expert witness.

A Doctor of Chiropractic, for all legal purposes, shall be considered an expert in his field and, when properly qualified, may testify in a court of law as to:

(1)   The etiology, diagnosis, prognosis, and disability, including anatomical, neurological, physiological, and pathological considerations within the scope of chiropractic, as defined in G.S. 90-151; and

(2)   The physiological dynamics of contiguous spinal structures which can cause neurological disturbances, the chiropractic procedure preparatory to, and complementary to the correction thereof, by an adjustment of the articulations of the vertebral column and other articulations. (1977, c. 1109, s. 3; 1989, c. 555, s. 1.)

§ 90-157.3. Ownership of chiropractic practices limited.

(a) Each partner in a partnership that is engaged in the practice of chiropractic shall be licensed under this Article.

(b) Each general partner in a limited partnership that is engaged in the practice of chiropractic and each limited partner who takes part in the control of the practice shall be licensed under this Article.

(c) The provisions of Chapter 55B of the General Statutes shall apply to all business corporations organized under Chapter 55 of the General Statutes and engaged in the practice of chiropractic. (1999-430, s. 2.)

Article 9.

Nurse Practice Act.

§§ 90-158 through 90-171.18: Recodified as §§ 90-171.19 through 90-171.47.

§ 90-171.19. Legislative findings.

The General Assembly of North Carolina finds that mandatory licensure of all who engage in the practice of nursing is necessary to ensure minimum standards of competency and to provide the public safe nursing care. (1981, c. 360, s. 1.)

§ 90-171.20. Definitions.

As used in this Article, unless the context requires otherwise:

(1) "Board" means the North Carolina Board of Nursing.

(2) "Health care provider" means any licensed health care professional and any agent or employee of any health care institution, health care insurer, health

care professional school, or a member of any allied health profession. For purposes of this Article, a person enrolled in a program that prepares the person to be a licensed health care professional or an allied health professional shall be deemed a health care provider.

(3) "License" means a permit issued by the Board to practice nursing as a registered nurse or as a licensed practical nurse, including a renewal thereof.

(4) "Nursing" is a dynamic discipline which includes the assessing, caring, counseling, teaching, referring and implementing of prescribed treatment in the maintenance of health, prevention and management of illness, injury, disability or the achievement of a dignified death. It is ministering to; assisting; and sustained, vigilant, and continuous care of those acutely or chronically ill; supervising patients during convalescence and rehabilitation; the supportive and restorative care given to maintain the optimum health level of individuals, groups, and communities; the supervision, teaching, and evaluation of those who perform or are preparing to perform these functions; and the administration of nursing programs and nursing services. For purposes of this Article, the administration of required lethal substances or any assistance whatsoever rendered with an execution under Article 19 of Chapter 15 of the General Statutes does not constitute nursing.

(5) "Nursing program" means any educational program in North Carolina offering to prepare persons to meet the educational requirements for licensure under this Article.

(6) "Person" means an individual, corporation, partnership, association, unit of government, or other legal entity.

(7) The "practice of nursing by a registered nurse" consists of the following 10 components:

a. Assessing the patient's physical and mental health, including the patient's reaction to illnesses and treatment regimens.

b. Recording and reporting the results of the nursing assessment.

c. Planning, initiating, delivering, and evaluating appropriate nursing acts.

d. Teaching, assigning, delegating to or supervising other personnel in implementing the treatment regimen.

e. Collaborating with other health care providers in determining the appropriate health care for a patient but, subject to the provisions of G.S. 90-18.2, not prescribing a medical treatment regimen or making a medical diagnosis, except under supervision of a licensed physician.

f. Implementing the treatment and pharmaceutical regimen prescribed by any person authorized by State law to prescribe the regimen.

g. Providing teaching and counseling about the patient's health.

h. Reporting and recording the plan for care, nursing care given, and the patient's response to that care.

i. Supervising, teaching, and evaluating those who perform or are preparing to perform nursing functions and administering nursing programs and nursing services.

j. Providing for the maintenance of safe and effective nursing care, whether rendered directly or indirectly.

(8) The "practice of nursing by a licensed practical nurse" consists of the following seven components:

a. Participating in the assessment of the patient's physical and mental health, including the patient's reaction to illnesses and treatment regimens.

b. Recording and reporting the results of the nursing assessment.

c. Participating in implementing the health care plan developed by the registered nurse and/or prescribed by any person authorized by State law to prescribe such a plan, by performing tasks assigned or delegated by and performed under the supervision or under orders or directions of a registered nurse, physician licensed to practice medicine, dentist, or other person authorized by State law to provide the supervision.

c1. Assigning or delegating nursing interventions to other qualified personnel under the supervision of the registered nurse.

d. Participating in the teaching and counseling of patients as assigned by a registered nurse, physician, or other qualified professional licensed to practice in North Carolina.

e. Reporting and recording the nursing care rendered and the patient's response to that care.

f. Maintaining safe and effective nursing care, whether rendered directly or indirectly. (1981, c. 360, s. 1; 2001-98, s. 1; 2013-154, s. 1(d).)

§ 90-171.21. Board of Nursing; composition; selection; vacancies; qualifications; term of office; compensation.

(a) The Board shall consist of 14 members. Eight members shall be registered nurses. Three members shall be licensed practical nurses. Three members shall be representatives of the public.

(b) Selection. - The North Carolina Board of Nursing shall conduct an election each year to fill vacancies of nurse members of the Board scheduled to occur during the next year. Nominations of candidates for election of registered nurse members shall be made by written petition signed by not less than 10 registered nurses eligible to vote in the election. Nominations of candidates for election of licensed practical nurse members shall be made by written petition signed by not less than 10 licensed practical nurses eligible to vote in the election. Every licensed registered nurse holding an active license shall be eligible to vote in the election of registered nurse board members. Every licensed practical nurse holding an active license shall be eligible to vote in the election of licensed practical nurse board members. The list of nominations shall be filed with the Board after January 1 of the year in which the election is to be held and no later than midnight of the first day of April of such year. Before preparing ballots, the Board shall notify each person who has been duly nominated of the person's nomination and request permission to enter the person's name on the ballot. A member of the Board who is nominated for reelection and who does not withdraw the member's name from the ballot is disqualified to participate in conducting the election. Elected members shall begin their term of office on January 1 of the year following their election.

Nominations of persons to serve as public members of the Board may be made to the Governor or the General Assembly by any citizen or group within the State. The Governor shall appoint one public member to the Board, and the General Assembly shall appoint two public members to the Board. Of the public members appointed by the General Assembly, one shall be appointed by the General Assembly upon the recommendation of the President Pro Tempore of the Senate, and one shall be appointed by the General Assembly upon the recommendation of the Speaker of the House of Representatives.

Board members shall be commissioned by the Governor upon their election or appointment.

(c) Vacancies. - All unexpired terms of Board members appointed by the General Assembly shall be filled within 45 days after the term is vacated. The Governor shall fill all other unexpired terms on the Board within 30 days after the term is vacated. For vacancies of registered nurse or licensed practical nurse members, the Governor shall appoint the person who received the next highest number of votes to those elected members at the most recent election for board members. Appointees shall serve the remainder of the unexpired term and until their successors have been duly elected or appointed and qualified.

(d) Qualifications. - Of the eight registered nurse members on the Board, one shall be a nurse administrator employed by a hospital or a hospital system, who shall be accountable for the administration of nursing services and not directly involved in patient care; one shall be an individual who meets the requirements to practice as a certified registered nurse anesthetist, a certified nurse midwife, a clinical nurse specialist, or a nurse practitioner; two shall be staff nurses, defined as individuals who are primarily involved in direct patient care regardless of practice setting; one shall be an at-large registered nurse who meets the requirements of sub-subdivisions (1) a., a1., and b. of this subsection, but is not currently an educator in a program leading to licensure or any other degree-granting program; and three shall be nurse educators. Minimum ongoing employment requirements for every registered nurse and licensed practical nurse shall include continuous employment equal to or greater than fifty percent (50%) of a full-time position that meets the criteria for the specified Board member position. Of the three nurse educators, one shall be a practical nurse educator, one shall be an associate degree or diploma nurse educator, and one shall be a baccalaureate or higher degree nurse educator. All nurse educators shall meet the minimum education requirement as established by the Board's education program standards for nurse faculty. Candidates eligible for election to the Board as nurse educators are not eligible for election as the at-large member.

(1) Except for the at-large member, every registered nurse member shall meet the following criteria:

a. Hold a current, unencumbered license to practice as a registered nurse in North Carolina.

a1. Be a resident of North Carolina.

b. Have a minimum of five years of experience as a registered nurse.

c. Have been engaged continuously in a position that meets the criteria for the specified Board position for at least three years immediately preceding election.

d. Show evidence that the employer of the registered nurse is aware that the nurse intends to serve on the Board.

(2) Every licensed practical nurse member shall meet the following criteria:

a. Hold a current, unencumbered license to practice as a licensed practical nurse in North Carolina.

a1. Be a resident of North Carolina.

c. Have a minimum of five years of experience as a licensed practical nurse.

d. Have been engaged continuously in the position of a licensed practical nurse for at least three years immediately preceding election.

e. Show evidence that the employer of the licensed practical nurse is aware that the nurse intends to serve on the Board.

(3) A public member appointed by the Governor shall not be a provider of health services or employed in the health services field. No public member appointed by the Governor or person in the public member's immediate family as defined by G.S. 90-405(8) shall be currently employed as a licensed nurse or been previously employed as a licensed nurse.

(4) The nurse practitioner, nurse anesthetist, nurse midwife, or clinical nurse specialist member shall be recognized by the Board as a registered nurse who meets the following criteria:

a. Has graduated from or completed a graduate level advanced practice nursing education program accredited by a national accrediting body.

b. Maintains current certification or recertification from a national credentialing body approved by the Board or meets other requirements established by rules adopted by the Board.

c. Practices in a manner consistent with rules adopted by the Board and other applicable law.

(e) Term. - Members of the Board shall serve four-year staggered terms. No member shall serve more than two consecutive four-year terms or eight consecutive years after January 1, 2005.

(f) Removal. - The Board may remove any of its members for neglect of duty, incompetence, or unprofessional conduct. A member subject to disciplinary proceedings shall be disqualified from Board business until the charges are resolved.

(g) Reimbursement. - Board members are entitled to receive compensation and reimbursement as authorized by G.S. 93B-5. (1981, c. 360, s. 1; c. 852, s. 1; 1987, c. 651, s. 2; 1991, c. 643, s. 1; 1991 (Reg. Sess., 1992), c. 1011, s. 3; 1997-456, s. 27; 2001-98, s. 2; 2003-146, s. 1; 2004-199, s. 26(a); 2006-264, s. 47.)

§ 90-171.22. Officers.

The officers of the Board shall be a chair, a vice-chair, and any other officers the Board considers necessary. All officers shall be elected annually by the Board for terms of one year and shall serve until their successors have been elected and qualified. (1981, c. 360, s. 1; 2003-146, s. 2.)

§ 90-171.23. Duties, powers, and meetings.

(a) Meetings. The Board shall hold at least two meetings each year to transact its business. The Board shall adopt rules with respect to calling, holding, and conducting regular and special meetings and attendance at meetings. The majority of the Board members constitutes a quorum.

(b) Duties, powers. The Board is empowered to:

(1) Administer this Article.

(2) Issue its interpretations of this Article.

(3) Adopt, amend or repeal rules and regulations as may be necessary to carry out the provisions of this Article.

(4) Establish qualifications of, employ, and set the compensation of an executive officer who shall be a registered nurse and who shall not be a member of the Board.

(5) Employ and fix the compensation of other personnel that the Board determines are necessary to carry into effect this Article and incur other expenses necessary to effectuate this Article.

(6) Examine, license, and renew the licenses of duly qualified applicants for licensure.

(7) Cause the prosecution of all persons violating this Article.

(8) Establish standards to be met by the students, and to pertain to faculty, curricula, facilities, resources, and administration for any nursing program as provided in G.S. 90-171.38.

(9) Review all nursing programs at least every eight years or more often as considered necessary by the Board or program director.

(10) Grant or deny approval for nursing programs as provided in G.S. 90-171.39.

(11) Upon request, grant or deny approval of continuing education programs for nurses as provided in G.S. 90-171.42.

(12) Keep a record of all proceedings and make an annual summary of all actions available.

(13) Appoint, as necessary, advisory committees which may include persons other than Board members to deal with any issue under study.

(14) Appoint and maintain a subcommittee of the Board to work jointly with the subcommittee of the North Carolina Medical Board to develop rules and regulations to govern the performance of medical acts by registered nurses and to determine reasonable fees to accompany an application for approval or renewal of such approval as provided in G.S. 90-8.2. The fees and rules developed by this subcommittee shall govern the performance of medical acts by registered nurses and shall become effective when they have been adopted by both Boards.

(15) Recommend and collect such fees for licensure, license renewal, examinations and reexaminations as it deems necessary for fulfilling the purposes of this Article.

(16) Adopt a seal containing the name of the Board for use on all certificates, licenses, and official reports issued by it.

(17) Enter into interstate compacts to facilitate the practice and regulation of nursing.

(18) Establish programs for aiding in the recovery and rehabilitation of nurses who experience chemical addiction or abuse or mental or physical disabilities and programs for monitoring such nurses for safe practice.

(18a) Establish programs for aiding in the remediation of nurses who experience practice deficiencies.

(19) Request that the Department of Justice conduct criminal history record checks of applicants for licensure pursuant to G.S. 114-19.11.

(20) Adopt rules requiring an applicant to submit to the Board evidence of the applicant's continuing competence in the practice of nursing at the time of license renewal or reinstatement.

(21) Proceed in accordance with G.S. 90-171.37A, notwithstanding G.S. 150B-40(b), when conducting a contested case hearing in accordance with Article 3A of Chapter 150B of the General Statutes.

(22) Designate one or more of its employees to serve papers or subpoenas issued by the Board. Service under this subdivision is permitted in addition to any other methods of service permitted by law.

(23) Acquire, hold, rent, encumber, alienate, and otherwise deal with real property in the same manner as a private person or corporation, subject only to approval of the Governor and the Council of State. Collateral pledged by the Board for an encumbrance is limited to the assets, income, and revenues of the Board.

(24) Order the production of any records concerning the practice of nursing relevant to a complaint received by the Board or an inquiry or investigation conducted by or on behalf of the Board. (1981, c. 360, s. 1; c. 665, s. 2; c. 852, s. 4; 1995, c. 94, s. 28; 1997-491, s. 1; 1999-291, s. 1; 2001-98, s. 3; 2001-371, s. 3; 2003-146, s. 3; 2005-186, s. 1; 2007-148, s. 1; 2009-133, s. 1.)

§ 90-171.24. Executive director.

The executive director shall perform the duties prescribed by the Board and serve as secretary/treasurer to the Board. (1981, c. 360, s. 1; 1993, c. 198, s. 1; 2009-133, s. 2.)

§ 90-171.25. Custody and use of funds.

The executive director shall deposit in financial institutions designated by the Board as official depositories all fees payable to the Board. The funds shall be deposited in the name of the Board and shall be used to pay all expenses incurred by the Board in carrying out the purposes of this Article. (1981, c. 360, s. 1; 1993, c. 198, s. 2; c. 257, s. 4; 1995, c. 509, s. 41.)

§ 90-171.26. The Board may accept contributions, etc.

The Board may accept grants, contributions, devises, and gifts which shall be kept in a separate fund and shall be used by it to enhance the practice of nursing. (1981, c. 360, s. 1; 2011-284, s. 63.)

§ 90-171.27. Expenses payable from fees collected by Board.

(a) All salaries, compensation, and expenses incurred or allowed for the purposes of carrying out this Article shall be paid by the Board exclusively out of the fees received by the Board as authorized by this Article, or funds received from other sources. In no case shall any salary, expense, or other obligation of the Board be charged against the treasury of the State of North Carolina. All moneys and receipts shall be kept in a special fund by and for the use of the Board for the exclusive purpose of carrying out the provisions of this Article.

(b) (See editor's note for initial fee) The schedule of fees shall not exceed the following rates:

Application for examination leading to certificate and license as registered nurse.. $75.00

Application for certificate and license as registered nurse by endorsement............. 150.00

Application for each re-examination leading to certificate and license as registered nurse.. 75.00

Renewal of license to practice as registered nurse (two-year period)...................... 100.00

Reinstatement of lapsed license to practice as a registered nurse and renewal fee.. 180.00

Application for examination leading to certificate and license as licensed practical nurse by examination... 75.00

Application for certificate and license as licensed practical nurse by endorsement. 150.00

Application for each re-examination leading to certificate and license as licensed practical nurse... 75.00

Renewal of license to practice as a licensed practical nurse (two-year period)........ 100.00

Reinstatement of lapsed license to practice as a licensed practical nurse and renewal fee.. 180.00

(See editor's note for initial fee) Application fee for retired registered nurse status or retired licensed practical nurse status............... ....50.00

Reinstatement of retired registered nurse to practice as a registered nurse or a retired licensed practical nurse to practice as a licensed practical nurse (two-year period).. ..... 100.00

Reasonable charge for duplication services and materials.

A fee for an item listed in this schedule shall not increase from one year to the next by more than twenty percent (20%).

(c)   No refund of fees will be made.

(d)   The Board may assess costs of disciplinary action against a nurse found in violation of the North Carolina Nursing Practice Act. (1947, c. 1091, s. 1; 1953, c. 750; c. 1199, ss. 1, 4; 1955, c. 1266, ss. 2, 3; 1961, c. 431, s. 2; 1965, c. 578, s. 1; 1971, c. 534; 1981, c. 360, s. 1; c. 661; 1987, c. 651, s. 1; 1997-384, s. 1; 2003-29, s. 2.)

§ 90-171.28. Nurses registered under previous law.

On June 30, 1981, any nurse who holds a license to practice nursing as a registered nurse or licensed practical nurse, issued by a competent authority pursuant to laws providing for the licensure of nurses in North Carolina, shall be deemed to be licensed under the provisions of this Article, but such person shall otherwise comply with the provisions of this Article including those provisions governing licensure renewal. (1953, c. 1199, s. 1; 1965, c. 578, s. 1; 1981, c. 360, s. 1.)

§ 90-171.29. Qualifications of applicants for examination.

In order to be eligible for licensure by examination, the applicant shall make a written application to the Board on forms furnished by the Board and shall submit to the Board an application fee and written evidence, verified by oath, sufficient to satisfy the Board that the applicant has graduated from a course of study approved by the Board and is mentally and physically competent to practice nursing. (1947, c. 1091, s. 1; 1953, c. 750; c. 1199, ss. 1, 4; 1955, c. 1266, s. 2; 1961, c. 431, s. 2; 1965, c. 578, s. 1; 1973, c. 93, s. 4; 1981, c. 360, s. 1.)

§ 90-171.30. Licensure by examination.

At least twice each year the Board shall give an examination, at the time and place it determines, to applicants for licensure to practice as a registered nurse or licensed practical nurse. The Board shall adopt rules, not inconsistent with this Article, governing qualifications of applicants, the conduct of applicants during the examination, and the conduct of the examination. The applicants shall be required to pass the examination required by the Board. The Board shall adopt rules which identify the criteria which must be met by an applicant in order to be issued a license. When the Board determines that an applicant has met those criteria, passed the required examination, submitted the required fee, and has demonstrated to the Board's satisfaction that he or she is mentally and physically competent to practice nursing, the Board shall issue a license to the applicant. (1947, c. 1091, s. 1; 1953, c. 1199, s. 1; 1965, c. 578, s. 1; 1981, c. 360, s. 1; 1991, c. 643, s. 2; 1993, c. 198, s. 3.)

§ 90-171.31. Reexamination.

Any applicant who fails to pass the first licensure examination may take subsequent examinations in accordance with the rules of the Board. (1981, c. 360, s. 1; 1993, c. 198, s. 4.)

§ 90-171.32. Qualifications for license as a registered nurse or a licensed practical nurse without examination.

The Board may, without examination, issue a license to an applicant who is duly licensed as a registered nurse or licensed practical nurse under the laws of another state, territory of the United States, the District of Columbia, or foreign country when that jurisdiction's requirements for licensure as a registered nurse or a licensed practical nurse, as the case may be, are substantially equivalent to or exceed those of the State of North Carolina at the time the applicant was initially licensed, and when, in the Board's opinion, the applicant is competent to practice nursing in this State. The Board may require such applicant to prove competence and qualifications to practice as a registered nurse or licensed practical nurse in North Carolina. (1947, c. 1091, s. 1; 1953, c. 1199, s. 1; 1961, c. 431, s. 2; 1965, c. 578, s. 1; 1981, c. 360, s. 1.)

§ 90-171.33. Temporary license.

(a)   Until the implementation of the computer-adaptive licensure examination, the Board may issue a nonrenewable temporary license to persons who are applying for licensure under G.S. 90-171.30, and who are scheduled for the licensure examination at the first opportunity after graduation, for a period not to exceed the lesser of nine months or the date of applicant's notification of the results of the licensure examination. The Board shall revoke the temporary license of any person who does not take the examination as scheduled, or who has failed the examination for licensure as provided by this act.

(b)   Upon implementation of the computer-adaptive licensure examination, no temporary licenses will be issued to persons who are applying for licensure under G.S. 90-171.30.

(c) The Board may issue a nonrenewable temporary license to persons applying for licensure under G.S. 90-171.32 for a period not to exceed the lesser of six months or until the Board determines whether the applicant is qualified to practice nursing in North Carolina. Temporary licensees may perform patient-care services within limits defined by the Board. In defining these limits, the Board shall consider the ability of the temporary licensee to safely and properly carry out patient-care services. Temporary licensees shall be held to the standard of care of a fully licensed nurse. (1981, c. 360, s. 1; 1991, c. 643, s. 3; 1993, c. 198, s. 5.)

§ 90-171.34. Licensure renewal.

Every unencumbered license, except temporary license, issued under this Article shall be renewed for two years. On or before the date the current license expires, every person who desires to continue to practice nursing shall apply for licensure renewal to the Board on forms furnished by the Board and shall also file the required fee. Failure to renew the license before the expiration date shall result in automatic forfeiture of the right to practice nursing in North Carolina until such time that the license has been reinstated. (1981, c. 360, s. 1; 1993, c. 198, s. 6; 2009-133, s. 3.)

§ 90-171.35. Reinstatement.

A licensee who has allowed license to lapse by failure to renew as herein provided may apply for reinstatement on a form provided by the Board. The Board shall require the applicant to return the completed application with the required fee and to furnish a statement of the reason for failure to apply for renewal prior to the deadline. If the license has lapsed for at least five years, the Board shall require the applicant to complete satisfactorily a refresher course approved by the Board, or provide proof of active licensure within the past five years in another jurisdiction. The Board may require any applicant for reinstatement to satisfy the Board that the license should be reinstated. If, in the opinion of the Board, the applicant has so satisfied the Board, it shall issue a renewal of license to practice nursing, or it shall issue a license to practice nursing for a limited time. (1981, c. 360, s. 1; 1993, c. 198, s. 7.)

§ 90-171.36. Inactive list.

(a)   When a licensee submits a request for inactive status, the Board shall issue to the licensee a statement of inactive status and shall place the licensee's name on the inactive list. While on the inactive list, the person shall not be subjected to renewal requirements and shall not practice nursing in North Carolina.

(b)   When such person desires to be removed from the inactive list and returned to the active list within five years of being placed on inactive status, an application shall be submitted to the Board on a form furnished by the Board and the fee shall be paid for license renewal. The Board shall require evidence of competency to resume the practice of nursing before returning the applicant to active status. If the person has been on the inactive list for more than five years, the applicant must satisfactorily complete a refresher course approved by the Board or provide proof of active licensure within the past five years in another jurisdiction. (1981, c. 360, s. 1; 1993, c. 198, s. 8.)

§ 90-171.36A. Retired nurse status; reinstatement.

(a)   After a registered nurse or a licensed practical nurse has retired, upon payment of the one-time fee required by G.S. 90-171.27(b), the Board may issue a special license to a registered nurse or licensed practical nurse in recognition of the nurse's retired status.

(b)   If a retired registered nurse or licensed practical nurse wishes to return to the practice of nursing, the retired nurse shall apply for reinstatement on a form provided by the Board and satisfy any requirements the Board deems necessary to reinstate the license. (2003-29, s. 1.)

§ 90-171.37. Revocation, discipline, suspension, probation, or denial of licensure.

The Board may initiate an investigation upon receipt of information about any practice that might violate any provision of this Article or any rule or regulation promulgated by the Board. In accordance with the provisions of Chapter 150B of the General Statutes, the Board shall have the power and authority to: (i) refuse to issue a license to practice nursing; (ii) refuse to issue a certificate of renewal of a license to practice nursing; (iii) revoke or suspend a license to practice nursing; and (iv) invoke other such disciplinary measures, censure, or probative terms against a licensee as it deems fit and proper; in any instance or instances in which the Board is satisfied that the applicant or licensee:

(1) Has given false information or has withheld material information from the Board in procuring or attempting to procure a license to practice nursing.

(2) Has been convicted of or pleaded guilty or nolo contendere to any crime which indicates that the nurse is unfit or incompetent to practice nursing or that the nurse has deceived or defrauded the public.

(3) Has a mental or physical disability or uses any drug to a degree that interferes with his or her fitness to practice nursing.

(4) Engages in conduct that endangers the public health.

(5) Is unfit or incompetent to practice nursing by reason of deliberate or negligent acts or omissions regardless of whether actual injury to the patient is established.

(6) Engages in conduct that deceives, defrauds, or harms the public in the course of professional activities or services.

(7) Has violated any provision of this Article.

(8) Has willfully violated any rules enacted by the Board.

The Board may take any of the actions specified above in this section when a registered nurse approved to perform medical acts has violated rules governing the performance of medical acts by a registered nurse; provided this shall not interfere with the authority of the North Carolina Medical Board to enforce rules and regulations governing the performance of medical acts by a registered nurse.

The Board may reinstate a revoked license, revoke censure or probative terms, or remove other licensure restrictions when it finds that the reasons for revocation, censure or probative terms, or other licensure restrictions no longer exist and that the nurse or applicant can reasonably be expected to safely and properly practice nursing. (1981, c. 360, s. 1; c. 852, s. 3; 1987, c. 827, s. 1; 1991, c. 643, s. 4; 1991 (Reg. Sess., 1992), c. 1030, s. 22; 1995, c. 94, s. 29; 2001-98, s. 4; 2009-133, s. 4.)

§ 90-171.37A. Use of hearing committee and depositions.

(a) The Board, in its discretion, may designate in writing three or more of its members to conduct hearings as a hearing committee to take evidence. A majority of the hearing committee shall be licensed nurses.

(b) Evidence and testimony may be presented at hearings before the Board or a hearing committee in the form of depositions before any person authorized to administer oaths in accordance with the procedure for the taking of depositions in civil actions in the superior court.

(c) The hearing committee shall submit a recommended decision that contains findings of fact and conclusions of law to the Board. Before the Board makes a final decision, it shall give each party an opportunity to file written exceptions to the recommended decision made by the hearing committee and to present oral arguments to the Board. A majority of the qualified members present and voting of the full Board shall issue a final decision. (2007-148, s. 2.)

§ 90-171.38. Standards for nursing programs.

(a) A nursing program may be operated under the authority of a general hospital, or an approved post-secondary educational institution. The Board shall establish, revise, or repeal standards for nursing programs. These standards shall specify program requirements, curricula, faculty, students, facilities, resources, administration, and describe the approval process. Any institution desiring to establish a nursing program shall apply to the Board and submit satisfactory evidence that it will meet the standards established by the Board. Those standards shall be designed to ensure that graduates of those programs have the education necessary to safely and competently practice nursing.

(b) Any individual, organization, association, corporation, or institution may establish a program for the purpose of training or educating any registered nurse licensed under G.S. 90-171.30, 90-171.32, or 90-171.33 in the skills, procedures, and techniques necessary to conduct examinations for the purpose of collecting evidence from the victims of first-degree rape as defined in G.S. 14-27.2, second-degree rape as defined in G.S. 14-27.3, statutory rape as defined in G.S. 14-27.7A, first-degree sexual offense as defined in G.S. 14-27.4, second-degree sexual offense as defined in G.S. 14-27.5 or attempted first-degree or second-degree rape or attempted first-degree or second-degree sexual offense. The Board, pursuant to G.S. 90-171.23(b)(14), shall establish, revise, or repeal standards for any such program. Any individual, organization, association, corporation, or institution which desires to establish a program under this subsection shall apply to the Board and submit satisfactory evidence that it will meet the standards prescribed by the Board. (1981, c. 360, s. 1; 1987, c. 827, s. 1; 1991, c. 643, s. 5; 1997-375, s. 1; 2003-146, s. 4; 2009-133, s. 5.)

§ 90-171.39. Approval.

The Board shall designate persons to survey proposed nursing programs, including the clinical facilities. The persons designated by the Board shall submit a written report of the survey to the Board. If in the opinion of the Board the standards for approved nursing education are met, the program shall be given approval. (1981, c. 360, s. 1.)

§ 90-171.40. Ongoing approval.

The Board shall review all nursing programs in the State at least every eight years or more often as considered necessary. If the Board determines that any approved nursing program does not meet or maintain the standards required by the Board, the Board shall give written notice specifying the deficiencies to the institution responsible for the program. The Board shall withdraw approval from a program that fails to correct deficiencies within a reasonable time. The Board shall publish annually a list of nursing programs in this State showing their approval status. (1981, c. 360, s. 1; 2003-146, s. 5.)

§ 90-171.41. Baccalaureate in nursing candidate credits.

Every graduate of a diploma or associate degree school of nursing in this State who has passed the registered nurse examination shall, upon admission to any State-supported institution of higher learning offering baccalaureate education in nursing, be granted credit for previous experience in the diploma or associate degree school of nursing on an individual basis by the utilization of the most effective method of evaluation to the end that the applicant shall receive optimum credit and that upon graduation the applicant will have earned the baccalaureate degree in nursing. (1969, c. 547, s. 1; 1981, c. 360, s. 1.)

§ 90-171.42. Continuing education programs.

(a) Upon request, the Board shall grant approval to continuing education programs upon a finding that the program offers an educational experience designed to enhance the practice of nursing.

(b) If the program offers to teach nurses to perform advance skills, the Board may grant approval for the program and the performance of the advanced skills by those successfully completing the program when it finds that the nature of the procedures taught in the program and the program facilities and faculty are such that a nurse successfully completing the program can reasonably be expected to carry out those procedures safely and competently. (1981, c. 360, s. 1; 1991, c. 643, s. 6.)

§ 90-171.43. License required.

No person shall practice or offer to practice as a registered nurse or licensed practical nurse, or use the word "nurse" as a title for herself or himself, or use an abbreviation to indicate that the person is a registered nurse or licensed practical nurse, unless the person is currently licensed as a registered nurse or licensed practical nurse as provided by this Article. If the word "nurse" is part of a longer title, such as "nurse's aide", a person who is entitled to use that title shall use the entire title and may not abbreviate the title to "nurse". This Article shall not, however, be construed to prohibit or limit the following:

(1) The performance by any person of any act for which that person holds a license issued pursuant to North Carolina law;

(2)   The clinical practice by students enrolled in approved nursing programs, continuing education programs, or refresher courses under the supervision of qualified faculty;

(3)   The performance of nursing performed by persons who hold a temporary license issued pursuant to G.S. 90-171.33;

(4)   The delegation to any person, including a member of the patient's family, by a physician licensed to practice medicine in North Carolina, a licensed dentist or registered nurse of those patient-care services which are routine, repetitive, limited in scope that do not require the professional judgment of a registered nurse or licensed practical nurse;

(5)   Assistance by any person in the case of emergency.

Any person permitted to practice nursing without a license as provided in subdivision (2) or (3) of this section shall be held to the same standard of care as any licensed nurse. (1981, c. 360, s. 1; 1993, c. 198, s. 9; 1999-320, s. 2.)

§ 90-171.43A. Mandatory employer verification of licensure status.

(a)   Before hiring a registered nurse or a licensed practical nurse in North Carolina, a health care facility shall verify that the applicant has a current, valid license to practice nursing pursuant to G.S. 90-171.43.

(b)   For purposes of this section, "health care facility" means:

(1)   Facilities described in G.S. 131E-256(b).

(2)   Public health departments, physicians' offices, ambulatory care facilities, and rural health clinics. (2003-146, s. 6.)

§ 90-171.44. Prohibited acts.

It shall be a violation of this Article, and subject to action under G.S. 90-171.37, for any person to:

(1) Sell, fraudulently obtain, or fraudulently furnish any nursing diploma or aid or abet therein.

(2) Practice nursing under cover of any fraudulently obtained license.

(3) Practice nursing without a license. This subdivision shall not be construed to prohibit any licensed registered nurse who has successfully completed a program established under G.S. 90-171.38(b) from conducting medical examinations or performing procedures to collect evidence from the victims of offenses described in that subsection.

(4) Conduct a nursing program or a refresher course for activation of a license, that is not approved by the Board.

(5) Employ unlicensed persons to practice nursing. (1981, c. 360, s. 1; 1991, c. 643, s. 7; 1993, c. 198, s. 10; 1997-375, s. 2.)

§ 90-171.45. Violation of Article.

The violation of any provision of this Article, except G.S. 90-171.47, shall be a Class 1 misdemeanor. (1981, c. 360, s. 1; 1993, c. 539, s. 632; 1994, Ex. Sess., c. 24, s. 14(c).)

§ 90-171.46. Injunctive authority.

The Board may apply to the superior court for an injunction to prevent violations of this Article or of any rules enacted pursuant thereto. The court is empowered to grant such injunctions regardless of whether criminal prosecution or other action has been or may be instituted as a result of such violation. (1981, c. 360, s. 1.)

§ 90-171.47. Reports: immunity from suit.

Any person who has reasonable cause to suspect misconduct or incapacity of a licensee or who has reasonable cause to suspect that any person is in violation of this Article, including those actions specified in G.S. 90-171.37(1) through (8), G.S. 90-171.43, and G.S. 90-171.44, shall report the relevant facts to the Board. Upon receipt of such charge or upon its own initiative, the Board may give notice of an administrative hearing or may, after diligent investigation, dismiss unfounded charges. Any person making a report pursuant to this section shall be immune from any criminal prosecution or civil liability resulting therefrom unless such person knew the report was false or acted in reckless disregard of whether the report was false. (1981, c. 360, s. 1; 1991, c. 643, s. 8; 1993, c. 198, s. 11.)

Vision Books Order Form

Fax Orders:	1-980-299-5965
Phone Orders:	1-704-898-0770
E-mail Orders:	www.visionbooks.org
Mail Orders:	Vision Books, LLC P.O. Box 42406 Charlotte, NC 28215

Shipp To:
Name_____
Address_____
City_____State_____Zip_____
Phone_____Fax_____
Email_____@_____

Bill To: We can bill a third party on your behalf.
Name_____
Address_____
City_____State_____Zip_____
Phone___(_____)_____Fax_____
Email_____@_____

Pamphlet Number ($15.00 Each)	Qty	Total Cost
_____	_____	_____
_____	_____	_____
_____	_____	_____
_____	_____	_____
_____	_____	_____
_____	_____	_____
_____	_____	_____
_____	_____	_____
Full Volume Set 1-92	92 Pamphlets	1,380.00

Free Shipping Shipping & Handling on Full Volume Orders
Add $1.00 Shipping & Handling per pamphlet $_____

Total Cost $_____

Thank you for your support. Management!

DID YOU ENJOY THIS BOOK?

Vision Books, LLC would like to hear from you! If you or someone you know has been fasely imprisoned, we would like to hear your story. If the 'North Carolina Criminal Law and Procedure' has had an effect in your life or if you have suggestions, we would like to hear from you. Send your letters to:

Vision Books, LLC
Attn: Staff Writers
P.O. Box 42406
Charlotte, NC 28215
Email: staff@visionbooks.org

Order Additional Copies:

Fax Orders: 1-980-299-5965

Phone Orders: 1-704-898-0770

E-mail Orders: www.visionbooks.org

Mail Orders: Vision Books, LLC
                       P.O. Box 42406
                       Charlotte, NC 28215

www.ingramcontent.com/pod-product-compliance
Lightning Source LLC
Chambersburg PA
CBHW051628170526
45167CB00001B/98